MOMPRENEURS®

*A Mother's Practical Step-by-Step
Guide to Work-at-Home Success*

MOMPRENEURS®

A Mother's Practical Step-by-Step Guide to Work-at-Home Success

Patricia Cobe
and
Ellen H. Parlapiano

A PERIGEE BOOK

A Perigee Book
Published by The Berkley Publishing Group
A division of Penguin Putnam Inc.
375 Hudson Street
New York, New York 10014

Copyright © 1996, 2002 by Ellen H. Parlapiano and Patricia Cobe
Text design by Irving Perkins Associates
Cover design by Jill Boltin
Cover photos © Tony Stone

First edition: September 1996
Revised edition: June 2002

Visit our website at www.penguinputnam.com

Library of Congress Cataloging-in-Publication Data

Cobe, Patricia
    Mompreneurs : a mother's practical step-by-step guide to work-at-home success /
Patricia Cobe and Ellen H. Parlapiano.
        p.   cm.
    "A Perigee book."
    Rev. ed. of: Mompreneurs / Ellen H. Parlapiano and Patricia Cobe, 1996.
    Includes index
    ISBN 0-399-52758-3
    1. Home-based businesses—United States—Management.   2. Home labor—United
States.   3. Self-employed women—United States.   4. Mothers—Employment—United
States.   5. Work and family—United States.   6. Women employees—United States.
I. Parlapiano, Ellen H. Mompreneurs.   II. Title.

HD2336.U5P366   2002
658'.041—dc21   2001056036

Printed in the United States of America

10   9   8   7   6   5   4   3   2   1

To my children, Matthew and Amy: Without you, I'd never have discovered the joys of mompreneurship. And to my husband, Bob—my equal partner in parenting. Thanks for being by my side every step of the way.

EP

To my three "guys," Elliott, Josh, and Matt: You helped me realize my dreams and become the mompreneur I am today. Thanks for your inspiration and support.

PC

Contents

Acknowledgments

As one of the moms in our survey so beautifully stated, the key to work-at-home success is to "surround yourself with upbeat people who believe in your possibilities." From the beginning stages of this book, we've been surrounded by people who had confidence in us and our message. We couldn't have written this book without their support and encouragement.

We thank our agent, Carla Glasser, for urging us to hurry up and write our book proposal, and then for waiting nearly two years while we did just that. Her endless energy and enthusiasm did more than land us a book contract; it kept us motivated and on track throughout the long publishing process.

We appreciate the patient guidance of Sheila Curry Oakes, our hard-working editor at Perigee Books. Her sound suggestions helped shape and strengthen *Mompreneurs*®. We also extend our gratitude to Julie Merberg, our former editor, who had the vision to buy into our idea at the start.

We give our heartfelt thanks to all the mompreneurs who shared their stories with us. We are grateful for the time you took to answer our survey, our phone calls, and our e-mail notes. Your insights and anecdotes give this book special meaning, and your voices ring out on every page. We're proud to pass along your smart strategies and enlightening comments.

Most of all, we thank our families for coaching us through the birth of this book. Our husbands, Elliott Feldstein and Bob Parlapiano, were always there for us—whether to cook dinner, fold laundry, or provide last-minute child care. (And they never once complained about the round-the-clock phone calls or midnight e-mailing!) Our children—Josh and Matt Feldstein and Matthew and Amy Parlapiano—are the lively and loving sparks for our businesses and our book. And our mothers—Myrna Cobe and Helen Hausler—who were wonderful role models during the years when our ideas about family and work were evolving. Thank you for blessing our lives and leading us to discover this rewarding and flexible way to work.

Introduction: Mompreneurs®
Are Here to Stay!

In 1996, when we published the first edition of this book and popularized the word *mompreneur*®, working from home still wasn't viewed as a viable or lucrative employment option by those in the media or the corporate work world. But things sure have changed in a few short years! Since then, work-from-home moms have been prominently featured on TV commercials, selling a variety of products—from wireless and Internet services, to office supplies, to convenience foods. (And thankfully, these moms aren't always shown in their bedroom slippers!) As you flip through parenting and women's magazines these days (as well as news publications like *Time* and *Business Week*), you're also much more likely to see motivational stories about mothers who work from home. And there are a staggering number of organizations and websites now targeting the needs of this ever-growing and very special workforce. It's clear: Mompreneurs are finally getting the respect they deserve!

Today, 4½ million moms with kids under 18 work from home in some capacity, according to Joanne H. Pratt Associates, a research firm in Dallas, Texas. Moms are not only starting businesses in record numbers, but they're finding more opportunities to work from home without having to launch their own enterprises. Corporations across the nation are recognizing the importance of offering telecommuting positions and other flexible work options in order to attract and keep valued employees—many of whom are juggling career and family responsibilities.

Whether they're running home businesses or telecommuting for corporations large and small, mompreneurs have become more visible, more powerful, and more profitable. At last, the rest of the world is acknowledging what work-from-home moms have known to be true for years: It *is* possible to have a personally and financially rewarding career, without leaving home *or* sacrificing time with your kids.

MEET THE MILLENNIUM MOMPRENEUR®

We're amazed and inspired by the successful work-from-home mothers we meet every day through our speaking engagements, our Mompreneurs® online chats and message boards on iVillage.com's Work channel, our own website (www.mompreneursonline.com), and the interviews we conduct while researching and writing on entrepreneurial topics. These moms are carving out creative ways to stay at home with their children and contribute to the family income. Some are transferring their skills from the workplace into exciting home businesses. Teachers are setting up after-school homework clubs, secretaries are becoming event planners, and graphic artists are making it big as website designers. Others are tapping their talents and passions to find work-from-home opportunities. We've met a former marketing exec who now runs a specialty cookie business, an advertising copywriter who has taken up landscape gardening, and an occupational therapist who sells homemade soap. These are just some of the ways moms are turning their ingenuity into diverse and thriving home businesses.

"If you really want to work at home, you will find a way to do it!" says Mary Ann Chaneski, a mom of two from Emerson, New Jersey. She worked full-time in the fashion industry designing scarves and blouses before her kids arrived. Now she runs her own home-based design service, creating scarf patterns for Ellen Tracy and for Federated department stores' private line. "Never in my life have I felt more creative!" she says. "I don't have to worry about corporate paperwork or politics. I can just focus my energy on colors, designs, and most important, my kids," Chaneski says. "And I'm bringing home as much salary, if not more, than I did working full-time."

Though Chaneski admits to working many late nights during crunch periods, she also has weeks at a time without any deadlines, and she packs that downtime with plenty of kids-only activities. As demand for her services grows, Chaneski is already planning on delegating some of her workload to a colleague with similar talents. "That way I can allow my business to grow without neglecting my family or my current clients," she says.

Portland, Maine, mom Hannah Brazee Gregory had always dreamed of having her own business, but it took her a while to discover the mompreneur solution. Eight weeks after her son, Camden, was born, she had returned to her full-time job as a public relations representative and magazine editor at the local children's hospital. She and her husband needed the income, she reasoned. "After all, we were about to buy a house," Gregory remembers.

By the time Camden was a year old, Gregory had her house and a new, high-powered position at the hospital; but she also had a very sick little boy. Camden had developed serious asthma, triggered by the colds he was catching in day care. After countless emergency room visits, Gregory decided to quit her job and stay at home with Camden until she could nurse him back to health. "It had always been my dream to have my own business," she says. So she tapped her public relations experience and talents in writing and graphic design to launch Hannah Creative Communications, a home-based company that provides affordable publicity and advertising support to non-profit organizations. "I am my own boss, I make more money than I ever did working for someone else, and I spend so much time with my son," she says. Gregory's new venture is working out particularly well now that another baby boy has joined the family.

ENDLESS POSSIBILITIES

While a good number of mompreneurs convert previous job experience into work-from-home opportunities, many embark into uncharted territory. Former middle school math teacher Robin Magruder and her business partner, Alison Davis (who was a corporate human resources manager before her kids were born), first met while coordinating a group for stay-at-home moms in the Bardstown, Kentucky, area. The two became friends and discovered a mutual passion for scrapbooking. "We'd get together each Monday to put together our scrapbooks while our children played with each other," Magruder says. As they cut and pasted their family photos, the moms dreamed of a way to capitalize on their hobby. In May 2000 they launched CutoutCrazy, a crafts company that sells scrapbooking kits and supplies. They also teach scrapbook classes at local adult-education centers. "We've found a fun way to be home with our kids, enjoy adult stimulation, and introduce scrapbooking to others," Magruder says.

Heidi Kluzak of Taylor Falls, Minnesota, had been freelancing as a photo stylist for *Better Homes and Gardens* magazine when she stumbled upon a new business idea—quite literally by accident! When her toddler, Peter, took a tumble during a playdate, Kluzak kissed his "boo-boo" and watched his hurt and his tears instantly disappear. "Wow, the power of a mother's kiss!" Kluzak marveled. "If only we could bottle it!" agreed her friend. "The essence of a mother's bond with her child was captured for me in that moment," remembers Kluzak, now the mom of two. So this enterprising aficionado of aromatherapy and infant massage began brainstorming: though a mother's love obviously can't be put in a bottle, what about a product that celebrates a mother's healing touch?

With the aid of a chemist, Kluzak created Mom's Kiss in a Bottle, a line of therapeutic massage and bath products for babies, which is now sold through national chains, boutiques, gift shops, spas, mail-order catalogs, and online retailers. Each bottle is accompanied by a free booklet called *An Introduction to Infant Massage,* written by a leading expert in the field. "The timing was perfect for starting a business. I work at home so I can stay home with my kids," says Kluzak, who intends to expand the business more agressively once her children are older. "One day my kids will be moving out and I'll be moving computers into their rooms! In the meantime, I still get to go to their T-ball games and work on my own time!" Kluzak says.

WHY WORK AT HOME?

Through our original nationwide survey and our ongoing interaction with mompreneurs in both the "real" and "virtual" world, we've discovered that moms everywhere choose to work from home for the same basic reasons.

Freedom of Choice

For most mothers today, working is an economic necessity. A study by the U.S. Census Bureau reports that 59 percent of American moms with babies have jobs in the traditional labor force. Yet according to research by Public Agenda, a nonprofit public policy group, seven in ten parents of children under age five *want* to stay at home with their kids.

It used to be that moms had only two alternatives: stay at home and relinquish salary, or work outside the home and relinquish time with the kids. But mompreneurship broadens your options. You don't have to abandon your career aspirations or money-making potential just because you long to stay home with your children. Mompreneurship offers you the best of both worlds.

Sue Papach, of Whiting, Indiana, has certainly found sweet success working from home. When her first daughter was born, Papach gave up her career as a sportswriter for a large newspaper and devoted herself to full-time motherhood. But after baby number three came along, Papach found herself craving the fulfillment and income of a "paying job." She started a home-based career in direct sales and stuck with it for several years. By the time her fifth child arrived, she began to long for something more creative. "I was always giving handmade crafts and chocolates as gifts and party favors," she recalls. For her sister's bridal shower, Papach decorated the cake with her homemade chocolates. That day, she received two offers to do other showers and got at least ten more phone calls from folks interested in learning more about her work. Her new enterprise, Oh Sew Sweet! Inc. Personalized Gourmet Chocolates, was on its way. Today Papach designs handmade gourmet specialty chocolates for every occasion and ships orders nationwide. Her chocolate butterflies were even featured in *Brides* magazine! "I get to hug my kids whenever I want! I get to stop when they come home and listen to all their news. Working from home puts me in control and allows me to be the best mom I can be!" Papach says proudly.

Family Flexibility

"Women use self-employment to gain flexibility and control over their lives," says researcher Joanne Pratt in her 1999 SBA-sponsored study, *Homebased Business: The Hidden Economy*. "Flexibility is particularly important for women with children under six," she adds. Over 73 percent of self-employed women with young children work from home at least part of the time, according to Pratt's research.

Indeed, all the mompreneurs we've talked to—business owners and telecommuters alike—agree that working from home offers them unparalleled freedom to tend to family and career needs under the same roof. You can nurse your baby while you answer your e-mail, take time out of your work day to attend a Mommy and Me class with your toddler, or pick up a sick child from the school nurse's office—all without having to ask a boss for permission.

"I love the flexibility to work when *I* want to," says Theresa Rodriguez Farrisi, of Jackson Township, Pennsylvania. This mother of six children under age eleven runs a small, home-based business called Homekeepers Publishing and Music. From here, Rodriguez Farrisi sells self-published books on diapering and adoption alternatives as well as tapes featuring her singing traditional American and international lullabies. As if she's not already busy enough, this mompreneur also homeschools her children. "Because my kids are all so young, there would be no other way for me to work the many hours I do in any other setting and still be able to nurture and care for them at home," she says.

The Control Factor

Recent studies have proven that parents want more control over their time and their children's lives and are willing to sacrifice career advancement and earning power to get it. A poll released by the Radcliffe Public Policy Center revealed that 83 percent of women say that having a work schedule that allows enough time for family is more important than a high salary or job prestige. A Cornell University study of middle-income couples found that almost all of those with children scaled back their work commitments for the sake of their families, but that mothers were twice as likely as fathers to put the brakes on their careers after the children were born. There is also a growing mistrust of child care, particularly evident with young parents. The Public Agenda study says that 56 percent of parents with children under age five believe that no one can do as good a job of child-rearing as they can, and 70 percent believe that one parent should stay home with the kids.

By becoming a mompreneur you can have unprecedented control over your work schedule, your earning power, and your children's daily lives. The main reasons women cite for operating a home-based business are to be their own boss and earn an income, says Pratt. As a mompreneur, *you'll* decide where and when you work and how much you can charge for your services. You can limit the time your children spend in someone else's care. Plus, you can expand your business at your own pace! "Our goal is slow and steady growth," says Magruder of CutoutCrazy. "Currently, we both work only ten to twelve hours per week," she says, "but as our children get older and enter school we will be able to dedicate more time to the business, and it will grow even more. Right now, our children are our top priorities."

Every Day Is Take Your Child to Work Day

Mompreneurs have a unique opportunity to be dual role models for their children, both as businesswomen and mothers. Even if you're working just a few hours a week at building your home business, you are preserving an important part of your career identity and self-esteem. Your children will benefit from seeing you gain respect and financial reward at something you really enjoy doing. And you can foster entrepreneurial spirit and a strong work ethic in your children by letting them help you build your business. Beth Kalish, of Wauconda, Illinois, involved her children in her self-publishing business from the start. She named the company "Hanky Kids" for her two children and patterned the characters in *Your Baby's Day Out* and *My Big Day* after them. And they couldn't be prouder of mom. "Every time we go into a store that carries my books, my little ones will rearrange the merchandise to better show off my products," Kalish laughs. "The look of excitement on their faces when they see my books is just priceless!"

"My whole family is involved in this business!" says chocolate-maker Papach. Her younger kids can get out the molds, cut ribbons, and put labels on boxes, while her teens help prepare and pour the chocolate. "My kids are my best critics!" she says, and the older girls are instrumental in helping her design teen events like sweet sixteen parties and bar and bat mitzvahs. "By allowing my kids to help with the business, they get to feel responsible and needed," Papach adds. "It also helps them learn how to utilize their time and handle decision-making. We all encourage each other, and that builds confidence at an early age."

Technology Makes It Easier Than Ever!

We first started writing about home businesses in the mid-1990s, and believe us, there was plenty to say back then. But just a few years (and a new century!) later, it's clear that the Internet has truly revolutionized the work-from-home landscape. It's now possible to do business globally—without leaving the comfort of your home office. And the World Wide Web has opened up a wide world of new career opportunities. . . . from e-mailing, to virtual office support, website design, online travel planning, e-zine/e-book publishing, and more.

"The Internet was the perfect niche for my talents," says Papach of Oh Sew Sweet! Inc. Personalized Gourmet Chocolates. "By utilizing the Internet, I can reach a vast number of people with a small investment. Doing work off the Internet has helped widen my eyes to the vastness of this country and how small 'new technology' makes it feel," she says. Beth Kalish of Hanky Kids, who sells her books both online and off, echoes her sentiments, adding "I can work on my business at 2 A.M. or communicate with customers by e-mail in the middle of the afternoon—without them hearing my kids fighting in the background!" Other mompreneurs love the Internet for the sense of community it provides on those days when they feel so isolated working from home. They "meet" and exchange ideas, leads, and referrals in online chat rooms and message boards, forge alliances to create joint marketing efforts, and support each other through the personal and professional ups and downs that are an inevitable part of the work-from-home life.

Each day we hear from moms who sing the praises of working from home and the technology that makes it possible. "I'll never go back to the nine-to-five office world again!" proclaims Susan Cioffi, a home-based sales and marketing rep in the hosiery industry, who communicates with manufacturers and customers via e-mail, fax, and phone. Other mompreneurs agree, describing their work-from-home status as "guilt-free," "secure," "more balanced," "less conflicted," "relaxed," and "more productive."

Of course, technology can have its dark side! It's not so easy to stay upbeat when you're on a rush project and your computer is infected with a nasty virus or the server goes down for hours. But we'll help you through the good times and the bad. As work-from-home moms ourselves, we have weathered many crises—from computer crashes to sick kids on deadline day to floods, power outages, and other natural disasters. We'll even offer tips on how to concentrate on your business when the plumber is banging on the pipes or a hole is being drilled though your office wall to install yet another phone line!

This book is your work-from-home survival guide, covering every aspect of mompreneurship. You'll learn how to choose the right business, maximize earning power, maintain a professional image with children underfoot, and equip a kid-friendly office. Whether you are already working at home or just thinking about it, our book will offer you the inspiration, camaraderie, and hand-holding you need to get started and keep going.

LET US BE YOUR MENTORS

We have more than twenty-five years of work-from-home experience between us. Ellen discovered this flexible work style while on maternity leave from her job as a magazine editor after her first child was born. In fact, she was nursing baby Matthew when Pat, who was working from home as a project editor, called to offer Ellen her first freelance assignment. Ellen hadn't expected to jump back into work mode so soon, but because she was eager to test the work-from-home waters, she took the job. She found she loved freelancing and the freedom that came with it. Not long after that assignment, Ellen resigned from her full-time magazine job and officially launched her home-based writing business. She's watched it change and grow over the years along with her children, who are now approaching adolescence. Matthew and his sister Amy have provided their mom with lots of inspiration for the frequent parenting articles she writes and have offered valuable office help by assisting with filing and web research.

Pat became a work-from-home mom when she gave birth to her first son, Josh. She had been an on-staff magazine editor for eight years and felt this was the perfect time to try something new. By the time her second child, Matt, arrived four years later, her freelance writing and editing business was in full swing. Now that her children are older and more independent, she can devote more time to expanding her business, while still being there for those busy— and sometimes tough—teenage years. And now she has more freedom to leave her home office and accept jobs requiring her to work on-site for various corporations—cell phone always in hand to handle any business or family crises that may arise at home!

We are well acquainted with the perks and pitfalls of mompreneurship and are aware that it comes with some very real challenges. We've had to deal with kids who eavesdrop on business calls, neighbors who insist on stopping by to chat when our desks are piled high, friends who ask us to take their children for play dates on our workdays, and mothers working outside the home who don't believe we're working moms, too. Like all work-from-home moms, we've needed validation, support, and encouragement from time to time. We wrote this book to address the concerns that work-from-home moms find most essential: scheduling family time and work time into one short day, balancing the dual roles of "mommy" and "businesswoman," and finding cost-effective child-care options for those times you find it impossible to work with the kids underfoot.

Mompreneurs®, Second Edition: A Mother's Practical, Step-by-Step Guide to Work-at-Home Success is a one-stop source, delivering both hard-core business and practical on-the-job hints. It is jam-packed with the nuts and bolts of running a business from home. You'll learn how to formulate a business plan, balance your books, deduct legitimate expenses, and systematically manage your time. Our book will also answer questions that typical home-business books do not address, such as how to convince telephone callers that the screaming person in the background demanding help with his homework is really your secretary!

Best of all, this book is filled with words of wisdom from hundreds of successful mompreneurs we've interviewed by phone and e-mail. You'll even hear from some celebrity work-from-home moms in our "Mompreneur® Hall of Fame" sections.

WHEN MOMS TALK, WE LISTEN!

We've updated our original book to include the topics of most importance to today's moms. While the advice from many of the mompreneurs featured in our first edition still rings true, we've added some fresh tips and success strategies from work-at-homers we've recently met. And we offer you the latest resources for getting a home business off the ground and growing it successfully.

You Want Cash in a Flash!

Many of you have told us you don't want to run a business, but you still long to find a way to bring in some money while staying at home with your kids. So we've added a brand-new chapter called "Cash in a Flash!" It lists reputable ways for stay-at-home moms to earn a little extra money, as well as tips for getting started. The "Cash in a Flash!" chapter certainly won't make you rich, but it will help you contribute to the household income and save for perks like family vacations.

A Word to Dads

We know there are a lot of work-from-home fathers out there, too. We see you coaching soccer in the afternoon, we run into you picking up your kids from school, and we've met you on the Internet. And we're happy to see that in the few years since the first edition of this book was published, you have made your presence known through resources like Slowlane.com: The Online Resource for Stay-at-Home Dads (http://slowlane.com).

We don't mean to ignore you. It's just that work-from-home moms are the audience we know and understand best. Please don't feel slighted; our intentions are not at all meant to seem sexist. In fact, you will meet many dads throughout these pages who have partnered up with their wives to run successful enterprises from home. The anecdotes and information here are relevant to all parents who work from home!

YOU'RE ON YOUR WAY TO WORK-AT-HOME SUCCESS!

We're proud to give you a parents' home business guide you can truly call your own. Not only will we deliver the practical information you need, but we promise to provide the reassurance to venture forth and prosper. So turn the page and enter the wonderful—and profitable—work-at-home world.

1

Life as a Work-at-Home Mom

What's an average day in the life of a mompreneur really like? As writers, we create a work schedule at the beginning of each week and do our best to stick to it. Some days go very smoothly, and we actually accomplish most of what we set out to do, but other days turn out to be less than perfect. There's that call from the school nurse alerting us that one of our children has an earache and we have to come and get him right away. Or the contractor who is remodeling the bathroom knocks on the office door to say he has run out of tile and "Could you please drive to the tile store for another carton?" It seems that no two days are the same, which makes life as a mompreneur challenging but never boring.

The pace of your work-at-home routine will be set by the rhythm of your family and the type of business you're in. Take, for example, the contrasting work schedules of the two mompreneurs below.

Diana LeGere gets to her desk early so she can squeeze in some tasks while her three children are still sleeping. The Salt Lake City, Utah, mom runs an administrative support service called Executive Final Copy, which specializes in writing résumés and business-related documents for executives. After she gets her older children off to school, LeGere paces her work day around the needs of her youngest daughter, Amanda, working in spurts to make sure all her needs are met. "I take a couple of hours off to bathe and feed my little one, and then keep the phone close and check e-mail throughout the day," she says. But LeGere saves complicated projects for naptime and after Amanda is asleep for the night. "If I do need to be involved in a project while she's awake, I make sure she has a chance to rent her favorite movie or I take her somewhere special when I'm done." Amanda also has her own little desk so she can work beside her mom. "I love having her in my office with me—

whether it's for a hug or to help out!" LeGere says. And, she adds, "It's a good feeling to know that sometimes I can just close up shop and take Amanda to the park!"

Across the country in New York City, Andrea Disario begins her day like any other working mom. She races to get breakfast made, book bags packed, and her two boys ready for school. Three days a week, she's got to be out the door with them by 7:30, so she can drop off Michael, her oldest, at orchestra practice. Since Daniel's school doesn't start till 8, Mom takes him to Starbucks for a hot chocolate and special one-on-one time. She walks Daniel to school and then goes for a hike or jog around the Central Park Reservoir. By 9:30 she's hard at work—not in a high-rise office building, but in her Park Avenue apartment, where she runs her one-woman marketing consulting firm. She'll work nonstop till school lets out, when she picks up the kids and spends the rest of the afternoon shuttling them to extra-curricular activities. She takes along her cell phone and Palm Pilot so she can make productive use of her waiting time.

As you can see, these two mompreneurs lead very different work-at-home lives, yet the pleasures and challenges of their dual roles are the same. "I have balance in my life," says Disario, and I never have to miss a violin recital!

THE BEST OF BOTH WORLDS

Most mompreneurs wouldn't trade their lives for any other. Having a home business offers perks that are rare in the regular workforce—little things like the chance to meet the school bus or being there when your baby wakes up from his nap. Most women choose mompreneurship because it's the perfect balance between business and family life. But along with the best come some problems such as disruptive children, unexpected school closings, and equipment breakdowns with no on-site service availability. Every day you'll face tough work-at-home issues like staying motivated, disciplining yourself, battling isolation, separating work and family life, and struggling to be taken seriously by people who don't think you have a real job.

"Life is certainly more challenging now than it was in the traditional workforce," says Joan Grant-Gibbs, a New York City interior designer. Indeed, being a work-at-home mom requires some very special skills. In addition to being a business owner, you've also got to be part troubleshooter, part law-enforcer, part personal cheerleader, and part Mary Poppins.

In this chapter and throughout the book, we'll show you the different roles mompreneurs juggle and some of the strategies they've developed to keep themselves and their businesses going. Let's start by exploring what you'll need to qualify for the job.

Job Requirements

A Marketable Skill or Product

Can you offer something that other people will pay for? This can be a service like accounting, calligraphy, or personal shopping; or it could be a product such as a quilt, a secret sauce, or a dried flower arrangement. Like many mompreneurs, your home-based business could be related to previous job experience. For example, one mompreneur we met worked as a city planner before she formed a land-use consulting business. But it could also spring from a hobby or a longtime dream. "This was always a fantasy of mine," says Carol Guthrie, a former account executive, who started her landscape design business from a home office overlooking her garden in Darien, Connecticut.

If you're the inventive type, you might find that your children are the inspiration for a great product idea. When she was walking through a Dallas shopping mall with her preschooler and baby, Gail Frankel found she needed an extra pair of hands to hold her other son's drink. Instead of cloning herself, she invented the Stroll'r Hold'r, a device that clips onto the stroller bar and holds a cup and other loose objects. Now she has a booming juvenile products business.

There are many career opportunities for moms who want to work from home.

Self-Discipline

Since you won't have a boss looking over your shoulder, you must be able to work independently and stay focused despite distractions. That can be pretty hard to do when there are dishes in the sink or when you can hear that the baby's giving the sitter a hard time. Mompreneurs must learn to ignore household tasks and other time-zappers during business hours. "I give myself permission to have a sloppy house sometimes," says Kim Palmer, co-owner of a custom editorial and design firm in Minneapolis. Adds Karen LaBonte, a writer from Yorktown Heights, New York, "I say no to all the stuff that would suck up my work time and free time—like coffee klatches and church committees."

That's not to say that mompreneurs don't try to sneak in a little housework now and then. "I loved knowing that I could run a load of laundry while a job was printing out," says Marilyn Vaughn, a graphic designer and former work-at-home mom from New Hope, Pennsylvania. Susan Moores, a dietitian from St. Paul, Minnesota, enjoys the convenience of marinating the chicken she'll be grilling for dinner. But work-at-home moms have to be careful not

 like cleaning out the fridge or rearranging the closets.
 that if they want to turn a profit, they've got to be dili-
ng and protecting their work time. Throughout this book
elf-discipline secrets.

The Ability to Shift Gears Often

Adaptability is one of the keys to successful mompreneurship. When interruptions do occur, you'll need to get quickly back on track. We both found
it crucial to drop our nine-to-five mind-sets and learn to become comfortable working in spurts. It's quite common to work several short shifts a day,
rather than devoting eight straight hours to business projects. To gain flexibility, you have to be more flexible. This kind of arrangement requires constant switching back and forth between the roles of mommy and
professional.

A Solitary Work Style

Can you survive without the daily social interaction of colleagues? Working
at home can be lonely, so you'll need to have a self-directed personality
and a real love of toiling in solitude. Keep in mind that there are many
ways to combat the isolation. Scheduling lunches, phoning colleagues,
joining professional groups, chatting online, and networking with other
work-at-home moms are just a few ways you can stay connected to the outside world.

Good Organization Skills

It's important to plan your time well and establish a schedule that accommodates both your business and your children's needs. Otherwise, you could
find yourself struggling to finish a project on the morning you had set aside
for your Mommy and Me class, or you might be answering e-mails or taking
phone calls round-the-clock, another hazard of living where you work.

An Adequate Work Space

You'll need a place to do business, whether it's a small desk wedged into a
hallway or a separate room with a door. Which is preferable? It depends on
your line of work and the age of your kids. Diane Quinn, a quilter from

Springfield, Virginia, keeps her sewing machine in a corner of the family room so she can work while the kids watch TV. Lillian Vernon, the mail-order queen, got started on her kitchen table. If you have a job that requires lots of phone calling, concentration, and paperwork, you'll be better off with an office that's set apart from the main flow of the family, even if you have to share it with the washing machine and dryer.

Professionalism

No one's going to take you seriously if the *Sesame Street* theme song is playing in the background every time you answer a business call. You and your business must project a professional image. Separate phone lines, answering machines or voicemail systems, business cards, and letterhead are among the essentials you'll need to convince clients of your credibility. You'll also have to establish house rules and employ a few creative tricks to deter kids from interfering with the business.

"I was once on the phone with a big client when my two-year-old burst into my office, yelling, 'Mommy, I went potty!' " says Maureen LaMarca, a marketing consultant from Whitehouse Station, New Jersey. To discourage announcements of this sort, she began locking her office door and instructing her sitter to keep the kids out of her way when she was working. But since her office was on the main floor of the house, noise could still be a problem. "I stuffed towels underneath all the doors," she says, "so my clients wouldn't think I was running a day-care center."

MOMPRENEUR STATISTICS

What We Like Best About Working at Home

Seeing kids when I want to	31%
Flexibility	30%
Setting my own hours	19%
No commuting	9%
Being my own boss	4%

What We Like Least About Working at Home

Workday never ends	26%
Loneliness/isolation	24%
Distractions	16%
Lack of concentration	8%

MOMPRENEUR MYTHS AND FACTS

Mothers are usually first drawn to the world of mompreneurship by the romantic notion that they can rock the cradle and tend to business matters at the same time. If you're not prepared for the realities of work-at-home motherhood, you're sure to be disillusioned. It's important to know what you're getting into before you set up shop as a work-at-home mom. Here's a look at the myths and the facts.

> MYTH: You can have it all.
> FACT: You can't, but you can control what you have.

Freedom of choice is what mompreneurship is all about. You can decide which projects you take and when you're going to work on them. If you opt to work early mornings or late evenings, it's because you've chosen those times to work, not because some supervisor is telling you to do it. If you want to go on your son's class trip or need to run to the pediatrician's, you don't have to ask anyone's permission. "I needed more control over my personal life," says an entertainment marketing consultant in Westchester, New York, who's paired rock stars like Michael Jackson and Tina Turner with corporate advertisers. "I don't want to be forced to do things I don't want to do. With my business, I get to pick my projects."

The benefit of mompreneurship is that you can design your business around your family needs. You can scale back or increase your working hours as necessary. Many of the mompreneurs tell us that they work untraditional and sometimes erratic hours, but all agree that the trade-off is worth the chance to spend more time with their kids.

Be careful not to fall into the superwoman trap, thinking that you can work late nights every night. Just as you can't have it all, you can't do it all, either. Being superwoman might sound achievable before you have kids, but once you become a mom, your superwoman capabilities fly out the window.

> MYTH: You'll work while the kids play quietly at your feet.
> FACT: You're likely to need child care.

If you've got the kind of business that involves phone calls, intense concentration, tight deadlines, frequent meetings, or lots of client interaction, plan to get yourself some kind of child care, especially if your children are not yet in school. You'll get more done and you won't risk ignoring or snapping at your kids because you've got a project to finish. "I worked at home for several months after my first child was born," says Mary Williams, a network marketer in Lynwood, Washington. "After about three days, it became obvious I needed help or I wasn't going to get anything done." She lined up a teen sitter to come to her home a few hours a day, and it helped boost her business and her credibility. "I could tell people I'd call them at a certain time and be able to keep my promise," she says.

The majority of the mompreneurs we talked to told us they couldn't get by without some form of child care. Most of them count on school and part-time sitters to occupy their kids while they work, though some opt for house-keepers, live-in nannies, and au pairs. However, a good number of our research participants survive with no child care at all. "It's difficult a lot of times," says Cecille Hansen, a desktop publisher in Burbank, California, "but I always have to go back to the reason why I'm working at home—it's because of my daughter. She's my priority right now, at least until she starts school. Then I'll put more time into the business."

MYTH: **Your kids will be able to see you whenever they want.**
FACT: **You'll need to teach them to respect Mommy's work hours.**

Don't expect that you can work whenever you feel like it. It's necessary to establish regular business hours and then make sure your family honors your work time. It can be hard for children to understand that Mommy's home but not available to play with them. If you're firm and consistent from the start, they'll get the message. "I let my family and sitter know that unless it's life or death, I'm not to be disturbed while working," says writer Karen LaBonte.

A regular work routine has multiple benefits. First, it's easier to plan and complete your work tasks if you've allotted a certain amount of time for them every week. You can also help to prevent the problem of over-scheduling, because you're keeping your work time carefully regulated. And for those dry times when you need to drum up new business, having a work schedule gives you the opportunity to do effective marketing. Best of all, a regular work routine helps set boundaries between business and family life so you can block out the time you want to spend with your children and keep it separate and sacred.

MYTH: **You'll have so many household distractions that you'll never get any work done.**
FACT: **You'll be more productive than ever.**

It's amazing what you can fit into your life when you're a mompreneur. On any given day, you might find yourself packing lunch boxes; driving car pools; making twenty business calls; dropping off a work assignment; picking up a sick kid from school; squeezing in five more calls while the sick kid sleeps; dispensing Pedialyte to the sick kid, who has now thrown up all over the bed; and putting all those soiled sheets into the wash, while negotiating a new business assignment from your laundry room via your cordless phone. Mompreneurs are masters of making every second count. Besides, think of all the time you're actually saving by working at home. No longer will you have to fritter away precious moments commuting to your job, dealing with office politics, or attending annoying spur-of-the-moment meetings.

MYTH: You can make a full-time salary on part-time hours.
FACT: Your earning power depends on your type of business and how much time you can spend on it.

Many mompreneurs find that working at home is more lucrative than jobs they held in the traditional workforce. For example, women in fields such as law, marketing, advertising, computer consulting, and public relations have told us that they can often make as much or more per hour than they did before. However, you can't always expect to scale back your hours and still generate a full-time income. "Be realistic about how much time you'll be able to devote to your business and gauge your earning power against your priorities," notes Beverly Williams, founder of the American Association of Home Based Businesses. "Ask yourself the question, 'Why do I want to be home-based?' When the answer is 'Because I want to spend more time with my children,' that should be your priority rather than the amount of dollars you'll bring in," she says.

No matter what you earn, keep in mind that paychecks are bound to be erratic and that your income may fluctuate. You could make a bundle of money one month, then go several months more before you have additional cash flowing in. It's also important to factor in the overhead costs of your business. Yes, you'll be saving money on clothing and commuting costs, but you'll also be spending on start-up costs, insurance premiums, and other business expenses.

Even so, the beauty of mompreneurship is that you can control how much you make by the amount of work you pursue. You may cut back on business hours and projects when your kids are babies and then step up your efforts (and your billings) as they reach school age. Although you may not match a full-time salary at the beginning, you can catch up eventually. As time goes on, you may even find that it is possible to earn more and work less.

FINANCIAL PROS AND CONS OF WORKING AT HOME

FINANCIAL GAINS	FINANCIAL DRAWBACKS
Determining your own wages	Sporadic paychecks
No more worries about corporate downsizing	No more prepaid insurance plans

You save on commuting and clothing costs	You've got to lay out start-up money and overhead expenses
You can write off many of your business expenses	You have to pay business taxes

MYTH: You'll never have to leave the house.
FACT: Home-based shouldn't mean house-bound.

You might have the type of business that requires you to do the bulk of your work at other locations. For instance, we know a laboratory consultant who has her office at home but spends much of her work time in labs. She always makes sure she's home by three, however, so she can welcome her daughter from school and be available to help her with homework.

Even if every aspect of your business can be done from home, it's essential to get out regularly to promote yourself and network. Joining organizations, attending conferences, scheduling personal meetings with clients, and fraternizing with other work-at-home moms will help boost your professional image along with your self-esteem.

MOMPRENEUR PROS AND CONS

PERKS	PITFALLS
You get to be your own boss	You have bossy children in your workplace
No commuting	No transition time between work mode and Mommy mode
You can plan your work around your family's schedule	Work can monopolize family time if you're not careful
No more office politics	No more water cooler/coffee machine camaraderie
You rarely have to wear power suits, panty hose, or heels	Sweatpants and sneakers can quickly lose their appeal
The Internet links you to the business world without leaving home	Sometimes you don't leave home for days

have to ask ...o stay home with a sick child	It's harder to give yourself a sick day when you need it
With your office at home, you can be there for your kids when you need to	The kids know you're in the house, so they need you all the time
You can attend daytime school events	Other moms think you're a snob because you're always racing back to your desk
You don't have to deal with memos or useless meetings	You do have to put up with distractions from kids, neighbors, repair people, and telephone solicitors
You've found a way to successfully combine work and family life	Sometimes it seems that you're the only one who notices

SUCCESS SECRETS

How do mompreneurs keep going day after day, through paint jobs and play dates, sickness and snowstorms? According to the hundreds of work-at-home moms we talked to, it comes down to these four simple strategies.

Confidence

You must believe in yourself and cultivate an "I can do it" attitude. Since you'll be working in isolation a lot of the time, you've got to become your own cheering squad. Always remind yourself of your successes, especially on those impossible days when nothing seems to be going right. "I tell myself, 'You're talented, you've got a great track record, and you're doing a great service to your children,' " says Andrea Disario.

It's also important to share your accomplishments with your family and your clients. Confidence is contagious: When you have it, you'll pass it along to everyone around you. Clients will feel comfortable leaving their business in your hands, and family members will be supportive and proud of your achievements.

Persistence

Once you believe you can do it, you've got to stick with it. Persistence is an incredible power, and it's what you need to relentlessly pursue hot leads, land new business, negotiate fair fees, and endure through the tough times. "Never take no for an answer," advises mompreneur Constance Hallinan Lagan. "I cannot tell you how many times I've won contracts because I've politely followed up, again and again." Just don't give up, she stresses. There will be times you'll feel like packing it in, but motivation and determination will help you keep going, she says.

Flexibility

Every mompreneur knows that even the best-planned routines fall apart once in a while. It's usually on those days when you've got a big presentation to finish that your child wakes up with the flu. That's why a roll-with-the-punches outlook and a reliable back-up plan is essential. "I know to expect setbacks now, because I've been doing this for years," says Andrea Disario. "I look at it as crisis management." When one of her kids gets sick, she automatically shifts into damage control mode and somehow always manages to find a way to get the work done. "I consider my family my other main client, and when they're barking, I have to tend to them. That really calms me down," Disario says.

Humor

When you put work and kids under the same roof, madcap yet maddening events can occur. A little laughter will go a long way in diffusing potentially stressful situations. Let's face it, funny things like these just don't happen in a traditional office setting. Take, for example, the day Pat's toddler Matt flushed two pages of a client's proposal down the toilet. Or how about the time the sitter canceled and Ellen attempted to conduct an important phone interview with two-year-old Amy around? The child ran off with her pen and notepad and then managed to disconnect the telephone mike. Ellen only discovered this crushing fact later when she attempted to transcribe the tape and heard thirty minutes of complete silence.

Julie Pophal can now laugh about the time her kids conducted some kitchen-floor chemistry experiments while she was downstairs updating business records for her transcription service. "The kids at the time were upstairs watching a favorite movie and playing Little Red Riding Hood," explains the Madison, Wisconsin, mom. "I didn't hear any yelling or screaming, just a lot of excited oohs and aahs. Well, when I went upstairs, I was shocked to see a whole gallon of milk and a whole quart of orange juice dumped on the kitchen and hall floors, along with a small container of pudding mixed in for good measure. They had a small wooden car in the middle of this mixture and were truly enjoying themselves. I was horrified as I saw this glop of ooze next to the floorboards and seeping underneath a little bit. Also, it was completely under the refrigerator. What a mess! I spent the next hour cleaning it up—an hour I didn't have. Now I know why magazines recommend hiring a baby-sitter when you're doing your work and not being attentive to your kids."

MOMPRENEURS' TEN COMMANDMENTS

1. Set a work schedule and stick to it.

2. Just say no to all trivial things that threaten to invade your work and family time.

3. Stay away from the fridge.

4. Remain calm when setbacks occur. You will survive them.

5. Don't make a habit of working weekends.

6. Allow yourself to play hookey once in a while. At the very least, plan some personal time into your schedule—get a manicure, have lunch with a friend, or go to an exercise class.

7. Keep your answering machine on during nonbusiness hours.

8. Network, network, network.

9. Make sure you're charging enough for your services. You're worth it.

10. Don't give up. (And don't get discouraged when you occasionally break these commandments. We've all done it.)

MOMPRENEUR® HALL OF FAME

DEBBI FIELDS
Founder, President, and CEO of Mrs. Fields Cookies, Inc., Park City, Utah
Mother of Five

Many big businesses start out on the kitchen table, then eventually outgrow the home setting. Debbi Fields has a completely different recipe for success. She began outside her home, opening her first retail store in 1977. The bigger her company and her family grew, the more she found herself wanting to run things from her home base. Today, the cookie queen rules her multimillion-dollar empire from a home office right off her kitchen, just twenty minutes away from the corporate headquarters in Park City, Utah. This setup allows her to tend to business and the needs of her daughters. Working from home "gives me the chance to be home and be a mom, and yet at the same time take advantage of my kitchen and create new products," Fields says.

How does she do it? "Technology is the key," she says. Her phone and computer lines are all connected to the corporate headquarters, and she can talk to her employees via intercom whenever she needs to. "Even though I'm not there, people feel like I am," says Fields. Organization is also essential. Fields rises by 5:30 every morning to get a half-hour jump on her kids before they wake up for school. "If I don't get ahead of them, it's a nightmare," she says. While they're still sleeping, she clicks on her computer and in minutes downloads information on her 700-plus stores nationwide and overseas. As the kids get dressed, she exercises and reviews the data. Next, Fields makes breakfast and gets the kids off to school. "They're out of here by 7, and then my day begins," she says.

When the kids are home, Fields keeps them very involved in product development. Her junior taste-testers rate new recipes with a thumbs-up or a thumbs-down. "It's a very positive thing," she says. "They understand what I do and they feel like they're very much part of my life." When she can, she brings the kids with her on business trips. Fields once took her youngest daughter, McKenzie, to the taping of her dessert show. "She just loved it," Fields says. "But then I had to go out and buy her inordinate amounts of Play-Doh so she could go into the kitchen and make her own products, too." If taking the children on the road is impossible, Fields says she drops them off for a night or two with a sitter "who's like a grandma to us."

Working with kids around takes loads of patience, Fields cautions. "Your children are going to ask you to stop in the middle of something, and you are going to be taken away from your focus. Just expect that, and let the kids have their time when you can. If you can't be interrupted right then, let them know that you'll be there in twenty minutes and that you'll give them a solid thirty minutes of uninterrupted time," she advises. Make sure you enjoy the work you do, Fields adds. "I absolutely love creating products. To me it is not work, it is just plain fun. It's a wonderful balance to be able to do something you love and be near your kids."

2

Career Opportunities and Job Options

While some mothers consciously make the decision to start a home business, others find themselves doing it unintentionally. That was the case with both of us. When our first babies were born, we both took maternity leaves from our magazine jobs, with the feeling that we might return to full-time office jobs. Once we were home with our newborns, the nine-to-five corporate world started to seem less appealing. Full-time motherhood was not an entirely attractive option either; we still wanted the personal satisfaction and financial security of working. Freelance writing from home seemed like the perfect compromise.

We must admit we were scared at first. What if we got no work? What if we couldn't make more money than we were paying out in baby-sitting? What if we couldn't juggle the dual demands of motherhood and writing assignments? What if we missed the stimulation of the office? Through the years, at one time or another, all of these what-ifs happened. With a little ingenuity, a bit of good luck, and supportive husbands and children, we found ways to get past the what-ifs. In the long run, the positives have largely outweighed the negatives, and our decision turned out to be the right one for ourselves and our families. Most surprisingly, we no longer see mompreneurship as a temporary measure lasting only until we feel ready to reenter the corporate environment. It's simply another career move in our lives, one that can possibly lead to bigger and better things.

MAKING THE TRANSITION

Fear. No steady paycheck. A detour off the corporate ladder. Lack of motivation. Loneliness. These are the thoughts that go through many a working mother's head before she decides to take the plunge into mompreneurship. Even those who see their home business as a unique opportunity to fulfill a lifelong dream can have anxiety attacks and periods of self-doubt. While this sudden independence can be downright scary, it's something women are adept at handling. "Women are natural free agents," says Carole Hyatt, author of *Shifting Gears: How to Master Career Change and Find Work That's Right for You.* "They've always had to be flexible, juggling the personal and professional, going from career to parenthood and back again."

Does this sound like you? Before you hand in your resignation at your current job or spend thousands on state-of-the-art equipment, it might be wise to evaluate your strengths and weaknesses. To see how you stack up as a potential home business owner, check off the statements that apply to you:

- ✓ I'm well-organized.
- ✓ I can get things done in a chaotic environment.
- ✓ I don't hesitate to make decisions.
- ✓ I'm willing to lose money or break even for a while.
- ✓ I'm an independent kind of person.
- ✓ I'm not afraid of criticism and rejection.
- ✓ I don't worry too much about what the next day will bring.
- ✓ I have a good deal of patience and perseverance.
- ✓ I'm well-disciplined.
- ✓ I'm self-motivated and determined.
- ✓ I can usually come up with more than one solution to a problem.
- ✓ I have enough confidence in my expertise and ideas to sell myself and my product or service.
- ✓ I'm always willing to learn and branch out.

Don't be surprised if you checked off many of these statements. Everyday mothering demands that you possess most of these personality traits and hone these same skills just to survive the rigors of child-rearing. Just think about it. Any stay-at-home mom must know how to plan and structure her time, be flexible and roll with the punches, have a good deal of patience, juggle lots of balls at once, form her own buddy system or network, and appreciate the unexpected. That's why mothers make such good home-based entrepreneurs.

Motherhood can prepare you well for running a business, but there are a couple of other things to consider. According to Paul and Sarah Edwards, home business authors and recognized self-employment experts, the two most essential characteristics for success are a strong desire for a different lifestyle and the willingness to learn what you need to achieve it. We think perseverance is another necessary trait, especially when things get off to a slow start or suddenly come to a standstill. Not being afraid of hard work is important, too.

BEST HOME BUSINESS OPPORTUNITIES FOR MOMS

While there are many kinds of businesses that can be run successfully from home, some seem to be much better-suited to mothers. Through our research, survey results, and extensive interviews with mompreneurs, we've divided these mom-friendly businesses into general categories, listing more specific types of jobs under each. Although the traditional cottage industries of the past are still popular among mothers, they're losing ground to more service-oriented businesses.

Communications

Freelance writer and/or editor for magazines, newspapers, websites, book publishers, corporations, nonprofit organizations, and public relations and advertising agencies; publicist; desktop publisher; scriptwriter for film and TV; studio story editor; media trainer; book packager; indexer; teleconference coordinator.

Office Support/Secretarial Services

Word processor, medical transcriptionist, medical claims assistant, virtual assistant, scopist (court transcript editor), printer (stationery, business cards, brochures, etc.), clipping service, translator, proofreader, database manager.

Art

Graphic designer, website designer, calligrapher, photographer, video/TV/film producer, illustrator, fashion designer, teacher.

Education/Child Care

Tutor, child-care/day-care provider, nanny referral service, psychological tester, college admissions consultant, summer program/homeschooling advisor, coordinator of gifted and talented enrichment program, special education advocate, researcher, textbook writer.

Law

Attorney specializing in real estate, tax, trusts and estates, contracts, immigration, corporate law, probate, intellectual property, and other nontrial work; mediator in divorce/custody cases and other disputes.

Health

Physician, dentist, orthodontist, chiropractor, childbirth educator, elder care coordinator, home health care/nursing agency, aromatherapist, fitness instructor.

Financial Services

Bookkeeper, tax advisor, accountant, bill collector, auditor, investment counselor/stockbroker, estate planner, insurance underwriter or agent.

Computers

Software creator, system designer/analyst, troubleshooter/repair person for individual and corporate clients, programmer, data processor, tutor/trainer for adults and children, web host, website developer.

Human Resources

Employment counselor, career coach, headhunter, temporary help agency, work options consultant (negotiator for flextime, part-time, telecommuting, child care/elder care, etc.).

Management Consultant

Marketing and promotion expert, market researcher, management/sales trainer, corporate coach, spokesperson, seminar organizer and promoter, supervisor of think tank.

Sales/Manufacturing

Mail-order/catalog sales, direct sales, manufacturer's rep, importer-exporter, web retailer, e-commerce consultant, consignment sales.

Therapy

Speech and language pathologist, physical therapist, occupational therapist, music therapist, social worker/psychotherapist, clinical psychologist, diagnostic tester.

Food/Nutrition

Caterer, recipe developer, baker, dietitian, personal chef, cooking teacher, cookbook author, custom cake creator, inventor and/or marketer of specialty food product.

Entertainment

Talent scout/agent, children's party planner/performer (clown, magician, puppeteer, etc.), musician, tape/CD producer.

Home Improvement

Architect, interior decorator, landscape designer, urban planner, custom window treatment designer, upholsterer, furniture refinisher, stencil painter, organizer/efficiency expert, contractor referral service, real estate agent.

Party/Event Planning

Coordinator of services for weddings, bar/bat mitzvahs, reunions, conferences, trade shows, conventions, and charity events; invitation service; decorations (flower arrangements, balloons, table appointments); band/DJ agent; fund-raiser.

Personal Services

Masseuse, hair stylist/colorist, manicurist, makeup artist, facials, electrolysis/leg waxing, personal trainer, image consultant, personal shopper/errand runner, pet care (training, grooming, walking, sitting), maid/cleaning service, chaffeuring/car pool service, baby-sitting service, travel agent, corporate gift service/gift basket creator, tag sale coordinator, professional organizer, corporate concierge.

Crafts/Sewing

Quilter, potter, knitter, costume/uniform maker, custom dressmaker, jewelry maker, silk-screener, furniture maker, personalized clothing/gifts, fabric artist, weaver, baby products, soapmaker, candlemaker.

MOMPRENEUR STATISTIC

Is your business related to previous work done outside home?
Yes   72%
No   28%

BRINGING YOUR SKILLS HOME

If you've enjoyed your work and wish to continue in the same field, the most obvious option is to take your career home. Almost three-quarters of the mompreneurs we surveyed started a business related to their past job experience and skills. The paths that seem to meander rather easily to the home office setting are public relations, advertising, marketing, writing and editing, social work/therapy, graphic design, architecture, secretarial services, website development, interior decoration, dietetics, and accounting. Women working in these areas usually have a solid network of contacts that acts as a kind of safety net. Just one referral, plus an initial investment in some office equipment, can get the business off the ground fairly quickly.

Andrea Disario, with thirteen years as a public relations executive and magazine writer under her belt, had the background and connections to set up her own business at home when her first child was born. She outfitted her office, which is off the dining room of her home, with a computer, fax, and extra telephone line. Then she spread the word about her one-woman marketing communications agency throughout her personal and professional network. She secured one client, then another. "With a bit of luck and lots of hard work, I was soon creating and executing marketing communications programs for some of the biggest names in the tabletop industry," reports Disario. "I have also done projects for Liz Claiborne Shoes and Braun Personal Care products and was even asked to have my children pose for press photos for Parker Brothers toys." Now that both her boys are in school full-time, Disario can enlarge her client base and possibly expand her one-woman shop by hiring others.

Journalist Julie Zander found a clever way to take her researching and interviewing skills, along with her years of experience editing her newspaper's obituary column, in a completely new direction. This mom of two from Washington State is now a personal historian and runs a business called Chapters of Life Memory Books. In an effort to preserve family heritage, she helps individuals write their memoirs and record their oral histories on audio tape. Then she transcribes and edits the information and publishes it in a personalized hard-bound keepsake book. "When I edited obituaries for the newspaper, I often found myself turning to co-workers and saying, 'This person's life would make a wonderful story,'" Zander recalls. "I decided I want to help families capture those stories in book form before their loved ones die. It's the best legacy anyone can leave to future generations."

HOME-BASED SHOPS

Other types of expertise may need a bit more creativity to translate into a home-based business. What if you've always worked in retailing? Should you set up a store in your home?

Betsy Bober Polivy and Jane Gelbard found a more innovative (and legal) way to capitalize on their retail experience at home. For nine years, these two women owned a successful children's book store in New Rochelle, New York, called Once Upon a Time. They worked there through their children's infancies and early childhood years, but the long hours and pressures of juggling work and family finally got to be too much. "Instead of running my business, I found that my business ran my life," says Gelbard. So the partners gave up the store and started a book-related business in Polivy's basement. Still using their trademarked "Once Upon a Time," name and logo, they developed a multifaceted company that markets baby gift baskets of books for new parents, organizes book fairs for schools and religious institutions, and arranges author and illustrator visits to schools for signings and special programs. Through word of mouth, a little advertising, and direct mail, their customer base has grown to include corporations, nursery and elementary schools, synagogues, and many personal friends who are all out there rooting for them. They don't want that audience to get overwhelming, however. "I know this might sound crazy," says Polivy, "but I am not looking to have our business grow too much more. I need to work, but I love being at home and I never want it [the business] to take me away from my family again. This is perfect."

Direct sales is perhaps a more natural outgrowth of a career in retailing. In fact, some of America's best-known direct sales giants are major employers of mothers. Companies such as Discovery Toys, Tupperware, Avon, Amway, Mary Kay Cosmetics, Rexall Drugs, and Longaberger Baskets have long been hospitable to the flexible work schedules many mothers desire. More recently, the fashion industry has staged a rapid expansion into home-based sales, providing busy women a quick, stylish, and more relaxing alternative to shopping at the mall. The Carlisle Collection, The Worth Collection, and The Hanson Collection have been leaders in this area, offering mothers with a fashion sense and love of clothes a great chance to build a career in sales.

According to Linda Karesh, a sales consultant with The Worth Collection, "Companies like ours are providing solutions—we are making it possible for women to operate substantial businesses out of their homes and also have quality family life." Lynn Heritage, a sales consultant with Mary Kay Cosmetics, adds that mothers can make executive-level salaries in her field. Special skills are usually not necessary to enter direct sales, and most of the companies provide training sessions and/or kits prior to beginning. If you already have some retail experience, you may have a jump-start in this area.

CLASS ACTS

Teaching is another field that may seem difficult to bring home. Tutoring, giving art and music lessons, or preparing students for college boards have typically been money-making home-based opportunities for former educators, but some of the mompreneurs in our survey have forged ahead in different directions, building nontraditional businesses that generate more sizable incomes.

Barbara Dershowitz is a former high school English teacher who decided to try something different soon after her son was born. "Although I wouldn't trade motherhood for anything, by the time Adam was three months old, my brain had turned to spaghetti," she remembers. "I told my brother-in-law over dinner one night that if I wasn't going back to teaching in September, I would want to be a corporate communications consultant. I knew what was coming out of high school, what was graduating college, and I knew that, while these students might be brilliant, nobody was teaching them how to communicate effectively for business." Her brother-in-law answered, "You've saved enough money to see you through. Why don't you put a program together?" That encouragement was all it took. Using her curriculum expertise and mastery of the English language, Dershowitz composed a full-day corporate communication seminar called "The Business Communications Workshop." The seminar covered written communication skills for executives, including those all-important reports, letters, and memos.

Dershowitz's next task was to sell her idea to the corporate world. "With the baby literally at my breast, I sat at our dining room table with the Yellow Pages and called large companies," she relates. "I promised myself I would make twenty cold calls a day, and, of course, I got better at it as time passed. After making my twentieth call one day and receiving twenty rejections, I decided to make a twenty-first call and was asked by the large insurance company on the other end to come in and present." Dershowitz's business built slowly from there.

Today, Dershowitz still conducts her seminar but has diverged into several other directions. She now hosts a weekly public service radio show, writes a regular motivational column called "To Your Success" in a women's newsletter, produces written materials for corporations, and publishes her own books. With her typical boundless energy, she is constantly exploring new avenues, such as working toward her FCC operator's license.

Former teachers Dana Dahm and Tabatha Horstman harnessed their experience, desire to stay home with their kids, and entrepreneurial spirit to start a craft kit company called *TaDa*. "We were both looking to keep our preschoolers busy in the afternoon and came up with the idea of a color-themed craft activity for each day of the week, complete with a literature tie-in," says Dahm. When other parents saw what they were doing, they offered to pay the two moms to put together activity packets for them, and "Do-Ables" were born. Dahm and Horstman now offer many more Do-Ables themes and have since extended their line to include "Cut-Ables" and "Read-Ables." Through their presentations to various groups ("How to Enrich Your Child's Mind Without Losing Yours" is particularly popular!), other moms began expressing an interest in selling the kits, so the partners formed *TaDa Certified Consultants*. Each consultant gets a starter package with a presentation outline and a large selection of craft kits for her buy-in fee.

Other teachers have capitalized on their creativity and experience with children in slightly different ways. They've developed educational flash cards, software, and other materials; become children's party entertainers; started summer camp placement services; organized teen tours; developed outreach programs to take to schools; and set up after-school courses in their homes for gifted and

talented students. More recent at-home careers include online tutoring, and curriculum and course development policy consulting. In the near future, there
might be even more call for home education entrepreneurs. Gerald Celente,
director of the Trends Research Institute in Rhinebeck, New York, predicts that
the growing work-at-home trend will give rise to an upswing in homeschooling, a phenomenon that should reach one million families by the year 2005.

CONVERT YOUR SKILLS

How easily can you make the transition from working outside to inside
the home? See how these twelve home-based businesses were started by
moms who brought their job skills directly home:

FORMER JOB	CURRENT HOME-BASED BUSINESS
Social worker in a school for troubled youth	Private therapist for adolescents
Test kitchen director for large food company	Freelance recipe developer for cookbook publishers, magazines, and food companies
Associate with large law firm	Attorney specializing in immigration law
Pastry chef at restaurant	Custom cake baking/decorating
Registered nurse	Childbirth educator
Advertising executive	Direct marketing/market research
Human Resources director	Temporary employment agency/career counselor
Sales manager for clothing manufacturer	Manufacturers' rep for several hosiery companies
TV producer	Creator of children's videos/programming consultant
Conference/trade show coordinator	Special events planner
CPA	Freelance accountant/income tax preparer
Computer programmer	Website developer

Refining Your Résumé

Some of the mompreneurs who started businesses based on their past work experience had to update their skills and/or equipment in order to succeed. This was true of Eileen Crespin, a fine artist and designer who branched out into computer graphics. Although sales of her artwork had always added to the family funds, Crespin knew that income wouldn't be enough for herself and her three daughters when she got divorced. A long job hunt turned up nothing that would be worth it after child-care costs were covered. While looking for outside work, Crespin did discover a strong demand for computer graphics artists in the advertising business, so she decided to freelance from home.

Crespin was able to upgrade her computer with a $500 loan from ACCION of New Mexico, a nonprofit lending organization that makes loans to small businesses, many of which are home-based. She used the ACCION money to purchase additional memory capacity to accommodate the big drawing programs required in her work. Then she invested her own time in learning how to use the software. In the end, it was well worth it. "For me, this arrangement was great," says Crespin. "I was able to run my computer graphic design business without giving up my pastel painting, and I could provide a stable home environment for my children."

Julia Bayar, an interior designer and mother of three, had also studied art but felt she needed more specific training to become a self-employed designer. "I really didn't become interested in interior design until I owned my own cooperative apartment and was asked by some of my neighbors to help with their design problems," relates Bayar. "I then decided to try a few courses at Parsons School of Design to see if I liked it enough to start a business. I loved it."

That educational boost gave Bayar the know-how and courage to set up her own interior design company, which she subsequently moved to a room in her suburban home that used to be a second kitchen. She does both residential and commercial work and is often called upon to design apartment and hotel lobbies. One of her most enjoyable ventures is designing whimsical children's furniture, which is proudly tested by her own kids before getting a stamp of approval. The best part of Bayar's business? "I get to use my own home as a showroom."

A Shift in Direction

What about the almost 30 percent of mompreneurs in our survey who branched out into uncharted territory? For many, motherhood brought the chance to change their work style and realize a longtime dream. Carol

Guthrie, who previously worked in advertising, is a good example. "It was always a fantasy of mine that I might actually do something professionally that combined my love for and talent in architecture, drawing, and gardening," says this Connecticut mother. "When I had the luxury of staying home with my second child, I was able to spend time in my garden, which in time, became quite beautiful. People noticed and asked me to help with their gardens, and it snowballed." Once her home-based business looked promising, Guthrie went for additional training at the New York Botanical Garden, which gave her the knowledge and confidence to keep pursuing her dream and literally watch it grow into a lucrative business.

Eileen Lichtenstein was also able to land a dream job at home. This mother of two had experience teaching school and working in an office, but always had a love for and interest in dance. Once her daughters were both in nursery school, she opened Eileen's Dance and Exercise Studio in her home. "Before I started my business, the thing that saved my sanity was taking a daily class at the local dancing school, nursing baby in tow," says Lichtenstein. "There I learned the stress-release technique of progressive muscle relaxation that helped me maintain my equilibrium and relieve frustration. When I work with young mothers now in my Moving Meditation™ sessions, this technique is always a big hit."

In addition to stress management, Lichtenstein offers Rhythm-Robics™ and other fitness/dance classes, as well as one-on-one instruction. Because the classes are geared to the mind/body needs of mothers and baby-sitting is provided, Eileen's Dance and Exercise Studio is a popular place. "I vowed to provide child care in whatever business I ventured into," remembers Lichtenstein, "so it was a priority when I opened the studio. As a bonus, the wonderful lady who baby-sat my preschool children while I took the class years ago enrolled in my senior Moving Meditation classes."

Filling a Niche

Fitness was the focus of Nancy Coleman's home business, too, until her baby's drooling launched her into a totally unrelated field. It started when son Davis's pediatrician advised his mom to keep her boy's chest dry to avoid a lot of colds and bronchial infections. The traditional bib, which Coleman hoped would solve the problem, soon proved to be no solution at all. "When I put the bib around Davis's neck, he made a face and pulled at it," she says. "I didn't blame him. It has no style and is stiff and uncomfortable." Searching for an alternate solution and finding none, Coleman invented and hand-sewed one of her own. Called Cool Drool,™ it's a miniature version of the classic cotton bandanna scarf—a fashionable, comfortable, and convenient alternative that was a hit with babies and their parents alike.

To market her invention, Coleman created a mail-order company called

The Coleman Collection. "Knowing nothing about manufacturing a product, I proceeded to teach myself the business, acquire an 800 number, find a manufacturer, and put together a hang tag, brochure, and accounting system," says Coleman. "Since then, every day has been a challenge." Although Cool Drool took off, Coleman kept up with her exercise studio. The body work gave this California mompreneur some much-needed stress reduction on those days she felt especially overwhelmed by the strains of success.

OUT OF THE MOUTHS OF BABES

Motherhood has sparked the idea for a number of other home businesses. Give an imaginative, energetic woman a child or two, and she begins to think of a product or service that can enrich family life. In our survey, we heard from mompreneurs who created baby equipment, room accessories, toys, games, sports gear, clothing, computer software, music tapes/CDs, and other child-oriented products because there was nothing like it on the market. All these women have a hands-on working knowledge of their audience—one of the keys to building a successful business.

There were also those who saw that a particular service could really meet the needs of parents or children. Marguerite Tirelli is one such mompreneur. She noticed a void in the marketplace, came up with a good idea, and ran with it. With three young children of her own, Tirelli knew how exhausting those postpartum days can be for parents of newborns, and she wanted to share the coping skills she had acquired as a mother with other mothers. So she started Beyond Birth, a service that helps new moms and dads become human again. In many of the developed countries of the world, this nurturing tradition has been around for centuries. Women known as doulas are hired to help new mothers recuperate from labor and delivery and guide them through nursing, diapering, bathing, and other baby care basics.

Tirelli and her partner, Julietta Ackerman, thought American women were ready for this same kind of service—and more. "Ask anyone who's given birth," says Tirelli; "you don't need that extra set of baby booties or a sterling silver comb and brush set. What you really need is someone to get the groceries, wash the clothes, tidy the house, fix dinner, and hold the baby so you can take a shower or spend a little time with your older kids." Now that insurance companies are forcing hospitals to shorten overnight stays, new moms need postpartum services more than ever.

Beyond Birth has a staff of college-educated, fully insured professionals with varied backgrounds who are trained to handle CPR, infant emergencies, newborn care, and assistance with breast-feeding. The doula concept has really caught on as a substitute for the extended family of the past. Even if Grandma or another relative lives close by, she often has a job or interests of her own that make her unavailable to lend a hand. For many new mothers, an objective, calm, nonrelated helper is considerably less stressful than a relative.

The partners in Beyond Birth have backgrounds that have proven especially complementary. Tirelli formerly worked in marketing on Wall Street and in elementary education; she takes care of the scheduling and business side of the service. Ackerman has a master's in public health and is a certified childbirth instructor, giving her the expertise to train the doulas. Together, they have watched their business grow and prosper, as new parents continue to swell the birth rate and more and more mothers and health professionals realize the benefits of postpartum care.

Other service-oriented businesses are benefiting from this mini baby boom, too, often in some nontraditional ways. Enterprising moms have started child transporting businesses for working parents who can't carpool their kids to after-school activities; child safety inspection services find the danger spots in homes and suggest baby-proofing solutions; kids' birthday party businesses provide everything from invitations to entertainment to favors for rushed parents; and there are music and movement classes for tots.

JUMPING ON A TREND

Trends may come and go (think Beanie Babies!), but certain ideas and the markets they target stick around for more than enough time to spawn a lucrative, long-term business. (See "A Look Into the Crystal Ball," page 38.) While surfing the web, Melanie Westmoreland of Chattanooga, Tennessee, discovered many sites dedicated to parties and personalized products. The former accountant figured she could combine the two into a successful home business, and Candesigns was launched. Westmoreland began by purchasing candy and other products through wholesale outlets and creating personalized wrappers to enclose the goodies. Her edible favors were a hit at baby showers, fund-raisers, children's birthday parties, business meetings, and other events. Brides and grooms were particularly taken with Westmoreland's personalized wine labels, which add a special touch to a wedding reception. "Since baby announcements are a very large seller, I market my wrapper brochures or leave postcards at ob-gyn offices, birthing centers, and baby fairs," says Westmoreland. The mother of two boys has since developed a website to showcase her creations and sell her design templates (www.candy wrapperdesigns.com).

As a mom of three and the daughter of aging parents, Cindy Plawner knew firsthand what it was like to be part of the "sandwich generation," but she never realized her demographics would lead to a new business! Plawner was having lunch in a restaurant with her future partner, Elise Waxman, when the two noticed an elderly couple at the next table. The woman was having a bit of trouble keeping her napkin tucked into her collar, and all of a sudden, a "lightbulb" went off in Plawner's head: Why not create a napkin that will stay put? A short time later, Plawner came up with Gourmet Guard™—a soft, absorbent disposable napkin with a self-adhesive strip attached to its leakproof back. "It's better than a napkin . . . it sticks," is the product's slogan, and it's now being used in nursing homes, hospitals, and assisted-living facilities as well as by home health care workers. While word-of-mouth advertising has expanded the business, Plawner and Waxman are making a big effort to reach a larger population through supermarkets and websites featuring merchandise for senior citizens.

When you're talking about a business that delivers home-cooked dinners to your door five nights a week, your customers can range from harried working parents to on-the-go singles to the housebound elderly. Carroll Olson of Bellevue, Nebraska, caters (literally) to all three groups. Olson always loved to cook, and when she left her corporate job to care for her daughter, her friends encouraged her to start a catering business. "I didn't feel like investing in the commercial kitchen space required by the state, so I decided to start a personal chef service instead," Olson recalls. Using her family as "guinea pigs," she experimented with recipes, made a brochure on her computer, and began marketing Easy Elegance Personal Chef Service to dual-career families and busy working couples. Four years later, she had 100 clients!

A LOOK INTO THE CRYSTAL BALL

How can you spot a hot trend that will keep its sizzle without losing its fizzle? Through our research and various economic predictors, we've zeroed in on the home business possibilities that we believe will continue to boom and are of particular interest to mompreneurs:

- ✓ Time-saving services for singles and families (personal chef, neighborhood concierge, pet-sitter, personal organizer, transportation coordinator)
- ✓ Businesses targeting parents (products and services for tweens and teens as well as babies and younger children, enrichment programs, academic consultant, vacation planner, space utilization expert)
- ✓ Personalized gifts and products (invitations/birth announcements, party favors, gift baskets, trade show promotions)
- ✓ Services and products for the growing elderly population (relocation services, home health care agency, insurance record-keeping, errand-running, computer tutoring)
- ✓ Educational and workplace counseling (homeschooling coordinator, diversity trainer, work/family consultant, curriculum advisor)

✓ Technology (web developer/designer, troubleshooter, programming consultant, videoconference producer, webcaster)

TAPPING YOUR TALENTS

Many mompreneurs showed us how a passion can be turned into a profitable venture. Lauren Groveman, a former model and actress, always loved to cook and bake. When her three children were small, she began giving cooking classes in the kitchen of her Larchmont, New York, home. "I wanted to be close to my children and teach others, especially mothers, how to feed their families with flavorful, nourishing food," says Groveman. Through her wonderful recipes and engaging style, Groveman's ultimate goal was to help the average person fill her home with warmth and comfort. Her enthusiasm was so contagious and the food so delicious that Groveman was convinced to capture the essence of her classes in a cookbook. *Lauren Groveman Cooks for Family and Friends* was the result, accompanied by TV appearances, in-store demonstrations, and other publicity. This mompreneur's passion for cooking continues to fuel her expanding business; she's since launched a videotape series and appears regularly on television and radio.

Others banked on pleasurable hobbies or special talents to produce income. Until her first daughter was born, Diane Quinn worked as an administrator at the Metropolitan Life Insurance Company and enjoyed sewing and quilting in her spare time. "When I decided to start my own business," says Quinn, "this seemed like a good place to begin." So she claimed half of the family room as her workspace and put together a sampling of baby quilts, friendship quilts, and placemats to sell at weekend craft shows. (A few pieces were reserved as gifts for family and friends, too.) Word got around about the quality and beauty of Quinn's quilts, and soon the orders began coming in. She was even able to wholesale her wares to a few small stores in her area of Virginia.

Quinn's plans for the future include an expansion of her quilting business and a reduction in craft shows. "I hope to establish a line of items to sell primarily to craft shops and country stores," she says. "I hope to get so much work that I can hire other quilters, who are also moms, to do some of the sewing."

There were also those who cashed in on the skills they picked up in volunteer positions. Diane Black, a former vice president for mortgage lending at a large bank, stayed home when her son Michael was born. At the time, she was living in Florida near a large swimming facility that hosted a major national competition. A big meet was coming up, and Black, a swimmer herself, volunteered to help the national registrar process entries and registration information. The registrar retired soon after the event was over, and Black decided to go after her position. "I had a feel for the paperwork and good experience," she says, "so I made a competitive bid for the job and got it."

When the family moved to Atlanta, Georgia, the job went, too. Black became the national registrar for U.S. Masters Swimming, managing a database of 30,000 swimmers who compete in events all over the country. Her knack for handling such a massive mailing list gave Black the confidence to contact some of the small businesses in her area, and she began to do mailings for several retail stores as well. "After doing a 30,000-member list, it was nothing to take on a few mailings of 2,000 to 3,000 each," she says, "and I already had the software."

MAXIMIZING YOUR SKILLS

TYPE OF BUSINESS	RELEVANT UNSALARIED EXPERIENCE
Desktop publishing/word processing service	Produced church newsletter
Event planning/wedding consulting	Organized major fund-raising dinners for local hospital
Bookkeeping/auditing	Treasurer of PTA
Tag sale coordinator	Ran garage sales for Girl Scouts
Online athletic gear merchandiser	Soccer coach for daughter's team
Personal shopper	Spent leisure time bargain-hunting

OTHER ROUTES TO MOMPRENEURSHIP

For a few of our respondents, the home business more or less found the businesswoman. Beth Hilson is a case in point. While in her 20s, she was diagnosed with celiac disease (the inability to digest wheat, rye, oats, and barley). Determined to keep this from interfering with her eating enjoyment, she attended cooking classes, eventually turning to the culinary world to become a professional food writer and teacher. Hilson's expertise enabled her to develop tasty gluten-free recipes to help control her celiac disease, but she never shared these with colleagues in the food business nor told them about her special diet for fear it would diminish her credentials as a food professional.

As she was forced to watch her diet more carefully, Hilson developed an assortment of gluten-free mixes to make freshly baked breads and pastries for her personal use. Once in a while, she became bold enough to offer tastes of these to her professional peers. Their positive reviews and encouragement, along with the realization that other people with similar dietary problems might enjoy her mixes, gave Hilson the confidence to venture further. The result is The Gluten-Free Pantry, Inc., of Glastonbury, Connecticut, a mail-order and online company that offers baking mixes for such treats as bagels, breads, brownies, biscotti, and pancakes.

Judging from the overwhelming response and constant flow of fan mail, people with wheat allergies and celiac disease (estimated to be around half a million Americans) welcomed Hilson's appealing products with open arms. "It was obvious that I wasn't the only one who felt a real need for good gluten-free products," says this mompreneur. In fact, one of the biggest complaints she hears is that other family members have devoured the baked goods without realizing they were gluten-free. Hilson has clearly achieved her goal of "creating foods that make people feel truly pampered so they won't feel like cheating on their diets." These days, this goal is even more important to her. Hilson's son was diagnosed as being gluten-intolerant after she founded the business. "Being at home helps me manage his diet, too," she says. He's also lucky to have all those great after-school snacks at his beck and call!

Buying into an existing business is another option we've come across. Susan Rietano-Davey and her partner, Sue Glasspiegel, were in management positions at Xerox and Travelers Insurance Company, respectively, when they independently decided to find more flexible work arrangements to accommodate their children. They met through Flexible Resources, a Greenwich, Connecticut, consulting and recruiting firm also started by two mothers. The original founders thought Rietano-Davey and Glasspiegel would be the ideal pair to expand their operation into the Hartford area and central Connecticut, and it soon became a done deal.

"We complement each other perfectly," says Rietano-Davey. "We're the completion of each other's skills and talents." Rietano-Davey is strong in sales and marketing, staffing and recruiting, management training, and public speaking, while Glasspiegel excels in analytic problem-solving, policy writing, and human resources planning. Together, they offer two main services. As recruiters, they place experienced professionals in flexible work arrangements, including part-time, job-share, home-based, telecommuting, interim management, and project assignments. As consultants, they teach companies why and how to implement flexible work policies for their professional employees. One key to their success is that both women truly practice what they preach: They work part-time from home, job-share, and telecommute. Flexible Resources not only suits the partners' talents and schedules, it reflects their whole philosophy about balancing motherhood and career. "We're role models for a lot of the people we represent," says Rietano-Davey.

Placing professional women in jobs with greater flexibility is still a major part of the business. These days, however, Flexible Resources is also seeing a lot of retirees who want to return to the workforce part-time, as well as consultants who wish to supplement their steady clients with a little extra work. There are more and more combination positions coming up, too, with companies allowing employees to divide their time equally between home office and headquarters. The future looks bright, according to Glasspiegel. "There's more of an emphasis on contracting out to a contingent work force now than ever before." That can only mean more business for Flexible Resources.

SHOULD YOU GIVE UP YOUR DAY JOB?

Perhaps you're a mom with a nine-to-five job who is exhausted and disenchanted but still a little afraid of chucking it all for the uncertainty of working from home. You may want to consider testing the waters by becoming a part-time mompreneur, as Michelle Fischer did. She lives with her husband and young son in a lovely old home in rural Vermont, the perfect spot for a bed-and-breakfast. Since Fischer was a frequent hostess for out-of-town friends and family members, it didn't seem like much of a stretch to turn three rooms into guest rooms and start charging visitors for the accommodations. The area attracts tourists during all four seasons, so there's a good flow of business. Fischer is responsible for cooking breakfast in the morning before she leaves for work and also on weekends, and making sure the guest rooms are in order.

Part-time mompreneurship is a bit easier to pull off if you have a part-time job outside the home rather than a full-time one. Most moms who are in the workplace forty or more hours a week can barely squeeze another activity into their jam-packed schedules, much less make time to start a business. However, if you're very energetic and motivated, it can be done, especially if you choose one of the more adaptable businesses, like a bed-and-breakfast. A few other possibilities are crafts and sewing, research, planning weekend events, flower arranging, recipe development, new product testing, editing or indexing, and graphic design.

TEN BELIEVE-IT-OR-NOT HOME-BASED BUSINESSES
(FROM OUR SURVEY)

Costume maker for Colonial Williamsburg
Llama rancher and breeder
Fantasy pen pal and Santa letter service for kids
Booking agent and talent scout for rock groups
Flight tutor for pilots
Naturalist/environmental educator

Radio broadcaster
Marionette maker and puppeteer
Referral service for female impersonators
Personal historian

TOP TEN JOB CHOICES FOR MOMPRENEURS
(FROM OUR SURVEY)

Graphic design
Freelance writing/editing
Public relations
Personal services
Law
Crafts
Interior design/decorating
Direct sales
Office support services
Computer and web consulting

DIRECT SALES

The flexibility of working in direct sales has always attracted mothers, from the first Avon lady to the current crop of virtual party planners on the web. These days, this job option is more popular than ever, employing more than 10 million Americans, about 75 percent of whom are women, according to the latest figures from the Direct Selling Association, based in Washington, D.C. Many of the recruits who are joining the ranks are moms—college-educated women who would rather be selling than working as lawyers, teachers, or corporate executives. It makes sense. Companies like Discovery Toys, BeautiControl Cosmetics, and Tupperware are strong proponents of putting family first.

Whether the product is cosmetics, dresses, baskets, vitamins, household cleaners, jewelry, toys, or plastic containers, the concept is basically the same: Sales are made by taking the line directly to a buyer's home or hosting parties or trunk shows for a group of potential customers in a home or office setting. More and more consultants are also supplementing person-to-person sales by marketing on the web.

The salesperson usually works as an independent contractor, meaning that her income depends entirely on her volume of sales minus the portion given to the supervisor who recruited her. Financial rewards can extend beyond the expected commission package. Top earners can become managers, receiving a percentage of the dollars made by the associates they supervise. In addition, most of the companies offer very appealing incentive programs, including vacation trips, cash awards, and prizes, like Mary Kay's famous pink Cadillac. The road to riches is not entirely smooth. To achieve this type of success, a rep must log long hours, be extremely self-motivated and achievement-oriented, and be good at handling rejection. Mothers of younger children who are starting out seem to prefer to work ten to fifteen hours a week, gradually increasing their workload and income as their kids grow. (See chapter 10, "Cash in a Flash!" for part-time tips.)

Flexible hours are just one of the draws of direct sales. Kathryn Paczak, a Shaklee representative in Virginia, likes the idea that she can put her own business philosophies to work in her job selling ecologically safe, healthful products. "I can also choose my own co-workers and clients," says this mother of two. Paczack and other sales reps find that time-pressed mothers are often their most interested customers, and it's relatively easy to reach this audience from the network of parents they routinely interact with in play groups, at school, and in community activities. Another plus is that the structure of a direct sales company is already in place, making it simpler and less risky than starting a business from scratch. The start-up costs are fairly low, too. The initial investment ranges from about $50 to $500 for a sample kit and other materials, all of which can be earned back from one or two well-attended parties or several big sales.

Although moms can build a lucrative career in direct sales, it's important to proceed with caution. If you stick with the well-known companies that have a national sales force, you should be on safe ground. Before you sign up, however, read the firm's marketing plan and sales literature and find out about its buy-back policy. Then interview other mothers employed as sales reps to get a real-life picture of the job. All these precautions are even more crucial when considering a smaller or newer company or a web-based venture. Be especially alert to multilevel marketing plans and network marketing in which you must recruit other people into the company in order to recoup your investment and produce income. To make matters worse, some of these "pyramid" schemes involve products that are not easy to sell.

We're happy to report that the mompreneurs in our survey are very satisfied with their choice of direct sales. As Betsy Johns, a Discovery Toys consultant in Michigan, puts it, "I never dreamed that with an engineering degree I'd be selling toys. But I really liked the idea that I could work around my family's schedule and be my own boss." Johns has worked an average of twenty-five hours a week and always has new toys around for her two daughters to test.

FAMILY-FRIENDLY FRANCHISES

No, we're not suggesting you set up a Burger King in your kitchen, but we would like you to know that many home-based franchises do exist, and the numbers are growing every year. These buy-in businesses are primarily service-oriented, offering everything from computer tutoring to travel consulting to kitchen cabinet refacing to disc jockey booking to direct-mail advertising. Purchase prices can go from a low of $5,000 to up to $20,000 and more; in any case, a buyer should have enough of a nest egg to get by for three to six months without making a profit.

In their book *Megatrends for Women*, Patricia Aburdene and John Naisbitt report that companies seek out moms as franchise operators because they offer business experience, stability, and motivation. Many mothers are happy they've been sought out. Diane Bader of Cumming, Georgia, bought a Kinderdance franchise shortly after she became a new mother and has enjoyed watching it thrive through the arrivals of her second and third children. Kinderdance franchisees run the nuts and bolts of their businesses from home but venture out to teach developmental dance and gymnastics to children in local schools, child-care facilities, and community centers. Bader was trained in the company's unique dance and movement techniques at the Kinderdance headquarters in Melbourne, Florida, before she started up. She also learned the basics of bookkeeping and marketing to keep the business running.

On-the-job training is one of the advantages of buying a franchise. Others include brand name recognition; local, regional, and even national advertising strength; a blueprint for getting the business off the ground; and continued technical support and advice. The downside is that the franchisee must pay royalties on her gross sales to the parent company, ranging from 7 to 35 percent, as well as monthly advertising fees. Although low-cost, home-based franchises may seem like an ideal opportunity for mothers, some unscrupulous companies have taken advantage of women just because they're moms. Susan Kezios, head of Chicago-based Women in Franchising, Inc. (WIF), presents seminars across the country geared especially toward women, and mothers always make up a large part of her audiences. While she agrees that moms can be some of the best franchise customers, she cautions them to "beware of being preyed upon by franchisors who are specifically looking for mothers. The rewards they promise may be real, but there are also terrible home-based franchising failures." For these reasons and others, it's very important to carefully evaluate a franchise before you invest in it.

CHECKLIST FOR POTENTIAL FRANCHISEES

✓ You should obtain a "uniform franchise offering circular" from the franchisor you're interested in. This document provides the names, addresses, and phone numbers of past and present franchisees, as well as information about the financial health of the company. But this document is only a starting point. It does not contain all the information you'll need to evaluate the franchise.

✓ Contact a sizable number of former and current owners and gather details about their experiences with this particular franchise. Some points to question: What are the franchisee's gross and net sales; what kind of training, support, and protection can you expect from the franchisor; what is the competition in your area; and how does this business affect homelife? Susan Kezios of Women in Franchising warns that it's not uncommon for a company to promise a home-based franchisee that she can easily work part-time and earn big bucks, when the reality is that running most franchises is a full-time job or more.

✓ Before you sign any franchise contract, go over it carefully, preferably with a franchise attorney who will argue aggressively on your behalf in negotiations with the parent company.

✓ Get in touch with the Better Business Bureau and/or Attorney General's office in the state in which the parent company is located and in your home state to see if any complaints have been lodged. You may also want to try the American Franchisee Association in Chicago (1-800-334-4232, 1-312-431-0545 or www.franchisee.org) to see if any lawsuits or complaints have been made against the franchisor.

✓ Call The Franchise Hotline at 1-800-794-6722 to help you look into an opportunity or determine your compatibility for a home-based franchise.

Author and work-from-home consultant Alice Bredin warns that franchising is not for everyone. If you have an independent personality and want to bring a lot of your own ideas into the operation, you may be better off financially and emotionally starting your own business. "Entrepreneurs are more likely to choose a business they are passionate about," she says, "and may therefore have a better success rate and make more money than franchise owners." Furthermore, start-up costs may be lower or comparable to buying an inexpensive franchise, and all the profits can go back into your venture or into your own pocket. Before you sink your savings into a home-based franchise, do your homework and a bit of thinking about life as a franchisee.

TELECOMMUTING: THE CORPORATE CONNECTION

The International Data Corporation (IDC) defines a telecommuter as "a company-employed person who works part or full time at home during normal business hours." Via computer, e-mail, fax, and phone, these home-based workers communicate with the main office, which may be any type of business from a bank to a small insurance agency to a publishing house to industry giants like IBM and Sears Roebuck. In 2000, IDC counted the number of telecommuters at about nine million, more than half of whom work for small businesses.

It's no surprise that telecommuting is becoming a popular choice for moms, especially those who want to keep a toehold on the corporate ladder and a hand in family life. For many women, the idea first occurs to them when they're pregnant and thinking about their options. For others, it suddenly becomes an appealing choice toward the end of maternity leave or during those hectic first months back in the office. For stay-at-home moms, telecommuting is a way to re-enter the workforce (possibly with a former company) and still be there for the kids.

One Postpartum Solution

When Liz White was a newscaster for a radio station in New York City, she helped launch a unique telecommuting arrangement to accommodate the birth of her daughter, Emily. Not wanting to stop broadcasting when she was home on maternity leave, White had the station install a complete radio studio in her laundry room next to the kitchen in her suburban New Jersey home. "The MIX 105 Babylink had all the necessary tools for a postpartum broadcast studio: computer, news wire machines, modem, fax machine, radio console, tape player . . . and breast pump," reported White when she began. "Connected by phone lines to the station's main broadcast studios in Manhattan, I was able to air news reports and join my co-host, Jim Kerr, and the Morning Crew . . . from my home." Even though listeners could occasionally hear the family's basset hound barking in the background, the station's largely female audience identified strongly with White's balancing act and became even more loyal. It generated good publicity, too—Babylink was featured in action on NBC's *Today Show*.

How did White work out this innovative work-at-home solution? She credits her "sensitive, New Age" boss with much of its success. He was willing to go along with the idea after White presented a written proposal detailing the logistics and setting timetables for working at home. She was also able to enlist her husband's help. Since her show was on in the early morning and his job started later, Dad took care of Emily when Mom began broadcasting.

Then a neighbor took over the baby-sitting until White got off the air at 10 A.M. The arrangement worked out to everyone's advantage. White was able to be close to her baby while she continued to work, and the radio station had a more productive, loyal employee.

TELECOMMU-TIPS

- ✓ Present a written proposal with specific timetables to your boss. Determine how much postpartum time you'll need and how much time/ how many days per week you plan to work from home.
- ✓ Point out ways your telecommuting can benefit the boss: conservation of office space, saving a temp's salary to cover your position, etc.
- ✓ Investigate which companies—particularly the ones in your field—are family-friendly and include their policies in your proposal.
- ✓ Don't rely on e-mail for all your communication with the office. Check in at least a few times a week by phone to let your boss and co-workers know what you're up to and personalize your dealings.
- ✓ Schedule a lunch date or attend the occasional office party to maintain the relationships you've built at work. If you think it's appropriate, bring the baby in for a visit.

Setting Up a Satellite Office

When Minnesota travel agent Amy Rea delivered her first child, she approached her boss with the idea of working from home four days a week. Since she worked for a small agency, she had a feeling he would be flexible. To sell the concept, Rea drew up a plan pointing out all the positive ways her telecommuting would impact on the company: decreased absenteeism, greater productivity, and increased loyalty. She also voluntarily took a pay cut to help her employer "come around to the idea and be more willing to give it a chance," says Rea. Her strategy worked, and everything soon fell into place "because my husband is a technical whiz who figured out all the hardware/software issues," she reports. Her computer at home was networked to her office, so she could access the same information as everyone else at the agency. In fact, callers can't tell where she is unless they hear a child's voice in the background.

Telecommuting was a bit of an adjustment at first, but soon Rea wouldn't have it any other way. She works three days a week and is making more money than she did before she set up at home, pay cut notwithstanding. In the beginning, she was able to work around her baby's nap schedules for the most part, trying to keep her workload reasonable so she could pay attention to him when he was awake. "Most of my clients know that I work from home, and they think it's great," she says. "It's hard work, but worth every minute."

Making a Re-Entry

Although Kathleen Eschbach gave up her job as an insurance underwriter to become a full-time mom, in the back of her mind, she always had the image of herself as a career woman. To keep that image alive, she maintained contacts with co-workers and stayed abreast of changes in the industry. When the youngest of her three children started preschool, Eschbach felt she was ready to rekindle the career woman side of her identity, so she submitted her résumé to Flexible Resources, an agency specializing in part-time and alternative job opportunities, with the understanding that she wanted to work mostly from home. "I felt I could be choosy and was willing to wait for the right situation to come along," says Eschbach.

Her patience paid off. About eight months later, Eschbach was placed with an insurance company that understood telecommuting and valued her experience and skills. "My boss thought it was a wonderful setup; he does some of his work at home, too, and recognizes the importance of a parent being close to her children." Together, Eschbach and her employer redesigned the job slightly so she could focus on the parts best-suited to a home-based environment: reviewing claim data, making quotes on cases, figuring out ratings, and planning benefits. Others in the company take care of customer service and similar person-to-person work. Once every week or so, Eschbach goes in to headquarters, but day-to-day contact is accomplished through phone calls, fax, and e-mail.

Kathleen Eschbach somehow knew that working did not have to be an all-or-nothing proposition, even in the normally conservative insurance industry. "I felt there had to be something in between working outside the home and not working at all," she says. For her, it turned out to be one of the growing number of part-time telecommuting positions. Eschbach feels confident that "if it's there for me, it has to be there for others, too."

Working Out the Kinks

While most moms who telecommute are pleased with the arrangement, some have noticed drawbacks to being work-at-home employees rather than entrepreneurs. For example:

- ✓ Resentment from colleagues at the main office who think you're not really working because you're at home.

✓ The need to give more than 100 percent to your job because yours might be the first to go if there are layoffs.
✓ The fear that decreased visibility at the office can limit your chances for advancement and raises.
✓ The greater necessity for reliable child care. Telecommuters usually go into the office at least once a week and must have coverage for that day.

Experts do believe that as telecommuting becomes more widespread, these concerns (except for the child care) will fade into the background. In fact, it's predicted that the majority of twenty-first-century workers will be telecommuting at least one day a week. As Susan Rietano-Davey of Flexible Resources says, "There's a little piece of almost every job that can be done from home."

MOMPRENEUR® HALL OF FAME

FRAN SUSSNER RODGERS

Founder and CEO of Work/Family Directions, Watertown, Massachusetts

Mother of Two

Fran Sussner Rodgers was one of many working mothers trying to main-tain that delicate balance between career and family responsibilities. Then her eighteen-month-old daughter, Nicole, developed severe asthma, and the scales tipped. Rodgers began doing more and more of her educational consulting work from home so she would be there when Nicole needed her.

From the bedroom of her home, she created an enterprise that both reflected and solved one of the major concerns of business and the growing female workforce: finding quality care for young children. Rodgers's first big client was IBM, which was looking for a child-care referral service for its frequently transferred employees. With seed money from the computer giant, she was able to round up a team, cre-ate a national network of child-care agencies, develop a database, and get Work/Family Directions off the ground. Meanwhile, this mompre-neur was putting her ideas to the test in her own life. "Working from home was a crucial transition period for me. At the same time, I could both care for my family [which now included a second daughter] and work very hard at something I strongly believed in." The arrangement gave her more flexibility and control over her life, allowing her to work on issues she cared about deeply while capitalizing on her mothering and business skills.

Soon, other clients came to believe strongly in her ideas as well, and the company began fielding requests for other types of services. As the work overflowed from desk to bed, Rodgers realized it was time to move out. "I had to hire more people, and it would have been hard to have them all in my bedroom," she says. "I was also ready to make a physical break." When she moved her office into a new space, the company started moving into new areas, too. Elder care referral was added to the roster, followed by services to help parents deal with adoption, school achievement, college placement, adult disabilities, and personal issues such as creating a living will.

Work/Family Directions has counted such mega-companies as Xerox, DuPont, General Electric, FedEx, and AT&T among its clients. Their employees tap into what is known as the LifeWorks family resource service and the company's vast consultation and referral capability. In addition, clients are offered help in strategic labor force planning, instituting career and workplace flexibility, and other services designed to maximize employee productivity by helping workers better manage their career and family responsibilities.

Rodgers has turned what was previously an area haphazardly handled by social service agencies into a critical business issue. In the process, she has built a profitable company with millions of dollars in revenues. She has also brought these important work-life issues into the forefront by managing the American Business Collaboration for Quality Dependent Care, a corporate sector coalition that is investing more than $100 million to fund projects that support the dependent care needs of their employees. The future holds even more opportunities for growth, as demographics demand increased family-centered services. One of Rodgers's favorite quotes says it all: "We've always said we started out as a mission that became a business. Now we're a business with a mission."

3

Getting Down to Business

Ellen's first freelance job came unexpectedly, while she was still on maternity leave from her position as a magazine editor. She hadn't planned on working so soon, but she couldn't resist the chance to test the work-at-home waters. Ellen learned a lot from that first story assignment. She realized that while typing at the dining-room table might be okay in a pinch, she'd need to set aside her own special workspace, if she was going to be successful long-term. And she discovered that although she was able to get most of her research and editing done while little Matthew rocked in the swing, she'd need someone to watch him while she did the phone interviews and the writing. Most important, she learned that this new work style *was* for her, even if she wasn't quite prepared for it.

Pat's first assignment more or less fell into her lap, too. Her son was just three weeks old when an editor she knew called. Although she had really wanted to take a few months of maternity leave before seriously beginning freelancing, she accepted. "I didn't want my first opportunity to slip by," she remembers.

When the two of us started out, we really winged it for a while. We lived from assignment to assignment—no definite goals, no business plan, and very often, no contracts. Luck and good connections kept us just barely in the black. Now that we're seasoned home-based workers, we know that it's better to be more savvy about setting goals, checking out the competition, marketing ourselves, negotiating fees, investigating legalities, and taking other steps to assure success.

When To Open for Business

Is there ever an optimal time for a mom to start a home-based business? For us, it seemed logical to begin when we were on maternity leave with our first babies, but other mompreneurs in our survey decided to go this route at different times in their lives. Some even knew they wanted to work from home once they became parents and started before they became pregnant.

During Pregnancy

Anne Kyle, a freelance book and magazine writer from Ossining, New York, was laid off from her editorial job while she was pregnant. She was looking around for a similar job when an editor/friend asked her to write a freelance article. She discovered she liked being on her own, spread the word about her new endeavor, and a business was born.

During Infancy

Daria Price Bowman, a marketing communications consultant from New Hope, Pennsylvania, launched her business from her kitchen table immediately after the birth of her first daughter. Bowman continued in a field she had been working in and didn't want to lose her momentum and contacts.

During the Toddler Years

When her daughter turned eighteen months old, Karen Pickus, a food professional in New York City, decided to focus more of her attention on work she could do from home. As a freelance food stylist, she had previously spent most of her days in photographers' studios. Although Pickus still accepts food styling jobs, she started taking on more recipe development work that she can do out of her own kitchen.

In the Preschool Years

Lisa Marie Nelson, a juvenile music producer from California, began her business when her oldest child was in preschool. After a career in the television industry, she knew her personality and work style were not well-suited to the corporate environment. Instead of returning to that world, she went into business as an independent record producer, writing and composing contemporary music for kids.

When School Starts

Many mompreneurs wait until their last child enters kindergarten before setting up shop. This is a sensible time to start, since home businesses can usually be scheduled around school hours, and there's little or no need for supplemental child care. Susan Cioffi, a home-based manufacturer's rep in Scarsdale, New York, reversed roles once her three children were in school full-time. Cioffi worked in New York City's garment district throughout her children's early years and didn't decide to go out on her own until her youngest—a set of twins—were in fourth grade and fairly independent. Starting at this point also means an empty, quiet house to work in most of the day.

While some moms try to develop their businesses as their children grow, others decide to slow down a bit. One mompreneur in our survey worked long hours building up her public relations company when her children were small. She had a full-time, live-in nanny so she could work in her home office until 6 P.M. every day. Once her children reached school age, she found she wanted (and needed) to be more available to help with homework, take part in after-school activities, and just be involved in their lives. She scaled back her hours to 9 A.M. to 3 P.M. most days, and the family was happy with the arrangement.

WHAT ABOUT MATERNITY LEAVE?

If you're thinking of opening a home business after a baby comes along, you might be uncertain about how soon you should start up. If you've already been working at home and are expecting an addition to your family, you may wonder how much, if any, time to take off when the baby arrives. In both cases, we recommend that you give yourself as much time as you possibly can to recuperate from childbirth, bond with your newborn, catch up on your sleep, and ease the adjustment of any older siblings. Plan to take several weeks off, if you can. If you're already working at home, let your clients know in advance that you'll be unavailable for a while. Remember, you chose the work-at-home route to have more family flexibility, so allow yourself to enjoy it.

If you feel you must tend to business right away, do try to pare down your workload and get someone to help with the housekeeping. Susan Rietze, who runs a Vermont-based service business with her husband, worked right up to delivery and was back at her desk about a week later, but she had her husband/business partner as a backup, and she was able to nap when the baby did. She also recruited a friend to come and help with the housework. "Remember, you can't do it all," Rietze cautions, "and you're not defeated when you have help come in."

FROM SECRETARY TO WORD PROCESSING SERVICE

As a crackerjack typist for the United Nations General Assembly in New York City, Sandy Greene's job was fast-paced and unpredictable. She often had to be present at meetings during odd hours of the day or night to transcribe minutes or be on call during the weekends. Shortly before Greene became pregnant with her first child, she decided to leave the UN to start a typing business from her home in Eastchester, New York. The timing turned out to be great. She could start up, then continue the business once the baby was born. Her first customer, a mother, brought in her son's high school term paper, and that client spread the word about Greene's quick and accurate work. (This customer is still with her today.) Greene's business blossomed. Students whose college applications and papers she typed told their parents, and vice versa. Soon she counted an appraiser, accountant, lawyer, eye doctor, private investigator, and a couple of schools among her regular clients. She charges $6 per page (single-spaced) and $5 per page (double-spaced). "Since I'm fast, it made more sense not to charge by the hour," says Greene.

START-UP COSTS: About $4,000 for computer, printer fax, and dictaphone system. Advertising costs were $600 for ads in the community phone books and local newspaper.

BIGGEST WORK/FAMILY CHALLENGE: Clients tend to drop off jobs without much advance warning. "It's rare that the work has to be done right away," says Greene, "but I feel pressured to get it out of the way." Once she finishes a job, she frequently leaves it in her mailbox to be picked up. This led to a strange 12:30 A.M. call from the police one night. It seems that a client of Greene's, who lives nearby, went for a midnight jog and stopped by her house to pick up his typing from the mailbox. Someone must have seen him, thought he was a burglar, and called the police!

FIVE-YEAR PLAN: Greene loves her business and the fact that she's home-based. She expects to continue both and plans to resume advertising to attract more steady clients.

BEFORE YOU GET GOING

There are many important financial factors to consider before you become a mompreneur.

- ✓ If you're married, can the family survive on your husband's salary while you get the business going?
- ✓ If you're a single mom, will your business generate enough income to live on? Do you have enough to fall back on during those all-too-frequent times when paychecks come in sporadically?
- ✓ What will you do about health insurance? What other types of insurance will you need for your business?
- ✓ What kind of start-up costs will you have? (You can figure them out on our "Mompreneur Start-Up Checklist," page 57). How will you pay for them?
- ✓ What will your day-to-day overhead costs be? (Plot them on the "Mompreneur Start-Up Checklist" page 57). Can you afford them?
- ✓ Are you in the financial position to quit your current job to start up your business? Does it make more sense to keep working, start the business on the side, and then quit when it takes off?
- ✓ How many hours do you want to work?
- ✓ What will you do about child care?
- ✓ Where will your workspace be, and what kind of equipment do you need to put in it? (Don't forget to factor equipment costs into your start-up expenses.)
- ✓ How does your family feel about your business? Is your husband supportive of your plans? When you're starting a business, you need to surround yourself with positive people who believe in what you're doing. Sit down with your kids and talk about how life will change when you begin working at home. Point out the wonderful benefits such as more family time and the power to be your own boss, but also be honest about your expectations. Let kids know that they're going to have to be quiet sometimes when you're working. Be clear that working at home doesn't mean you're always going to be available to play with them. The more you include your family in your business plans, the better understanding they'll have of your new role.

MOMPRENEUR START-UP CHECKLIST

Use this worksheet to figure out your approximate business costs.

Start-Up Costs

Item   Cost

____ Office furniture   _____

____ Computer   _____

____ Printer   _____

____ Software   _____

____ Modem/DSL Line   _____

____ Fax machine   _____

____ Phone system   _____

____ Answering machine/voicemail/

answering service   _____

____ Phone line for business

(installation fee)   _____

____ Phone line for fax/modem

(installation fee)   _____

____ Manufacturing equipment   _____

____ Other equipment   _____

____ Equipment service contracts   _____

____ Manufacturing supplies   _____

____ Cost of warehouse/storage space   _____

____ Stationery   _____

____ Business cards   _____

____ Other marketing materials

(brochures, etc.)   _____

____ Fee for registering domain name   _____

____ Website design costs   _____

____ Advertising costs

Item	Cost
____ Permits/licenses	_____
____ Trademark/patent fees	_____
____ Business name registration fee	_____
____ Franchise start-up fee	_____
____ Direct sales sample kit	_____
____ Accountant's fee	_____
____ Attorney's fee	_____
____ Other	_____
TOTAL START-UP COSTS	_____

Overhead Costs

Item	Cost
____ Telephone/fax bill	_____
____ Internet Service Provider (ISP)	_____
____ Web hosting	_____
____ Merchant account fees	_____
____ Postage/shipping/freight	_____
____ Office supplies	_____
____ Manufacturing supplies	_____
____ Marketing and advertising	_____
____ Child care	_____
____ Travel expenses	_____
____ Dues for networking organizations	_____
____ Insurance premiums	_____
____ Business checking account	_____
____ Credit line and/or loan charges	_____
____ Employee salaries/benefits	_____
____ Taxes	_____
____ Books/publications/subscriptions	_____

Item	Cost
⎯⎯ Franchise royalties	⎯⎯⎯⎯⎯⎯⎯⎯
⎯⎯ Warehouse rental	⎯⎯⎯⎯⎯⎯⎯⎯
⎯⎯ Other	⎯⎯⎯⎯⎯⎯⎯⎯
TOTAL OVERHEAD COSTS	⎯⎯⎯⎯⎯⎯⎯⎯

THE MOMPRENEUR® START-UP PLAN

You've decided the time is right, and you know just the type of business you'll run. The next step is our simple Mompreneur® Start-Up Plan. Although many successful mompreneurs (including us) skipped a lot of these steps—and learned from the many mistakes made along the way—we think you'll save yourself a lot of time, grief, error, and second guessing if you follow this methodical plan. Of course, no start-up is foolproof, and your business, like most, is bound to evolve as you go along and become more experienced as a mompreneur. But these steps will help you become more confident from the beginning and will better prepare you for the upcoming work-at-home challenges.

Start-Up Step #1: Do Your Homework

Use the web to gather as much information as you can about your particular business. Read everything you can get your hands on and research similar businesses in your area to find out about your marketplace, your competition, and appropriate product prices or fees for your services. Get important feedback from potential clients and customers by networking on message boards and listservs related to your target market and by conducting online surveys. Find out what they like and dislike about your idea and what they'd be willing to pay for a product or service like yours.

General home-based business books, plus specific books and magazines on your particular trade are another good place to start. (See our Resources section on page 286 for suggestions.) There's an almost endless array of entrepreneurial and trade publications out there, and it's worth a trip to your local library to track them down. Nearby colleges sometimes have business development centers with libraries full of resources for entrepreneurs. Also try your local women's business development centers. (To find one near you, click on the SBA's Online Women's Business Center at www.onlinewbcorg.)

Don't be afraid to do some additional sleuthing to uncover the essential business clues you need. When Julie Pophal was trying to determine what she should charge for her transcription/word processing services, she got out her phone book and called secretarial agencies to see what their fees were. Then she came up with a rate that was a little lower so that she could be competitive. You need to get your facts before you can get on with the rest of your business plans.

WHERE TO GO FOR START-UP HELP

- ✓ American Association of Home Based Businesses; www.aahbb.org
- ✓ American Express Small Business Services; www.american express.com
- ✓ American Women's Economic Development Corporation; New York City; 917-368-6100
- ✓ Association of Small Business Development Centers; www.asbdc-us. org
- ✓ Center for Women's Business Research 202-638-3060; www.nfwbo.org
- ✓ The Entrepreneurial Edge from the Edward Lowe Foundation; www.lowe.org
- ✓ Homebased Working Moms; Austin, Texas; 512-266-0900; www. hbwm.com
- ✓ Mompreneurs® Online; www.mompreneursonline.com
- ✓ Online Women's Business Center; www.onlinewbc.org
- ✓ Service Corps. of Retired Executives (SCORE): Small Business Counseling; www.score.org
- ✓ U.S. Small Business Administration; www.sba.gov

Start-Up Step #2: Build Your Support Network

Talk to other home-based business owners, especially other mompreneurs. "Work-at-home mothers love to share business knowledge and strategies," says Maria Chilcote, a former vice president of a retail corporation who now runs a training and consulting firm from her home in Springfield, Virginia. "When I was in the corporate world, it was very hard to find women who wanted to share their business secrets or tips. Women were very territorial about what it took to get them where they are. But home-based working moms have found out that the secret of networking is to give, not to get. The getting comes later."

The best way to meet fellow work-at-homers is through entrepreneurial and home-based business organizations, trade associations, women's business groups, work-at-home networks, and online forums. By joining these types of groups, you can continue your business fact-finding while you mingle with people in your field. To find groups in your area, contact your local women's resource center (usually part of your county government) or chamber of commerce and local community colleges, which often have entrepreneurial centers. (See chapter 7 and the Resources section on page 286 for more leads.)

When you find someone who's doing the same thing as you, stick to them like glue, urges Chilcote. Ask plenty of questions about rates, pricing, common problems, and what they'd do over if they could.

If you'd like a little more hands-on expertise before you actually get your company up and running, consider signing up for a seminar or workshop on self-employment or running a home-based business. Many local colleges, business training and entrepreneurial centers, chambers of commerce, and other community organizations offer them. Courses like these are often filled with inspirational and practical advice and are a great way to get your specific questions answered.

Start-Up Step #3: Check Zoning Laws and Other Legalities

Make sure that you're legally allowed to run a business in your home. Many communities, particularly suburban areas, have zoning laws that prohibit or restrict home businesses. Regulations vary across the country, so it's important to check with your local government to see what's allowed in your area. Contact your city or county government and find out who you need to talk to about home-business regulations. (It's usually someone in the planning or building inspector's office.)

Just checking the zoning laws isn't enough. It's also essential to find out whether your homeowner's association or condo/co-op board has any covenants that restrict home businesses, notes Beverly Williams, founder of the American Association of Home Based Businesses. These supersede local zoning laws, so even if your county or city allows you to have a home business, you could still be limited.

According to work-at-home experts Paul and Sarah Edwards in their book *Working from Home,* "Irksome restrictions may limit the hours you can work and prohibit using your address in advertising, including Yellow Page listings, and using outside buildings, such as garages, for your offices." Communities might also have restrictions on increased traffic (such as delivery trucks or client's cars) or on-street parking, limits on the number of employees allowed to work with you, and bans on displaying outdoor signs on your property, the Edwardses say.

It's no secret that there are many home-based businesses operating without the proper authorization. Usually these are sole proprietors in professions that don't require a lot of in-home client meetings or truck deliveries. Some get away with it without a problem; others get in trouble when their neighbors get angry and report them. What happens if you're caught violating zoning laws? You could get fined or have your business closed down. We think it's better to be safe than sorry. A little checking up front can save you a lot of time and expense later. Whether you're operating legally or not, stay on the good side of your neighbors. They have the power to make or break your business.

In addition, it's important to research what kind of trademarks, licenses, or permits your business will need and whether or not it's necessary to register your business name. Again, your county government will be of help here, but it's also beneficial to check with your federal and state governments to make sure that you're meeting all their business requirements. If you'll be running a food business, you'll need the go-ahead from your local Board of Health, and you'll have to conform to its regulations. Don't forget about liability insurance. You'll need extra to protect against lawsuits from dissatisfied customers and to cover you in the event a client or delivery person is injured on your property. Make sure, too, that your homeowner's policy covers your expensive office equipment. If you're uncertain about the other necessary legal steps required for your business, it's wise to consult an attorney for advice.

Talk to your accountant and decide on a structure for your business. Will you be a sole proprietor, like the majority of novice mompreneurs, or will you opt to form a partnership, corporation, or limited liability corporation (LLC)? You'll hear all about these choices in chapter 8.

Ask your accountant how often you'll need to pay your business taxes and what kind of financial records you'll need to keep. Your accountant can tell you how to go about getting a tax ID number and will be knowledgeable of the current IRS regulations and what qualifies as a valid business deduction. This is essential to know at start-up time because you're likely to be investing in some expensive equipment and will want to know how much of it will be tax-deductible. "My accountant will tell me, 'Buy this now, because next year you won't be able to write this off,'" says Maria Chilcote.

We'll be giving you more information on zoning, licensing, incorporating, insurance, trademarks, tax requirements, and other legalities in chapter 8.

Start-Up Step #4: Claim Your Name

Choose a business name that's catchy and conveys your mission. Then register it with your county, city, or state government (see chapter 8 for more details) and reserve it as a domain name.

A word of caution: Just because a domain name is available doesn't mean you have the right to use it as your business name. Before you register any business names you should do a trademark search to make sure that it does not infringe on someone else's trademark. (You can do a preliminary trademark search at www.uspto.gov or www.nameprotect.com.) If it hasn't been trademarked, register as many forms of the domain name as you can afford with domain registration sites such as Verisign.com. We know mompreneurs who even register misspelled versions of their domain names so there's no chance of another business having a "confusingly similar" web address.

Though pricey, trademarks are becoming increasingly important in the Internet age as a protective measure. A trademark will prevent others from using your business or product names for a similar purpose in U.S. commerce. Any name, logo, symbol, or slogan used to market a product or service can be trademarked, as long as it is "distinctive," rather than merely "descriptive." (For example, Mompreneurs® is unique and distinctive, while "work-at-home mom" is merely descriptive.) If you have a unique business name that has not already been trademarked by someone else, and if you plan to offer your services or products outside your home state, you should strongly consider filing for a federal trademark with the U.S. Patent and Trademark Office at www.uspto.gov. (We'll give you more details on this in chapter 8, as well.)

MOMMY'S SPECIAL HELPER

As an at-home mom in 1990, former stockbroker Carol Gamble noticed that whenever she was cooking, her eighteen-month-old daughter Hanna insisted, "Me do!" Gamble wanted to encourage Hanna's independence but couldn't find a way for her reach the counter and sink safely. "If I put her on a chair, she'd topple right off," recalls the Shreveport, Louisiana, mom. She searched stores for a step stool with protective sides but found nothing the right height. So she created one herself.

Inspired by the design of her backyard toddler slide—which she'd actually dragged into the kitchen for Hanna to stand on—Gamble had a graphic artist sketch her vision for what she'd come to call the "Learning Tower." She took the drawing to a local carpenter, who built a sturdy tip-proof wooden platform with railings. It had three adjustable levels so it could grow with Hanna. That very first "Learning Tower" was big and bulky, but it worked. After spending most of the 1990s fine-tuning the Learning Tower and shopping it to buyers at the annual Juvenile Products Manufacturers Show in Dallas, Texas, Gamble finally landed in the "Natural Baby Catalog" in fall of 1998. The Learning Tower was named "one of the top 100 products of 1998" in the syndicated "Dr. Toy" newspaper column, and is now available in many catalogs, including "Leaps and Bounds" and "Sensational Beginnings," retailing for about $159. It can also be purchased at Gamble's website, Littlepartners.com.

In May of 2001, Gamble licensed the Learning Tower to Guidecraft, a manufacturer of children's wooden furniture. "Licensing was exactly what I had hoped for," says Gamble. "Sales had grown so much, that doing everything on my own became too much to handle." Now, Guidecraft takes care of manufacturing and distribution and marketing, and Gamble receives a percentage of all sales.

START-UP COSTS: Getting the product on the market took nearly ten years and $100,000 in patents, prototypes, redesign, safety testing, liability insurance, and marketing costs for ads, brochures. and tradeshow fees.

BIGGEST WORK/FAMILY CHALLENGE: Gamble "went back to the drawing board so many times" to find screws that wouldn't come loose and be swallowed and clamps that couldn't catch fingers. The Learning Tower had to be evaluated for safety issues like stability and possibility of head entrapment before retailers would agree to carry it, and each design change required new testing at an independent safety laboratory. "There's no room for human error with a juvenile product," Gamble says. But "I have wonderful memories of the time Hanna and I spent trying out the Learning Tower as we made bread and cookies and salads," she adds. "Hanna gained early on the knowledge and joy that she was welcome in the kitchen." Any time and money spent on helping other children experience that same feeling is well worth it, Gamble says.

FIVE-YEAR PLAN: To boost sales and profits, and build a presence in retail stores. So far Gamble has been putting any money she makes right back into building the business. But she's optimistic that her company will soon be in the black. "My biggest reward is seeing the joy and wonder of a child helping in the kitchen and knowing that I'm helping to make that possible."

Start-Up Step #5: Write a Business Plan

You may already be thinking, "I don't need a business plan. That's only for businesses that require major financing." We thought the same thing when we started up. "All we have to do is get some equipment and some writing assignments, and we'll be on our way," we thought. But as we look back on those early days, we realize that a simple set of goals for our family and our work lives could have helped us guide our business better. With a business plan, we would have made wiser decisions about the type of work we took and what we charged for our services.

Many mompreneurs are "intimidated by business plans because we think they have to be these complicated documents with long-range financial projections," says Maria Chilcote, who runs a training and consulting firm from her home. It's true that you will need this kind of financial information if you're going to get a business loan, but most of us can get by with a much simpler business plan. Why do we need one at all? "A business plan is a road map for where you want your business to go and how you're going to get it there," says Beverly Williams, founder of the American Association of Home Based Businesses. "It doesn't have to be long," she adds. A business plan can be just a few short sentences in a notebook defining your business and your major goals for it. Don't worry about being locked into these goals forever. Business plans usually evolve as the company grows, and you'll probably revise your business plan many times as the years go by.

Chilcote suggests you first think about who you are, what makes your business different, and whether you have a market niche. Then see if you can describe your organization and what it does in one sentence. For example, the first sentence in her business plan is: "I'm Maria Chilcote of The Training Emporium, a firm that specializes in training and consulting for organizations and small businesses."

Think about your main business goals, says Chilcote. Where would you like your business to be in the next three months? Six months? A year from now? How much would you like to be making? Write these goals down and then think about how you're going to reach them. Don't forget to factor your family responsibilities into your plan. Be realistic about how much time you can actually devote to business. For example, if you're counting on spending two full days with your baby every work week, write down: "I will work approximately twenty hours a week, on Mondays, Wednesdays, and Fridays, and will spend the other two days with Amy." Then describe how you'll accomplish this. "I will get a baby-sitter on Mondays, Wednesdays, and Fridays for approximately seven hours a day. I will not work on Tuesdays or Thursdays, and I will put my answering machine on to screen my calls on those days." If you will be using a business plan to get financing, you'll want to take these family goals off the copy you give to the bank or loan agency.

Next is marketing. How will you get your clients or find your customers? Will you advertise? What kind of promotional materials will you need? What other ways can you promote yourself and your business? All these things should be included on your business plan.

To attract business, you'll need professional-looking promotional materials, such as business cards, letterhead, and envelopes. You may also want to print some flyers or brochures describing your product or services. Spring for the very best marketing materials you can afford, urges Chilcote, but don't think you have to settle for no-frills business cards or brochures just because you're on a budget. You can get high-quality promotional materials without going broke. We'll show you how in, "Budget Start-Up Strategies," page 77.

Financial projections are not necessary on your business plan if you're not trying to get a loan. However, we think it will be helpful to plot out a few money matters to help you control your financial future. You've probably already charted many of these costs on your "Mompreneurs® Start-Up Checklist." Jot down your start-up costs (equipment, marketing expenses, advertising costs, etc.) and log in your day-to-day operating expenses. If you're a manufacturer (making something by hand or machinery), you'll also need a manufacturing plan, emphasizes Barbara Brabec in her book, *Homemade Money*. Brabec says that your manufacturing plan should contain a "description of required equipment and facilities; how and where raw materials will be obtained; their estimated cost; how/where you will store/inventory them; and labor and overhead costs involved in the manufacturing process."

We think the most important financial facts you can list on your business plan are how much you'll charge for your services or product and when and by how much you will budge from that price. It's natural to want to do everything you can to attract clients and customers. Unfortunately, however, many mompreneurs (us included) are too quick to drop their prices when trying to land new clients. It's fine to offer discounts once in a while, but you should have a clear idea of how low you are willing to go. By putting this down on paper, you'll be in a better bargaining position when people try to whittle down your prices.

If you're going to get a loan for your business, you will need something more complex than what we've shown you. You'll also need more accurate financial projections if you're a single mom or if you plan to have a staff. If that's the case, see the financial data portion of our "Building Your Business Plan" box below. We also recommend you get some basic books on writing a business plan (your library or bookstore offers plenty) and check out some of the business plan computer software on the market.

BUILDING YOUR BUSINESS PLAN

Most business plans have the same basic components. We've worked out a simple outline you can follow. You can also use the online SBA Business Plan Tutorials (www.sbaonline.sba.gov) or the business plan template from the Edward Lowe Foundation (www.lowe.org).

DESCRIPTION OF BUSINESS: Is it a sole proprietorship, partnership, or corporation? Is it a merchandising, manufacturing, or service business? Why will it be profitable?

PRODUCT/SERVICE: What are you selling? What benefits are you selling? What sets your goods and services apart from the competition?

THE MARKETS: Who are your customers/clients? How will you attract, hold, and increase your market share? How do you price your products or services?

THE COMPETITION: Who are your nearest direct and indirect competitors? How are their businesses similar to and different from yours? What have you learned from their operations?

THE LOCATION: Where will your business be located? Why have you chosen your home as your base of operations? Why is this a desirable location? What kind of space do you have? What kind do you need?

MANAGEMENT: How does your background/work experience help you in this business? What are your strengths and weaknesses in running a business? Will you need other personnel from time to time (bookkeeper, secretary, attorney)?

FINANCIAL DATA: If you are applying for a loan, you'll need to add these elements to your business plan:

Forecasted income statement. Should show projected profits and losses for three to five years. Start-ups should research similar existing businesses to get an average.

Cash flow projection. Should show how much cash your business will need, when it will be needed, and where the cash will come from. Cash flow projections can be used to create a budget for your business.

Balance sheet. Records the cash position (liquidity) of the business and the owner's equity at a given point in time.

We suggest enlisting the services of an accountant to put together this financial data, especially if you're seeking financing for a new business.

WHAT ARE YOU WORTH?

Pricing your service or product is one of the trickiest parts of running a home business. To help determine her fees, Joanna Hayes, a CPA and work-at-home mom from Tustin, California, used her financial expertise to devise an exercise that can help steer you in the right direction.

"When I started my practice, I made a list of all the benefits I had received in my previous position as an employee," she says, "and I assigned a dollar value to them." She then jotted down her former salary, all the expenses she would incur in her own new business, and the tax benefits she would receive as a home-based worker. Adding and subtracting, Hayes computed the total dollar amount or salary she would need to come up with on her own.

To set an hourly fee, she divided that dollar amount by the number of billable hours she would have, minus the time it would take to do administrative tasks. For example, your goal may be to work 1,000 hours per year (about 20 hours a week), and you estimate spending 150 of those hours on administrative tasks for which you can't charge. Hayes explains, "To figure out an hourly rate that would make me financially 'whole' with my former position,

I divided that same dollar amount from above by 850 hours. I then took that number and compared it to the market rate for my services." Fortunately, Hayes's computations worked out in her favor, and she is making more money being self-employed at home than working for someone else. Her final bit of advice: "Be able to quantify, in dollar terms, everything that can be quantified."

SETTING A FAIR FEE OR PRICE

FOR SERVICE-ORIENTED BUSINESSES: Should you bill per hour, per day, or per project? Generally speaking, if you're a fast worker and the task before you is not overly difficult, you'll make more by setting a flat fee for the project. To determine this figure, set an hourly rate and estimate how long it will take you to finish the job, building in a cushion of extra time. If the work or client is unfamiliar, double your estimated time and figure out your fee from there, suggests Hayes. Don't forget to build in thinking time. Some people get their best ideas while showering or driving their car.

If there are parts of a project that can gobble up your time (lots of phone calls, meetings, rewrites, etc.), an hourly fee makes more sense, but remember to bill for all work performed, recommends Hayes. "It's easy to forget to add in fifteen minutes here and there, but if you don't track it, your day will be lost. I don't charge for five-minute phone calls, but I will charge a client who makes three five-minute calls to me in one morning," she adds.

Daily fees are usually negotiated if you're asked to be on-site for a project. For example, an editor or publicist may come into an office to tackle a big writing job or press campaign, or an event planner may be needed to oversee a conference at a hotel. It's also common to charge by the day if you're holding a focus group in your home or developing recipes in your kitchen. The simple way to calculate a daily fee is to multiply your hourly rate by eight. However, if you're booked to work several days or on a regular basis for a client, it's good protocol to offer a discount and round off your figure.

FOR PRODUCT-ORIENTED BUSINESSES: When pricing a product, there's a bit more to consider. Here's a standard formula the Edwards recommend that home-based businesses use to determine initial price:

total material costs + overhead +
minimum profit + retail margin = retail price

Barbara Brabec's *Homemade Money* goes into much greater detail on product pricing.

Whether you're selling a service or a product, it's wise to reevaluate your prices every six months to a year. If you find the competition raising their fees, maybe you should be doing the same. If the cost of materials or your overhead suddenly shoots up, your prices should reflect those increases. Conversely, if business is slacking off, it may be because you're overcharging.

Step-Up Step #6: Obtain Necessary Financing

Your completed "Mompreneur® Start-Up Checklist" gives you an idea of how much money you're going to need to invest up front. Where are you going to get that money? If your start-up costs are relatively low—and most mompreneurships fall into this category—your personal savings account and credit cards are likely to be your best financing sources.

Terri Reed, a Virginia-based home seamstress who creates historic costumes for Colonial Williamsburg and custom-made wedding attire for clients in her area, spent approximately $2,500 of her own money to start her business. She put it toward a new sewing machine, a serger and cabinet, business cards, business license and name registration costs, and sample dresses. For her word processing equipment, Tracy Rios borrowed $4,000 from her parents and supplemented that with $1,000 of her own. When she started her freelance writing business, former newspaperwoman Julie Fanselow of Twin Falls, Idaho, purchased her $2,500 computer system by credit card and paid it off over two years or so. Dallas inventor Gail Frankel drained her family savings account of $50,000 to finance Stroll'r Hold'r, a convenient catch-all that clips onto the back of a baby's stroller.

When start-up costs are substantial, you may need to get a loan for your business. Obtaining one is not always a simple matter, particularly for female home-based business owners. "Women may have a harder time getting financing because they tend to go into service-oriented businesses with no hard assets," says Sharon Hadary, executive director of the Center for Women's Business Research. Though funding opportunities for women-owned businesses have grown, mompreneurs still report difficulties in obtaining bank loans. Many have mentioned that they perceived some degree of gender-based discrimination from loan officers and venture capitalists. Despite this, women-owned businesses are growing dramatically and have become a powerful and expanding economic force.

That's because "women are relationship-oriented," says Hadary, and they have learned to capitalize on these skills when dealing with bankers. When looking for a loan, she suggests you begin by researching the various banks in your area. "Interview bankers to find out what type of businesses they're interested in and then choose the one best-suited to your business," Hadary says. Once you've narrowed down a receptive bank, put your personal accounts into that bank and continue developing a relationship with the banker, she says. Take him or her to lunch and discuss your idea. Listen to the banker's suggestions, and tailor your business plan to reflect them. "You want to make your banker feel like your advisor, like part of your business," says Hadary. Don't be surprised if you're asked to pledge your personal assets to secure the loan, she adds. "Banks need collateral—whether they're processing a loan for $10,000 or $100,000."

WHERE TO GO FOR A LOAN

BANKERS THAT BELIEVE IN WOMEN: Mompreneurs with a solid business plan shouldn't be afraid to go directly to a bank for a loan. Institutions like Bank of America, Bank One, and Fleet are particularly supportive of women-owned businesses. And don't rule out your personal bank— especially if you've been doing business there for a while.

THE U.S. SMALL BUSINESS ADMINISTRATION (SBA): Did you and your banker discuss SBA loans? This agency makes two basic types of loans to small businesses. A *guaranty loan* is made primarily by banks but guaranteed by the SBA for up to 90 percent of its value. Businesses can get loans up to $750,000, but most work-at-home moms don't require that much. You and your banker decide on the interest rates and payment schedule. An even more attractive idea is the LowDoc program, a joint bank/SBA venture in which small businesses can secure a loan of $150,000 or less. This program is attractive because it simplifies the application process, provides a rapid response, and better suits the needs of most mompreneurs. Some banks also offer an SBA-sponsored microloan program with loans of $25,000 or less. This pilot program is growing, so ask about it at your bank.

Larger *SBA-backed loans* are also available through many banks. The SBA Women's Loan Pre-Qualification Program helps you put together a solid loan application and backs you with a pre-qualification letter to take to banks. It's especially helpful for tough-to-finance home or service-based businesses.

SMALL BUSINESS INVESTMENT COMPANIES (SBICS): These are private, for-profit institutions sponsored by the SBA. These local companies lend money to or make equity investments in start-ups or small businesses. There are also Specialized Small Business Investment Companies (SSBICs) run by the SBA; both are amenable to requests by women.

STATE ECONOMIC DEVELOPMENT AGENCIES: You can tap these agencies for smaller amounts of money, and some are particularly interested in women and minorities. ACCION of New Mexico is one such agency that made loans to two of the mompreneurs in our book. Check your home state to see if a similar program is in effect.

Count-Me-In: To encourage women's economic independence, Count-Me-In has established a national loan fund for potential or current women business owners. Business loans, ranging from $500 to $10,000, and scholarships for business training and technical assistance will be given to qualifying women. You can apply online (www.count—me-in.org.).

Self-Employment and Enterprise Development (SEED) programs: Loans are available to unemployed workers. Instead of collecting unemployment insurance, you receive a lump sum to use to start a business. Counseling, training, and technical assistance are also part of the program. However, SEED programs are only available in a handful of states. To find out if your state offers one, call your state government or the United States Department of Labor in Washington, D.C. (www.dol.gov).

Small business development centers: These are springing up at colleges and universities as well as in community storefronts. For a directory of centers near you, check out the Association for Small Business Development Centers (www.asbac-us.org) and the SBA Online Women's Business Center (www.onlinewbc.org). While most centers focus on entrepreneurial training programs and advice, small sums of money are sometimes available, too. Even if loans are few and far between, these centers usually have well-stocked resources libraries and experts who can guide you toward potential lenders you may not know about.

Start-Up Step # 7: Market Yourself

Create a website and professional-looking business cards, letterhead, flyers, and/or brochures to promote your business. Then spread the word about your enterprise to everyone you know. We'll tell you exactly how to do this in chapter 7.

WHAT YOU NEED IN A WEBSITE

No matter what business you're in, a website is essential in these high-tech times. And it doesn't have to cost a fortune. You can start with a simple site and add extra features as your business grows. But here are the basics you'll need to consider from the start:

✓ **Clean design.** The simpler the design, the more usable the site. Aim for a good balance of text and graphics on your home page. Too much text looks boring, and too many graphics will slow downloading time. Avoid flashing images, huge fonts, garish colors, and jarring backgrounds.

✓ FAST LOADING TIME Don't clutter home pages with an abundance of graphics, animated or oversized images, plug-ins, or pop-up windows. These take longer to load, and you don't want viewers surfing off your site because it takes so long to bring up. Instead, place small thumbnail images in the home page; visitors can click on them to enlarge them for a better look.

✓ EASY NAVIGATION. Visitors should be able to find their way from your home page to other areas of your website without getting lost. Simple navigational bars or buttons, pull-down menus, and icons all help lead the way. A good rule of thumb: It should take no more than three clicks to get from any one page to another on your website.

✓ CONCISE, CATCHY CONTENT. A visually pleasing site may attract viewers the first couple times, but content is what will keep them coming back. Web users are looking for good information—that's the primary reason they log on in the first place. So present your content in a clear, well-written format without being too wordy. Even if your website is mainly a catalog of products, give visitors a little extra information (such as tips or related articles) along with the product descriptions.

✓ INTERACTIVITY. Find ways to make visitors feel like they're active participants in your site. Surveys, quizzes, contests, and newsletters are all relatively easy to include and help personalize the surfing experience for guests. A simple feedback area is another way to encourage interaction.

✓ SHOESTRING STRATEGIES. Many mompreneurs choose to design their own websites, using templates and tools provided online at sites like AOL Hometown, Yahoo!'s Geocities, Lycos' Angelfire, iVillage.com, or other free providers. Others opt to learn HTML code and design a site from scratch. Or you may decide to use the help of a skilled web designer. For do-it-yourselfers, web design has a bit of a learning curve, but once you master the technology, you can update your site easily and cheaply. What you ultimately choose to do depends on your energy level, time constraints, and pocketbook.

Start-Up Step #8: Set Up Your Workspace

You've got to have your own personal work space, whether it's an upstairs room with a door, a converted apartment closet, or a tiny corner of the family room. What's most important is that you select a location that fits your space availability and suits your family and business needs. For example, if you live in an apartment, you may have to settle for a hallway nook instead of the converted bedroom that many homeowners are lucky enough to work in. Need to keep an eye on the kids while you work? Then station yourself in view of the children's play areas. Are you on the phone a lot with stuffy clients who won't appreciate noisy kids in the background? Then that office with a door might be a necessity. Pick the space that best works for you, and fill it with the equipment, furnishings, and storage materials that you need to run smoothly.

BREEDING A BUSINESS IDEA

"Ever since I was four years old, I've wanted to raise llamas," says Barbara Coffman, a former bookkeeper who runs Cloud Peak Llamas from her fifty-acre ranch in Story, Wyoming. It wasn't until 1987, however, when she was a stay-at-home mom with two young daughters, that she finally got her first pet llama. Soon after, she bought five more and began a family backpacking tour service, loading up the llamas and taking tourists on guided trips into the mountains. That business lasted for five years, during which time Coffman also became involved in breeding. Today, she has a lucrative ranching business dedicated exclusively to breeding and showing llamas, miniature donkeys, fainting goats, and guanacos (a cousin of the llama). Her exotic animals command big bucks from buyers as far away as Louisiana. "Technology makes it possible for me to do business anywhere in the United States without leaving home," Coffman says. How does she communicate with customers? Via her high-tech phone, fax, and computer system, conveniently located—where else?—in the barn.

START-UP COST: The initial costs for Coffman's tour business totaled about $10,000, which paid for the llamas, the backpacking equipment, and any insurance premiums.

BIGGEST WORK/FAMILY CHALLENGE: "The winters in Wyoming. Working in a foot of snow when it's twenty below zero is physically and mentally stressful."

FIVE-YEAR PLAN: The divorced Coffman has remarried. Her new husband is a livestock nutritionist who raises quarter horses. Together they'll be building a new barn and getting involved in animal training, as well as expanding the breeding business.

Start-Up Step #9: Establish Your Record-Keeping System

If you've followed Start-Up Step #3, your accountant has already told you what kind of important records you need for tax purposes, but you're the one responsible for keeping track of everything from expenditures to profits. Take the time now to come up with a way to organize all your business records. It will save you a lot of hunting for bills and receipts later on.

"No company can survive without a bookkeeping system. And life has become too complicated for shoe boxes to work anymore," says Geraldine A. Larkin in her book, *Woman to Woman: Street Smarts for Women Entrepreneurs*. Though Larkin strongly recommends hiring a bookkeeper, we feel this is an unrealistic option for most mompreneurs in the beginning stages of their business. Larkin's book also offers an easy "eight part system" for women who want to handle the books themselves. Since not all of Larkin's components will be necessary for the mompreneur, we've highlighted the ones that we think will be most beneficial for accurate record-keeping below. Financial computer software programs such as Quicken®, Peachtree Accounting®, Quickbooks®, and MYOB® can help simplify many of these steps.

A SEPARATE CHECKING ACCOUNT FOR BUSINESS: Don't use your personal checks to pay for business expenses. A separate checking account used just for business expenditures helps you look more professional and simplifies your record-keeping.

A LOG OF EXPENSES: Keep a running record of what you're spending on phone bills, fax bills, supplies, travel, vendors, and other business disbursements.

A RECORD OF SALES/BILLS AND RECEIPTS: Keep a journal or file for tracking what you've billed or sold and for noting when people have paid you.

A GENERAL LEDGER: You'll need this if your business requires preparing monthly financial statements.

INVENTORY RECORDS: If you have inventory, you'll need to check it periodically to keep track of what you really have.

PAYROLL RECORDS: These are only necessary if you have employees. Your accountant can tell you the best way to set this up.

Start-Up Step #10: Schedule Your Office Hours

Determine the exact hours and days you'll be working every week, and do your best to stick to them. Remember, if you were in the traditional workforce, you'd have a starting and a quitting time. It should be no different when you work at home. Sure, your hours are going to vary from time to time, and you're bound to put in your share of late nights and weekends when the kids get sick, but if you've set boundaries for your work life, it will be easier to keep family and business demands from overlapping.

Start-Up Step #11: Line Up Your Child Care

If you're going to use child care, start searching for your Mary Poppins.

Start-Up Step #12: Open for Business

Jump in and get going. Don't get discouraged if you get rejected during your cold calls or your marketing attempts. "The most important thing to remember is that when you are turned down, people are not rejecting you as a person. They just happen not to want or need your services at that time," says Maria Chilcote. Adds Terri Reed, Virginia-based seamstress, "You never know whether you'll succeed unless you try." So keep plugging away, and business will be booming before you know it.

FLEXING YOUR MONEY MUSCLE

Money: We know we want it, but we're not always so good at getting what we deserve. "I think negotiating for money is one of the hardest things," says Debi Hamuka-Falkenham, a graphic artist in Seymour, Connecticut. "It's tough to be confident without sounding arrogant, especially, I think, for a woman," adds Julie Fanselow, a freelance writer. "But it's necessary."

If you want to maximize your earning power and be taken seriously as a businesswoman, you've got to become more assertive about money matters. Here are some tips on how to do that from other mompreneurs:

KNOW YOUR VALUE AND TELL YOURSELF YOU'RE WORTH IT: "You must be confident and believe you are worth the price you are asking for," stresses Jane Boyd, a Canadian work-family consultant. Adds Terri Reed, "At first I found it tough to get the fees I deserved for my work because I didn't think a custom-made dress would command a very high price. I have changed my thinking about the value of my services, and now feel I get what I deserve."

CHARGE A COMPETITIVE PRICE, BUT DON'T SELL YOURSELF SHORT: "Don't prostitute yourself," cautions Maria Chilcote, who runs a training and consulting firm from her home in Springfield, Virginia. Keep in mind that a bargain-basement pricing strategy can actually backfire, chasing business away rather than attracting it. "At first, I set my prices well below the competitors, thinking it would bring me extra business," says Reed. "But I found instead that most people don't feel they will get a quality product if your price is too low."

DON'T BACK DOWN, BUT IF YOU DO, TELL CLIENTS IT'S ONE-TIME ONLY: "Initially, many people will just want to get the job and will underbid themselves into a hole," notes Nancy Danahy, a graphic designer. "While that's okay for a first job for a client, be frank if they offer you more work at the same rate. Say, 'I'd love to take on more work from you, but I found I lost money on the last job. Could we renegotiate the fee?' If the work is contingent on the lowest fee possible, you'll have to make a hard decision. In my field, sometimes the artistic reward and good samples are payment enough, but not for many jobs."

PUT IT IN WRITING: Protect yourself with a written contract or proposal that clearly states the service or product you're providing, when you expect to deliver it, how much you are getting paid for it, and when the payment is due, says Chilcote. Then make sure the agreement is signed and dated by you and your client. "When I make a proposal, I am very careful to explain what is and what is not covered in my fee," says Boyd. "That way there are no gray areas, and I can be sure that when I have to ask for extra money, I am justified."

ASK FOR A DEPOSIT OR ADVANCE: "I never have unpaid fees because the client must pay before they get their dress," says Reed. "To avoid any unpleasant situations, I ask the client to pay half the fee before I even start the work. I do this to make sure the client's check clears the bank before I spend any significant amount of time on that project."

BE CHOOSY ABOUT THE JOBS YOU TAKE: You may do it once, but you don't have to continue working for a client who underpays or takes advantage of your services, says New York writer Lisa Iannucci. She's learned that small businesses don't always pay freelance writers when they should, so she's not as likely to work for them anymore. "I keep reminding myself that I'm worth the money, and that I no longer have to prove myself." Be realistic, too, about whether or not certain jobs are worth your effort. When she first started freelancing, Ellen agreed to write a new product story on ceiling fans, even though she knew nothing about them. The piece wound up taking her ten times longer than stories in her area of expertise (parenting), yet she was paid the same rate. She learned the hard way that writing on a subject you know and love is much more cost-effective than exploring unfamiliar topics that don't interest you.

BE A PEST ABOUT UNPAID FEES: "My biggest problem is getting paid in a reasonable amount of time," says Sandra Chute, a copyeditor in Alexandria, Virginia. "Many people just don't pay me until I've sent an overdue invoice and then made a follow-up call about it." When clients don't pay up, e-mail or fax them overdue notices, and follow those up with phone calls. "I once did a party for a client and her check bounced," says Deborah Mumford, a naturalist who runs an environmental education program in Purdys, New York. "When the second check finally came, it was for the wrong amount. So I had my husband call and say he was the bookkeeper. Meanwhile, I said to myself, 'You should really be doing this.' But somehow I just felt that he had more clout."

If you're a member of a professional group, see if they have a grievance committee that will go to bat for you, suggests Iannucci. And if all else fails, and you're owed a significant amount, bring the client to court.

BUDGET START-UP STRATEGIES

BARTER: Trade services with other people who can help you. For example, Lisa Marie Nelson, a children's songwriter and record producer in California, did some free writing for ABC. In return, she got to use their recording studio for her productions. Maria Chilcote drove a neighbor's daughter to school every day in exchange for free baby-sitting. You can barter for just about anything, from printing services to warehouse space to computer consulting.

PURCHASE USED OFFICE EQUIPMENT: "I found these wonderful chairs at a used office furniture store," says Jackie Iglehart, a mompreneur and former editor of a monthly newsletter on personal finance. With the help of her local computer consultant, she was also able to find a great secondhand computer that was perfect for her needs. She also saved by leasing a copy machine, using fluorescent lighting rather than incandescent bulbs, and buying a carpet remnant instead of wall-to-wall carpet.

BUY SUPPLIES WHOLESALE: Don't pay list price for crafts materials or other supplies you may need for your business, says Iglehart. If you have a tax ID number, you'll be able to purchase what you need though wholesalers, she says. Look through mail-order catalogs, too, for discounted office supplies.

DESIGN YOUR OWN MARKETING MATERIALS OR USE A DESKTOP PUBLISHER: You can save a lot of money by utilizing desktop publishing instead of a traditional print shop, points out Chilcote. If you can't do it yourself, she says, find someone who can. You bring the design ideas and the fancy paper, which you can buy in smaller quantities and for affordable prices through discount paper catalogs, and the desktop publisher does the rest.

BUY AS YOU GROW: Make do with what you can until you get established. "I worked at the dining room table on an ancient word processor, and as I made money, I invested in furniture and a computer," says mom Sandra Chute. "My rule was no debt."

MOMPRENEUR® HALL OF FAME

Lane Nemeth
Founder of Discovery Toys, Inc., Martinez, California
Mother of One

When Lane Nemeth started her business, the only thing she was really clear on was her vision. "I knew I wanted to help parents understand the importance of playing with their children and give them high-quality toys that would be educational as well as entertaining," she says. Other than that, "I really had no idea what I was getting into."

As a former day-care center director, Nemeth had the early childhood education background to help her achieve her mission. She knew that the kind of learning toys she had in mind were available to educators but not to the general public. It was her parenting experience that launched her into action. She wanted safe, long-lasting, nonviolent toys for her baby, Tara. When she couldn't find them in any store, she decided to market them herself.

Next came the real challenge: tracking down the toys to sell. "I wrote to about 200 American toy manufacturers from the Thomas Register and thought that, of course, the world was simply waiting for my great new idea," Nemeth recalls. Unfortunately, she only got two responses, "and neither was anything I was interested in," she says. Then she heard about a small local toy show in Los Angeles. With $5,000 in her pocket, borrowed from her grandmother, and with an old friend along for support, she flew from San Francisco to Los Angeles. "I remember getting to the airport in L.A. and picking up the luggage and saying, 'Now what am I supposed to do?' "

Nemeth only found about forty toys on that trip, but they were enough to get her on her way. In 1978, she started Discovery Toys from her garage in Martinez, California. The business grew so quickly that there were soon toys everywhere: in the kitchen, the living room, and even the bedroom. After just a few short months, using more borrowed capital from family and friends, Nemeth found it necessary to move into warehouse-office space.

Instead of selling the toys at retail, Nemeth had independent salespeople pitch them directly to parents through home demonstrations. In that first year, she had a sales force of three. Today, Discovery Toys has over 30,000 independent contractors, most of whom are mothers with young children.

Nemeth has had her share of stumbling blocks along the way. "I've made every mistake that is humanly possible," she says. She also has fought many biases. "When I went to sign the lease on my first warehouse, the man would not allow me to sign it because my husband had to sign it. I was really furious. But it was fun to go back many years later and say, 'Remember me?'"

Nemeth notes that motherhood has prepared her well for tough business challenges. "Mothering taught me that you really need to listen to people, and you need to have patience and respect," she says. "When your child spills milk, you don't say, 'Oh, you horrible person, you spilled your milk.' You say, 'Oh, gee whiz, look at this white thing we have on the floor. Let's mop it up together.'" It's just as important to do that when you're a boss, she says. When someone makes a mistake, it's great if you can say, "Oh, let's mop this up together and see what we can learn," she says. "I use my mothering skills in my business every day. And when I'm in my 'good mother' mode, I'm a very good boss. When I lose my 'good mother' face, I can be a real pain."

4

Child Care

As brand-new mothers, we believed we could easily work our writing assignments around the baby's nap schedule. Our fantasy went something like this: "Newborns sleep for stretches of three hours or more, waking only to eat and be changed. That means I can work at least six hours a day and still have time to bond with my baby."

Of course, the reality turned out to be quite different. We quickly learned how unpredictable babies can be. Ours, like most, didn't nap by the book. Sometimes they'd take several short snoozes, leaving us little time to get a project under way. Other days they'd sleep for long stretches, yet always wake up when we got that important call. To our surprise, they weren't always content to hang out in the infant seat, swing, or playpen while we tapped away at our computers. When they were cooperative, we'd worry that we were neglecting them.

As they grew to be active toddlers and preschoolers, we found it even harder to focus on our kids and our work simultaneously. We had to face up to another fact of mompreneurship: If you've got a job that requires lots of phone work and concentration, you'll need some sort of child care to help you stay sane and guilt-free.

MULTIPLE CHOICES FOR MOMPRENEURS

We discovered that there are a wide variety of child-care options available to work-at-home moms, and between us, we've tried just about all of them. As a mompreneur, you'll also find yourself sampling many different types of child-care arrangements over the years as your kids and your business grow.

Of the hundreds of mompreneurs we talked to, 89 percent said they relied on some form of child care. These methods ranged from the traditional (in-home sitters, family day care, school programs, and the like) to the innovative (sitter-sharing, baby-sitting co-ops, and other imaginative systems). Many of the moms we polled used a combination plan, pairing different types of child-care programs (such as schools and mother's helpers) to give them the coverage they needed to get their work done.

Does It Pay to Use Child Care?

Being able to afford child care can be a big dilemma for work-at-homers. If you're just starting up and are uncertain about your earning power, it may seem unprofitable to pay someone to watch the kids. Even if you've already got a thriving business, child-care costs can quickly drain your profits. Still, the majority of mompreneurs we talked to considered child care a necessary expense because it buys them the chance to give both the kids and the business the undivided attention they need. "For me, having reliable child care is not a luxury, it's a flat-out requirement," says Lisa Dillon, a technical writer in Portland, Oregon.

If you're worried about whether child care is really worth it, here are some ways to help put your mind at ease.

Consider It an Investment in Your Future

Child care is a little like college tuition. It can be expensive, but it paves the way for your success later on. "Sometimes I felt like my baby-sitter made more than me," says Theresa Kump, a Larchmont, New York, writer who no longer needs child care now that her kids are in school. But without a sitter, Kump says she never would have gotten her business up and running. The money she shelled out for sitting enabled her to become well established as a freelancer. By the time both kids were in school for a full day, Kump had a broad client base and fewer child-care costs.

Don't Feel Guilty About It

You may think that using child care defeats the purpose of being home with the kids, but there's not much point to working at home if you spend most of your time telling children, "Not now, Mommy's busy." Child care actually helps you gain more control of your work time so that during your off hours, kids have you all to themselves. Vermont-based graphic designer Karen McCloud says the leisurely breakfasts and special lunch breaks she shared with her preschoolers every day wouldn't have been possible without her in-home sitter. "We'd hang out and wait for the sitter to arrive in the morning, and then I'd come down at lunchtime, and we'd read and talk until it was time for me to go back to work," McCloud says. "There was no rushing and no pressure, and we all valued and looked forward to that time together."

Explore Low-Cost Options

There are lots of affordable child-care choices out there; you just have to know where to look for them. Mary Williams, a network marketer from Lynnwood, Washington, streamlined her child-care costs by hiring a local teen who was trying to get started baby-sitting. "She was willing to take less to get the experience," Williams says, "and I could be here if anything happened, plus breast-feed on demand."

WHAT'S THE RIGHT CHILD CARE FOR YOU?

IF YOU . . .	YOUR BEST BETS ARE . . .
Plan to work partial days or just a few days a week	Family members, part-time in-home sitters or family day-care providers, nursery schools, tot drops, Parent's Day Out programs, baby-sitting co-ops, sitter-sharing, trade-off sitting
Need full days to work	In-home caregivers, live-in nannies, au pairs, day-care centers, family day care, housekeepers
Need to supplement school hours	After-school programs, family members, teen sitters/ mother's helpers, camps, play dates, housekeepers
Need someone to drive the kids around	Family members, nannies, au pairs, other moms
Travel or attend evening meetings often	Family members, live-in nannies, au pairs

IF YOU . . .	YOUR BEST BETS ARE . . .
Don't have an office that's set apart from the main flow of the family	Away-from-home caregivers like family day care, day-care centers, tot drops, Parent's Day Out programs, school and after-school programs
Are on a tight budget	Family members, teen sitters/mother's helpers, family day care, baby-sitting co-ops, sitter sharing, play dates, trade-off sitting, on-call sitters, kids fend-for-themselves incentive program
Often have to see clients at home	Away-from-home caregivers like family day care, day-care centers, school programs

ASSESSING YOUR NEEDS

Before you begin exploring all your child-care options, have a clear idea of what you require in a caregiver. Sit down and think about the ages and the needs of your children. Consider your type of business and the kind of work schedule you'll keep. Will you want to work every day or just a few days a week? Can you get by working mornings or afternoons, or do you need full days? Also take an honest look at your temperament and personality. Are you focused enough to work while the kids are with an in-house sitter, or will you be more productive if you drop them off somewhere? What other skills are important to you? Do you need someone who can drive? Are you interested in someone who can do light housework?

When Ellen's kids were babies, she was lucky to have her mother-in-law living nearby. Grandma came and watched the kids three days a week while Ellen churned out articles from an upstairs bedroom. That gave Ellen two whole days a week off, which she happily spent playing with baby Matthew while her answering machine screened her calls. Pat didn't have nearby relatives who could baby-sit, so she opted for a neighborhood day-care center two days a week, supplemented by a grandmotherly baby-sitter when her first son was an infant and toddler. Once son number two was born, it became more convenient and cost-effective to hire a live-in au pair.

Setting your own schedule allows you to be more flexible and creative about the kind of child care you choose. You may only want someone three days a week. Maybe you'll need a sitter for a few hours every day. Perhaps you'll opt for live-in help who can cook and clean, too. If your kids are in school and you work a nine-to-three day, a summer setup and a few well-planned play dates may be all you need to supplement the academic calendar.

No matter which type of child-care arrangements you pick at first, your requirements are bound to change as your children grow older. When her kids were babies, Mary Gillett, a Michigan writer and marketing communication consultant, had in-house help several afternoons a week. As they grew, she shifted to a neighborhood day-care home, then a preschool. Now that the kids are in school full-time, she has a sitter pick them up a few days a week so she can wrap up her work by late afternoon.

REVIEWING YOUR CHILD-CARE OPTIONS

There are three main types of child care: in-home, where somebody comes to you; family day care, where your child is watched in someone else's home; and center-based programs such as schools, day-care centers, and after-school programs. Within these main groups there are a variety of specific options for you to consider. If you're like most of us, you'll find yourself mixing and matching various child-care options over time to create your own customized plan. We've found work-at-home moms to be extremely clever about the combination plans they come up with. That's because mompreneurship gives you freedom of choice and opens you up to an array of part-time or full-time options to suit every stage of your family and business life. For a complete list of child-care referral services and resource organizations, turn to chapter 11.

CAN YOU DO IT WITHOUT A SITTER?

Take this quick quiz to see if you can get by without formal child care. If you answer yes to most of these questions, you may be able to pull it off. (For strategies on surviving without child care, turn to the end of this chapter.)

1. Are your kids in school full-time? ____ Yes   ____ No

2. If your kids are young, are they easy to manage and good at entertaining themselves? ____ Yes   ____ No

3. Do you do the type of work that can be easily interrupted? ____ Yes   ____ No

4. Can you get most of your work done in the early mornings or late evenings while your kids are asleep? If so, will you have the stamina to keep up this kind of schedule? ___ Yes ___ No

5. Does your business require very little phone time? ___ Yes ___ No

6. Does your business require very few face-to-face meetings? ___ Yes ___ No

7. Are you calm and patient and able to put up with constant interruptions from the kids? ___ Yes ___ No

8. Are you in a laid-back profession where clients are apt to be more kid-tolerant than those in more formal fields? ___ Yes ___ No

9. Will you be able to bring your kids with you when you pick up or drop off work? ___ Yes ___ No

10. Are you in the kind of field (such as toy-selling or children's fashions) where having the kids around is actually a plus? ___ Yes ___ No

11. Do you have a business partner who can keep the ball rolling when you're in a bind? ___ Yes ___ No

12. Is your office within view of the kids' play areas? ___ Yes ___ No

TRADITIONAL CHILD-CARE CHOICES

Child-care costs vary widely, depending upon where you live and the amount of experience the caregiver has. Child-care costs are typically higher in urban areas. On the following pages, we've tried to give ball-park ranges of child-care costs wherever possible. Keep in mind that these are rough approximations only.

Postpartum Helpers

Looking for someone to help out during your first few weeks home with a new baby? A doula may be just what you need. Doulas are caregivers who come into your home to help you during the first six weeks after you give birth. Unlike baby nurses of generations past, doulas address the needs of the new mom rather than the infant. The doula's tasks might include reading a story to an older sibling, picking up the dry cleaning, folding the laundry, and doing some cooking and grocery shopping. Many doulas have backgrounds as nurses, childbirth educators, teachers, lactation consultants, or social workers and most have families of their own.

"If you're expecting a baby and already run a business from home, a doula can help you meet the multiple demands of the newborn and the business," says mompreneur Marguerite Tirelli, founder of Beyond Birth, Inc., a New York doula service.

BEST FOR: Newborns

THE GOING RATE: About $20 an hour, with a 12-hour minimum

BENEFITS:
- ✓ A great option if you've already got a home business and don't plan to take maternity leave
- ✓ Someone to help you run the household while you tend to both baby and business
- ✓ Offers lots of emotional support and confidence-boosting
- ✓ Gift certificates available from many doula agencies (easy for close friends or family members to treat you to this service)

DRAWBACKS:
- ✓ Extremely expensive
- ✓ Only available the first six weeks postpartum

Family Members

If your husband works odd hours, you might rely on him for your primary child care. Kim Palmer's spouse, Jim Kern, is a newspaperman who works nights, so he's able to care for their kids in the mornings and early afternoons while she runs her Minneapolis publishing firm. Laura Mathisen, a copywriter in Spokane, Washington, relies on both her husband and her in-laws for baby-sitting care. "It's a good system," she says, and it allows her to put in as many as fifty hours a week for just the price of treating Grandma and Grandpa to a few dinners out.

Older children can also be recruited to sit for their younger siblings during the after-school hours and on school holidays and vacations. Try to use this as a stopgap measure, not your main source of child care.

BEST FOR: All ages

THE GOING RATE: Usually free or for minimal charge. You can also show your appreciation with small gifts, dinners out, and other little luxuries.

BENEFITS:
   ✓ Children and family members spend special time together.
   ✓ Reliable.
   ✓ Low- or no-cost.
   ✓ No references to check.

DRAWBACKS:
   ✓ Difficult being boss to family members.
   ✓ Relatives may have a different child-rearing style.
   ✓ If the kids are in your home, it will be more difficult for you to stay on task.
   ✓ If the caregiver is your husband, you may feel like you're sometimes missing out on important family time.

PUTTING SIBLINGS IN CHARGE

If you have preteen or teenage children, they may be able to take charge of their younger siblings once in a while after school. When she had to run out for a quick demo, Marsha Swainston, a Sterling Manager for Discovery Toys in Lenexa, Kansas, occasionally asked her teenager to watch her younger brother. "I only did it in a pinch, and I made sure it was only for short periods. And I was always reachable by cell phone," Swainston says.

If you're considering giving your children child-care responsibilities, be respectful of the older child's social and private needs. Treat this as a favor, not a requirement. Limit kids' sitting hours so they don't become overburdened or resentful. Offer to compensate them for helping you out. This might mean paying them an hourly rate or awarding them special privileges, such as dinner out or a night at the movies. Swainston's daughter received some very special perks for helping her mom run the business. "She got to come along on the family vacations that are part of the Discovery Toys incentive plan," says Swainston. "We've been to Hawaii, Cancun, China, and Hong Kong."

Are your kids ready to take on child-care responsibilities? Ask yourself these important questions:

✓ Do your children get along well?
✓ Will you be in the house most of the time or close by and easily reached in case of emergency?
✓ Will the baby-sitting cut into children's homework time or extracurricular activities?
✓ Will the kids be able to play quietly or work together on activities like homework or crafts projects?

Live-Out, In-Home Caregivers

Someone (not a relative) cares for your kids in your home, either full-time or part-time. The caregiver does not live with you. In-home caregivers might be young mothers with children of their own, grandma types with grown kids, or high school or college students. You'll often hear in-home caregivers referred to as nannies, baby-sitters, and mothers' helpers, and these names are often used interchangeably. Technically, nannies usually have formal child-care schooling or extensive experience. A baby-sitter is generally someone without special training, who may or may not have previous experience caring for kids. Mother's helpers are preteens and teens who provide care while you're in the house after school and during holidays and vacations. Housekeepers are another type of in-home child care, but we're going to talk about them separately.

Most mompreneurs seem to prefer having their in-home caregivers come part-time. Technical writer Lisa Dillon had a nanny come to her home in Portland, Oregon, four days a week from 9 A.M. to 2 P.M. At $6.50 an hour, it wasn't cheap, she says, but it allowed her to work a pretty full schedule and have the flexibility to arrange for client meetings. Betsy Johns, a Discovery Toys consultant from Portage, Michigan, paid a local youth about $10 a week to come a few afternoons after school. If you'd rather work mornings, you might be able to find a college student or senior citizen who's available.

Another part-time idea is to check with child-care agencies in your area to see if they offer nanny-sharing programs, where two or three families share the caregiver. "It's basically like a private day-care center that rotates from home to home on a weekly or monthly basis," says Dillon, who's considered this method but hasn't yet tried it out.

BEST FOR: Infants and toddlers

THE GOING RATE: Anywhere from around $3 to $8 an hour for preteen or teen sitters; up to $10 an hour or more for more experienced sitters; $11 to $15 an hour for professional nannies

BENEFITS:
- ✓ You have more control over how children spend their day.
- ✓ Kids get individualized attention and stay in familiar surroundings.
- ✓ The caregiver comes to you.
- ✓ You can take quick breaks with your children.
- ✓ Kids' naps, mealtimes, and other daily rituals won't be disrupted.

DRAWBACKS:
- ✓ It's distracting, and the kids might have a hard time leaving you alone.
- ✓ It's expensive.
- ✓ There's a high turnover rate.
- ✓ You're stuck when the caregiver can't come.
- ✓ It can be hard to delegate all responsibility to a sitter when you're home and available.

Live-In Nannies

Live-in nannies reside in your home and may have some professional training, such as a diploma from a nanny school. Their responsibilities can include preparing the children's meals, organizing their daily events, supervising play dates, and shuttling kids to and from school and extracurricular activities. "I have always felt that a live-in is best, since my hours can be erratic," says Kitty Ault, an event planner in Westchester, New York.

BEST FOR: Infants, toddlers, and preschoolers

THE GOING RATE: Anywhere from around $200 to $500 per week or more

BENEFITS:
- ✓ Same as for live-out, in-home caregivers, plus . . .
- ✓ You've got someone there for the kids if your business requires traveling or evening meetings.
- ✓ They may do cooking or light cleaning.

DRAWBACKS:
- ✓ You lose your privacy.
- ✓ It's one of the most expensive options.
- ✓ It's distracting, and the kids might have a hard time leaving you alone.
- ✓ It can be hard to delegate responsibility to someone else when you're home and available.

Au Pairs

Another type of live-in caregiver, au pairs are usually young European or American women under the age of twenty-five. They live with you up to one year in exchange for airfare, housing, and a weekly salary. Au pairs may work no more than forty-five hours a week. You'll need to provide them with a separate bedroom and weekends off. If they drive, they'll be available to taxi children back and forth, but you'll need to provide the vehicle. For the names of agencies that can help place you with an au pair, turn to chapter 11.

BEST FOR: Preschoolers and grade-schoolers

THE GOING RATE: About $125 a week, plus room and board, plus a fee (averaging about $4,000) to the au pair agency to cover the caregiver's cost of transportation, health insurance, and administrative costs

BENEFITS:
- ✓ Same as for live-out, in-home caregiver, plus . . .
- ✓ They're young and energetic.
- ✓ It's less expensive than a live-in nanny.

DRAWBACKS:
- ✓ There could be a language barrier, and au pairs may get homesick.
- ✓ They're often inexperienced in dealing with babies.
- ✓ They only stay for one year.
- ✓ You lose your privacy.
- ✓ It's distracting, and the kids have a hard time leaving you alone.
- ✓ When you're home and available, it can be hard to delegate responsibility to someone else.

Housekeeper

This in-home caregiver handles both child-care duties and household chores such as cooking, cleaning, and running errands. They can work part- or full-time, and may live in or out.

BEST FOR: All ages

THE GOING RATE: Anywhere from $5 to $10 an hour or more

BENEFITS:
- ✓ You get a hand with housework.
- ✓ Someone's around to let the kids in from school if you have to attend an outside meeting.

DRAWBACKS:
- ✓ They may not have child-care experience.
- ✓ Taking care of children and housework can be an overwhelming task for some people.

Family Day Care

Your children are cared for in someone else's home, often by mothers who have their own children there, too. Some day-care providers take only one family at a time, while others run more formal businesses that welcome groups of children. The group size in family day care is always small (usually between four and twelve children), with two or more adult caregivers often available for every six kids.

You'll most likely be responsible for getting your kids to the day-care home, although sometimes you can find caregivers who are willing to pick your kids up from school. Maureen LaMarca, a New Jersey marketing consultant, who used family day care in the after-school hours, was lucky enough to find a provider right on the bus route. Her kids were dropped there every afternoon, and all LaMarca had to do was pick them up.

BEST FOR: Infants, toddlers, and preschoolers

THE GOING RATE: Anywhere from around $3 to $5 an hour or more

BENEFITS:
- ✓ Homey, intimate, family-like setting.
- ✓ Kids get to interact with other children.
- ✓ An economical option.
- ✓ With the kids out of the house, you can work in peace.

DRAWBACKS:
- ✓ Your kids are exposed to other children's germs.
- ✓ You're stuck if the caregiver or your child gets sick.
- ✓ Many family day-care providers are not licensed or regulated.

THINKING OF STARTING YOUR OWN FAMILY DAY-CARE BUSINESS?

Is running a home day-care business a tempting solution to your child-care dilemma? It's a way to have a rewarding career and make money without having to hire a sitter for your own kids, but being a family day-care provider isn't for everyone. Here are some important questions to ask yourself before you make the decision:

Do you absolutely love taking care of children? "Your heart has to really be in this," advises Cheryl Mucciolo, a day-care provider in Hopewell Junction, New York. "Sometimes people think it's easy, and say, 'Oh, I think I'll take in a couple of kids and earn some money,' but those children are going to be with you from morning till night, and you really have to be dedicated to them."

Are you prepared to be on-call round-the-clock? The job goes on well after you've said good-bye to the last child at the day's end. "Parents call you at all hours," says Deborah Eaton, a family child-care provider in San Diego and former president of the National Association for Family Child Care. You are the child's home away from home and the parents' main connection to what's happening during the day, adds Mucciolo. Parents will want your support, your feedback, and your advice—and you have to be there for them, no matter what the hour, she says.

Are you willing to divide the time you spend with your own children? A day-care business can take over your homelife. Your children will have to share their mommy and their personal space with other kids. If you have younger children, assure them that you'll protect their personal belongings, Eaton suggests. For example, keep their rooms and favorite toys off-limits to the other children. If you're planning to have older kids assist you in the business, offer them a small stipend for their help. Most important, find ways to keep your own kids from getting lost in the crowd. "Sometimes you want to favor your own children, but it's just not fair to the rest of the group," says Mucciolo, so you've got to set aside one-on-one time with them after everyone else is gone and do your best to make the nights and weekends special, she says. "Sometimes it's the littlest things—like a private talk or snuggling up for a family movie or a quick trip out for ice cream—that show your kids that they're important, too," Mucciolo says.

Do you have the space? Make sure you've got areas you can set aside to accommodate a group of children of varying ages. Do you have room for cribs, changing tables, and activity and eating spots? Will you be able to keep the business set apart from your main living areas? Mucciolo has a separate in-law apartment used just for the day-care business. "It helps me to physically shut the door on work at the end of the day," she says.

Day-Care Centers

You bring kids to a child-care facility, where they're grouped according to age and cared for by staff members trained in early education. Centers may be privately owned or operated by nonprofit organizations such as churches, synagogues, public schools, and community groups.

BEST FOR: Preschoolers

THE GOING RATE: Around $3.00 an hour or more

BENEFITS:
- ✓ Reliable—centers are usually open on holidays and will get a substitute when caregivers are sick.
- ✓ Usually one of the most affordable options.

DRAWBACKS:
- ✓ Children receive little individual attention.
- ✓ Children are exposed to other kids' germs.
- ✓ You're stuck when your child gets sick.

Tot Drops

Also commonly called Stay and Plays, these are group drop-off programs where you can take your children on a first-come, first-served basis. They're often run by churches, nursery schools, and community organizations, and they usually accept kids for up to three hours at a time.

BEST FOR: Toddlers and preschoolers

THE GOING RATE: Around $3 to $6 an hour

BENEFITS:
- ✓ A good place to go when you just need a few hours of childcare.
- ✓ Great backup when your regular child care falls through.
- ✓ Your child gets to play with other kids.

DRAWBACKS:
- ✓ There may not be room at the tot drop on the day you need it.
- ✓ Your children will be exposed to other kids' germs.
- ✓ The makeup of the group changes from day to day, so there's no consistency for your child.

Parent's Day Out

Parent's Day Out, also known as Mother's Day Out or Children's Day Out, are group programs, often based in churches, nursery schools, or community centers, where you can drop off children who are too young for formal preschool. Kids usually attend one morning or afternoon a week, although some programs offer an extended day. You have to commit to the full session, which could last a semester or the entire school year.

BEST FOR: Toddlers and preschoolers

THE GOING RATE: Rates and programs vary too much to estimate. But in some areas, prices can be comparable to the cost of a half- or full-day of nursery school.

BENEFITS:
- ✓ You get a solid block of time in which to work every week.
- ✓ Your kids get to socialize with others.
- ✓ It's a good way to get kids ready for preschool.

DRAWBACKS:
- ✓ Parent's Day Out facilities are closed during the summer and school holidays.
- ✓ Your kids are exposed to other kids' germs.
- ✓ You're stuck if your child gets sick.

Nursery Schools

Preschool programs are often run by churches, synagogues, local Ys and other community organizations, and sometimes by colleges or universities. Most preschool programs group children in classes according to age, and some take children as young as two. The best ones will offer a variety of age-appropriate activities and play materials so that children can learn in a fun, relaxed way. Days and hours can vary, depending on the school you choose. Most only offer half-day programs (either mornings or afternoons), for anywhere from two to five days a week, but some provide extended-day programs, where kids are kept for a few extra hours in the afternoon. Full-day, five-day-a-week nursery school programs are also available and growing in number.

BEST FOR: Preschoolers

THE GOING RATE: Varies, according to program

BENEFITS:
- ✓ A safe environment supervised by teachers trained in early education.
- ✓ Children hone language, socialization, motor, and other important development skills.
- ✓ Reliable—when teachers are sick, schools hire a substitute.

DRAWBACKS:
- ✓ Good programs are often pricey, with a limited number of openings and long waiting lists.
- ✓ Limited hours, too many holidays, and a very short school year.
- ✓ Children are exposed to other kids' germs.
- ✓ You're stuck if your child gets sick.

Full-Time School: Grade School, Middle School, High School

Since a typical school day runs from around 8 A.M. to 3 P.M., this is usually the main source of child care for mompreneurs with kids ages six and up.

BEST FOR: School-age kids

THE GOING RATE: Free, if public school; tuitions vary for private schools

BENEFITS:
✓ Finally, five full days to work!

DRAWBACKS:
✓ What do you do on holidays, school vacations, and snow days?

After-School Programs

If school is your main form of child care, this can be a good way to get in some extra work time. After-school clubs and other extracurricular activities like sports, scouts, or dance lessons are often offered by local Ys, boys and girls clubs, community centers, and churches and synagogues, as well as in private facilities, such as dance studios and karate schools. Some nursery schools and day-care centers also offer after-school or extended-day programs.

BEST FOR: School-age children

THE GOING RATE: The cost of extracurricular programs varies widely, according to the type of activity. School-based clubs are often run by PTAs and cost only a small fee.

BENEFITS:
✓ An inexpensive way to squeeze in extra work hours on school days.
✓ Kids learn new skills and make new friends.

DRAWBACKS:
✓ Limited hours.
✓ Transportation is usually not provided.
✓ Can be a tiring day for younger children.

Summer Camps

Kids spend all or just part of their summer vacation at day camps or sleep-away programs, where they're exposed to a variety of recreational activities.

Day camps may offer partial-or full-day programs. In addition to private camps, there are often many fine programs offered by your community, local schools, churches, colleges, and nonprofit groups like YW/YCAs or Girl or Boy Scouts. Some communities also offer minicamps during winter and spring breaks.

BEST FOR: Preschool and school-age children

THE GOING RATE: Varies widely, depending on the type of camp and whether it's a day camp or sleep-away. Private camps will be more expensive than those run by a community or organization (such as Girl Scouts). Many camps offer scholarships or other types of financial assistance. Ask when requesting applications.

BENEFITS:
- ✓ Gives you summer child-care coverage.
- ✓ Kids learn new skills and make new friends.
- ✓ There are a variety of programs to choose from, so you can find one to suit your child's interests and your work schedule.

DRAWBACKS:
- ✓ Programs fill up quickly, and many require applications as early as February and March.
- ✓ Good camps can be costly.
- ✓ Transportation or lunch may not be provided or may cost extra.

SITTERS ON CALL

If your hours vary so much that it doesn't pay to commit to a permanent sitter, an on-call sitter who you can use on short notice is an option to explore. This is also a great backup plan to have for those days when your regular child-care arrangements get canceled. Here are some of the on-call systems other mompreneurs have found helpful.

FLEXIBLE FAMILY CARE: By spreading the word at nursery school, New York attorney and writer Julie Moran found a wonderful family day-care provider who was willing to take her kids on an as-needed basis. "Occasionally she was unavailable on the day I wanted, but most times she came through for me," Moran says. On busy weeks, Moran used her two or three times, while during slow periods, she often didn't need her at all.

THE BEEPER PLAN: As a childbirth coach, Cathy Gallagher never knew when she was going to have to rush to the hospital to assist clients who were in labor. "My husband was here for middle-of-the-night sitting, but I needed someone who could take the kids in the day-time," she says. So Gallagher and her business partner struck up an innovative deal with a local young mother. They gave her a beeper and paid her a monthly fee of $100 to be on call, whether she worked or not. Then they paid her an additional $5 an hour for the days she worked, which usually numbered about four times a month. When someone went into labor, Gallagher would beep the sitter and say, "I've got someone cooking—I'm going to need you," and the sitter would come right over. "It worked for all of us," Gallagher says. "Our sitter was guaranteed a monthly salary, and we had spontaneous child care we could count on."

SICK-CARE PROGRAMS: If your kids are home sick from school or day care and you've got a can't-miss deadline or meeting, you may find help at your local hospital. Some have Sniffles Clubs or other sick-care programs where you can send mildly ill kids for the day. Sue Noble, who now does typing from her home in Tuscaloosa, Alabama, occasionally used her nearby Children's Sick Room service when she was working nine to five. "Claire had her own room, own TV, own phone, a nurse to stay in the room with her to care for her every need, and lunch brought in on a tray. I was so envious," Noble says. Fees are usually hourly and will vary according to the part of the country you're in. Keep in mind that not all hospitals have this service and that sick-care programs will not accept kids with contagious diseases like chicken pox.

CORPORATE-SPONSORED EMERGENCY CHILD CARE: If you're lucky, your spouse's employer or the company for which you telecommute may provide backup child-care services. Ellen's husband worked for a company that had a child-care center in the building lobby for employees to use on an emergency basis. When the schools were closed or the sitter couldn't come, Ellen's kids commuted to work with their daddy, who dropped them off at the center before reporting to his desk. Some companies also have child-care referral services, which can send backup, in-home sitters on days your caregiver cancels.

BUDGET PLANS

Baby-Sitting Co-Ops

Baby-sitting co-ops are formed by neighborhood parents who agree to sit for each other on a regular basis. Co-ops can be small or large. When Marsha Swainston started hers in Lenexa, Kansas, only about ten families were involved. But it grew to include over twenty families. When you need a sitter, you choose from the names on the list of co-op participants. Instead of cash, you pay by tokens or tickets. Every family starts out with the same amount and then pays about one token (this varies according to the co-op) for each hour of sitting required per child. When your token supply runs low, you know it's time for you to pay back by contributing your baby-sitting services. Co-op parents set the rules and usually meet about once a month to tally up tokens and discuss problems. Sometimes co-ops will appoint a director to oversee and enforce policies. For example, Kathy Holstrom's Merrifield, Virginia, co-op picked a secretary to arrange and keep track of sitting appointments and monitor everyone's token allotments.

BEST FOR: All ages

THE GOING RATE: Free—it's a reciprocal arrangement.

BENEFITS:
- ✓ Your kids will be cared for by experienced parents.
- ✓ Your children will have playmates.
- ✓ You've got a wide range of sitters to choose from.
- ✓ It's free.
- ✓ You have a say in the co-op policies.

DRAWBACKS:
- ✓ Baby-sitting co-ops are difficult to find and form.
- ✓ You'll have to devote much of your free time to baby-sitting for others in the co-op.
- ✓ Your kids will be exposed to other children's germs.

Sitter-Sharing

Two moms pool their resources and hire an in-home baby-sitter, who they can share. One summer Marguerite Tirelli, owner of a postpartum care service, teamed up with another work-at-home mom and split the fee for an in-home sitter who watched both their kids three days a week, rotating from house to house. "It was great," said Tirelli. "Our kids got to play together, and we got solid blocks of time to work—sometimes in perfect quiet."

Another way to sitter-share is to hire a full-time person and then work out a schedule where you each use her on designated days. If you go this route, it's helpful to draw up an informal contract stating which days you'll be using the caregiver and how much each of you are responsible for paying.

BEST FOR: All ages

THE GOING RATE: Same as for in-home caregivers, although you may be able to negotiate a lower rate if you can guarantee the sitter a full week of work.

BENEFITS:
- ✓ It's easier to find full-time caregivers than part-time ones.
- ✓ It can be more economical than hiring a part-time caregiver.

DRAWBACKS:
- ✓ If your friends change their minds or their work plans, the arrangement will unravel.
- ✓ You cannot control whether the other moms treat caregivers fairly or pay them on time.

The Trade-Off Method

Two friends team up to care for each other's children in their homes on designated days. For this to work best, you and your friend should share similar parenting philosophies. A good relationship between the kids is also important.

BEST FOR: All ages

THE GOING RATE: Free—it's a reciprocal arrangement.

BENEFITS:
- ✓ No cost.
- ✓ Your kids have playmates.

DRAWBACKS:
- ✓ It cuts into your private time with your own children.

The Barter Plan

You find a neighbor or friend to watch your children in exchange for your services. For example, if you're a caterer, a home-cooked dinner might be the perfect payment. If sewing is your trade, perhaps you can show your appreciation with a custom-made outfit. Barbara Coffman, a rancher in Story, Wyoming, often did odd jobs for her friends who volunteered their baby-sitting services.

BEST FOR: All ages

THE GOING RATE: Just the price of your services and materials

BENEFITS:
- ✓ Free baby-sitting

DRAWBACKS:
- ✓ Friends and neighbors may feel taken advantage of if you make a habit of this.

The Play Date Solution

Arranging for your child to visit a playmate's house is a good way to get in a few extra hours during crunch times. Just be sure to reciprocate when you're not as busy. You may even be able to sneak in some work when you host a play date, especially if you have older children.

BEST FOR: School-age kids

THE GOING RATE: Free

BENEFITS:
- ✓ No cost.
- ✓ Kids get to play with their favorite friends.

DRAWBACKS:
- ✓ When it comes to payback time, you could find yourself with a play date at your house every day for a month.

The Kids-Fend-for-Themselves Incentive Program

Music teacher Roberta Young had been through so many sitters she decided to try something new. "I told my kids that I'd pay them if they could take good care of themselves while I'm in the next room with a student," she says. Rather than just put the older sibling in charge, this method makes each child responsible for his or her own behavior. Young set down some basic rules beforehand: such as: Stay inside, no fighting and no interruptions, and no one gets the money unless everyone complies. If you're considering this plan, make sure your kids are at least five years old, and only try this for short periods of time (an hour or less). Also be sure to stay within earshot of the kids at all times.

THE GOING RATE: Young paid each child $1 if they followed the basic rules, and she offered them bonus dollars for completing their homework, tidying up the house, and keeping the TV off.

BENEFITS:
- ✓ Encourages children to work cooperatively.
- ✓ Cheaper than a sitter.
- ✓ Teaches kids about money and earning power.

DRAWBACKS:
- ✓ Gives you a very limited time to work.
- ✓ Kids are unpredictable, and you can't count on them following the rules.

THE CHILD-CARE SEARCH

Seven Steps to Finding a Great Caregiver

Now that you've decided which type of child care is best for you, here's how to go about finding it.

TELL EVERYONE YOU KNOW

The best caregivers are often found through word of mouth. Ask everyone you can think of—friends, colleagues, relatives, teachers, pediatricians, church members, local shopkeepers, and other work-at-home moms—if they have any leads. "I've gotten very good care for my kids by asking around at churches," says Rosalyn Smith, a personal computer consultant in Showell, Maryland. Ellen found the best sitter she ever had by talking to the director at her son's nursery school.

Playgrounds, pools, and other local kid hangouts are also a hotbed of information, and it pays to chat with the moms and caregivers you meet there. They might be able to recommend good preschools or family day-care programs. You might even find a mother who has a part-time caregiver who needs more hours. You never know when a caregiver's situation might be changing, too: Perhaps the children will soon be entering school and won't need her any longer. Caregivers are also likely to have friends who are searching for baby-sitting jobs.

READ ADS AND SCHOOL AND COMMUNITY POSTINGS

Scour local papers, penny savers, and corporate and community newsletters for caregivers' ads. Also check the bulletin boards at churches, synagogues, schools, gyms, supermarkets, and doctors' offices.

PLACE AN AD OR A POSTING

High school and college employment centers are wonderful sources for finding part-time sitters, particularly if you need afternoon hours or help on school holidays and vacations. Idaho writer Julie Fanselow found her afternoon sitter by calling the local high school and talking with someone in the counselor's office. The counselor passed on her request for a reliable teen to a class in child care, where there was a young girl who was perfect for the job.

If you're looking for an older, mature person who can work mornings or early afternoons, try putting an ad in local church bulletins and community newsletters. Corporate newsletters and school bulletin boards are other great— and often free—places to post ads. Newspaper or penny saver ads will get you the most responses but will cost a small fee.

In your ad, be specific about your needs, listing the age of your kids as well as the hours and particular responsibilities required. When Ellen needed someone to pick up her kids from school a few days a week, she hung this ad on her daughter's nursery school bulletin board:

WANTED

Loving mom to care for my 3½-year-old, 2 afternoons a week (hours from about 11:45 to 5). Pick up from nursery school needed. Also must be available to meet my 6-year-old at bus stop (at 3) and care for him for rest of afternoon. Flexible days/hours. Opportunity for full days during holidays and vacations. Competitive salary.

Call Ellen—555-0000

GO THROUGH AN AGENCY

If you can't find a caregiver on your own or just don't have time to do the legwork, a child-care agency can help. For a fee, agencies will do the initial screening and send you a group of prospective caregivers to interview. (Placement fees vary according to the agency and where you live. Generally, fees range anywhere from around two to three weeks salary to a flat fee of $2,000, according to Michelle Erlich, author of *The Anxious Parents' Guide to Quality Childcare*.) If you go through an agency, find out what kind of background checks are done on caregivers and be sure to interview all applicants thoroughly before hiring. There are also some agencies that specialize in temporary child care and can provide sitters on an as-needed basis. These can be very helpful as a backup when your regular child-care arrangements fall through, though you won't always know the person that the service sends.

SCREEN AND INTERVIEW CANDIDATES

Once you've placed your ad or gathered a list of potential caregivers, it's time to begin the two-part interview process. First, do a preliminary screening over the phone to determine whether the applicants really suit your needs. Briefly go over the job requirements, caregivers' experience, salary, and any other issues of importance, such as where they live and whether they smoke or drive. Have a notebook on hand so you can record your reactions as you talk to each applicant. Eliminate anyone you feel uncomfortable with, and invite your best prospects for an interview at your home.

When you interview caregivers face-to-face, be prepared with a list of questions (see "The Interview: Important Questions to Ask" box, page 103, for samples) and a general idea of the type of person you want (mature and loving? young and energetic?). Have your children present during the interview so you can observe how the caregiver relates to them. Make notes to yourself as you talk. Remember, chemistry counts. Before the caregiver leaves, ask for a complete employment history and as many references as possible.

CHECK THE CAREGIVER'S REFERENCES

Call as many of the references as you can, and ask about the caregiver's duties, reliability, personality, discipline style, and relationship with the kids. Encourage the references to give you specific examples of things they liked or didn't like about the caregiver, and find out why she is no longer employed there.

You might also consider doing a more throrough background check on the applicant. Detective agencies can run a criminal record search for around $150 and a driver's record search for around $50.

MAKE YOUR FINAL SELECTION

Trust your gut instincts, and hire the person you're most comfortable with. Arrange for the caregiver to come for a little orientation session a day or two before the job actually begins. This gives everyone a chance to go over the new routine and offers kids a sneak preview of what life with their new sitter will be like. Don't forget to pay your caregiver for this orientation session.

THE INTERVIEW: IMPORTANT QUESTIONS TO ASK

Face-to-face interviews are your best opportunity to gather as much information as you can about potential caregivers. Try to ask open-ended questions that require explanation rather than yes or no answers, and see how the caregiver would react in various situations by posing rhetorical questions. For example, when discussing discipline style, ask questions like "What would you do if my child ran out in the street?" and "How do you handle it when kids won't share their toys?" Also clearly describe your expectations. If housework is involved, say so now and firm up the caregiver's specific responsibilities.

Here are some essential issues to cover and our suggested ways to phrase the questions:

- ✓ Tell me about your experience and the other jobs you've had.
- ✓ What are the age ranges of the kids you've cared for?
- ✓ How do you enjoy spending your day?
- ✓ What is your discipline style?
- ✓ What kinds of things do you enjoy doing with the kids?
- ✓ What do you usually do when the children nap?

If the caregiver will be working in your home, it's also helpful to address these questions:

✓ Have any of your previous employers worked in their homes? How did you like that?
✓ How do you feel about having me in the house while you work?
✓ How would you keep the kids from disturbing me?
✓ In the event that the kids got very noisy while I was working, how might you quiet them down?

CHOOSING FAMILY DAY-CARE HOMES, CHILD-CARE CENTERS, AND PRESCHOOLS

When you're selecting a family day-care home or a center-based program, there are several essential factors to keep in mind. The American Academy of Pediatrics (AAP) suggests you follow these guidelines when making your choice.

Ask About the Group Size and the Child/Staff Ratio

The child/staff ratio indicates how many caregivers there are in each group. Ideally, you want the smallest group you can find with the largest number of caregivers. The National Association for the Education of Young Children (NAEYC) recommends the following minimum standards for various age groups:

FROM BIRTH TO AGE ONE: A child/staff ratio of four to one: no more than eight children in a group, with two caregivers.

FROM AGES TWO TO TWO AND A HALF: A child/staff ratio of six to one: no more than twelve children in a group, with two caregivers.

FROM AGES TWO AND A HALF TO THREE: A child/staff ratio of seven to one: no more than fourteen children in a group, with two caregivers.

FROM AGES THREE TO FIVE: A child/staff ratio of ten to one: no more than twenty children in a group, with two caregivers.

Check That It's Licensed and/or Accredited

The Handbook of Child and Elder Care Resources, published by the Work and Family Program Center of the U.S. Department of Commerce, defines licensing and accreditation as follows:

State licensing indicates that minimum standards for health, safety, and child/staff ratios have been met and are periodically reviewed through inspections. Centers in churches or public schools could be exempt from state licensing in some states.

Accreditation means that the child-care provider has gone beyond the minimum standards and is voluntarily striving to achieve high-quality care. The National Academy of Early Childhood Programs, a division of the NAEYC, accredits early childhood programs, day-care centers, preschools, kindergartens, and after-school programs. The National Association for Family Day Care (NAFDC) accredits child-care homes.

Observe the Home or Center during Business Hours

The setting should be bright, cheery, and spacious, and the children should seem happy there.

Be Sure It's Clean

Check kitchens, bathrooms, and sleeping and diaper-changing areas.

Make Sure It's Safe

Everything—indoors and out—should be childproofed, and there should be a variety of age-appropriate toys, all in good condition. Play areas should be fenced in and well-supervised with safe, low-to-the-ground equipment and impact-resistant surfaces (like grass, sand, wood chips, or rubber mats).

Pay Close Attention to the Discipline Style and the Relationship Between the Caregivers and Children

Caregivers should be attentive and comforting and should discipline in a manner that's calm, gentle, and firm.

Inquire About the Sickness Policy

What happens when a child gets sick? Are there alternative arrangements available in the event the caregiver is ill?

Make Sure That Smoking is Banned

No one should be allowed to smoke during the hours that the children are there.

Be Sure It's Close to Home

You'll want to be able to get back to your desk quickly after dropping off the kids.

Follow Your Instincts

If your first reaction is that your child wouldn't be happy, it's not the right choice for you.

WHAT YOU NEED TO KNOW ABOUT CHILD-CARE LAWS

Though it's common practice to hire illegal aliens as caregivers and to pay in-home sitters or housekeepers off the books, be aware that this violates federal law. Here are the important laws and regulations you need to know about before you hire your caregiver:

Caregivers Need a Green Card

U.S. Immigration laws state that you can be fined (or even jailed) for hiring people who are not authorized to work in this country.

Sponsors Can't Hire Caregivers Until Work Authorization Is Official

To help foreign caregivers obtain their green cards, the U.S. Department of Immigration allows families to sponsor caregivers. Be aware, though, that sponsorship can take anywhere from five to fifteen years, and you are still not allowed to hire that person until the work authorization is officially granted. So while sponsorship seems like a great way to hold onto a terrific sitter, it's unrealistic for most families. If you want more information about the sponsorship process, we suggest you contact an attorney specializing in immigration law.

You Must Pay Taxes for In-Home Caregivers

According to the federal law known as the Nanny Tax, you are required to pay social security and medicare taxes for any domestic employees who earn $1,200 or more during a single calendar year. (You do not have to pay Social Security taxes for domestic workers under the age of eighteen, unless their principal occupation is household employment, so you need not worry about paying taxes for that high school kid who sits for you.) In addition, you're responsible for paying federal and state unemployment tax and any state-required workers' compensation and disability insurance. For more information about taxes and the paperwork required when filing, call 1-800-TAX-FORM (1-800-829-3676).

Life with Your Caregiver

You'll breathe a sigh of relief when you finally firm up your child care. Although your search is over, your work is not. Now you've got to focus on fostering a happy and honest relationship with your caregiver. After all, you'll want to keep that great child-care arrangement going as long as you can. Here's how to do it.

Secrets to a Lasting Relationship

RESPECT

Treat your caregiver like a valued family member, rather than a hired hand. Be fair and considerate, and don't load the caregiver with tasks that weren't in the original job description. For example, you can't expect your sitter to taxi the kids around, supervise play dates, or clean the house if you haven't discussed these issues previously. If you want to add new duties, discuss them with your caregiver first and offer additional stipends or incentives such as raises, bonus pay, or extra paid vacation days. "Until I had my first baby, I had underestimated how difficult it would be to find the perfect caregiver," says medical writer Mary Gillett. "Once that special caregiver is found, she is worth her weight in gold. Treat her well, with respect and with fairness, and expect the same in return."

REVIEW

It's important to monitor your child-care arrangements to make sure that everyone is happy with the way they're working out. Here, good communication is key, so talk to your caregiver regularly and encourage her input as well.

Always ask how the day went and find out whether there are any matters that need to be discussed or suggestions that the caregiver would like to make. By setting even five minutes aside every day to talk, you're showing your caregiver that you value her feelings and feedback. Be thoughtful, though, and don't schedule these talks when the sitter's off the clock; caregivers have personal lives, too.

REWARD

Show caregivers how much you appreciate them. Make it worth their while to stay with you long-term by offering yearly raises, Christmas bonuses, and paid vacation days. In addition to giving her housekeeper a yearly raise, Andrea Disario, a New York City marketing consultant, upped her housekeeper's salary when the second child came along. It's also nice to surprise your caregiver from time to time with small tokens like flowers or a coupon for a manicure. "If you can pay well and offer any kind of extra benefits, you will find it much easier to find someone reliable who will come to have a vested interest in your family and will be there to help you when emergencies occur," says Kim Selzman, an attorney in Shaker Heights, Ohio. "Because we always treated our baby-sitter well, she stayed with us for a number of years and would almost always come on a phone call, even if unscheduled."

What Your In-Home Caregiver Wants You to Know

We've talked a lot about the challenges of trying to work with the kids at home, even when they're occupied with a sitter. But it's also tough for the sitter to feel like she's in charge when we're coming out of our offices for impromptu snacks or hugs from the kids. The very flexibility we crave can be hard on the sitter and on the kids, who have to separate from us again each time we return to our desks.

We asked some in-home caregivers for their solutions to this dilemma. Here's what they had to say.

DON'T HOVER

Make your good-byes short and sweet. If you take breaks with the kids, make them short and schedule them into the day, so the children know when to expect them. For example, the daily ritual of lunch or snacks with Mommy is a nice treat and not as disruptive as surprise visits all day long. Though it's sometimes difficult, try your best to stay in your office when you hear the kids crying. If you don't let the caregiver do her job, no one is going to get much work done.

TREAT THE CAREGIVER LIKE A PARTNER, NOT A RIVAL

She's here to help you, not take over your role. Sometimes moms become resentful that while they're working, the kids and the sitter are sharing a special relationship. When you feel a little jealousy creeping in, tell yourself how lucky you are to have this flexible work style and remember that your caregiver is helping you make it all possible.

GIVE THE CAREGIVER SOME HOUSE RULES

Offer caregivers clear guidelines on when you are to be interrupted. Some mompreneurs don't want to be bothered unless it's an emergency, while others don't mind being summoned for quick questions or to witness children's first steps or words. It's also important to establish appropriate house noise levels and activities. Will you allow the kids to have play dates when you're working? Do you need kids to keep the volume down on the stereo and TV? Will you expect your caregiver to take the children out of the house as much as possible? The more your caregiver knows about your needs, the better job she can do.

When Your Caregiver is Grandma or Grandpa

Special challenges can arise when you rely on grandparents for child care. First of all, you're likely to share different child-rearing philosophies, which can lead to conflict. Grandma and Grandpa may be lenient on matters like nutrition or bedtimes, yet have strict notions about things like potty training and walking shoes. Feelings of competition can also occur, particularly if grandparents are constantly voicing words of wisdom while new moms learn the ropes. How do you reconcile your differences without causing family strife? Follow these tricks from other mompreneurs.

PICK YOUR BATTLES

Stand your ground on the issues that matter most to you and relax your standards on the rest. One New York mompreneur decided that safety and nutrition were of utmost importance, so she lobbied for window guards on her in-laws' upper-floor apartment, even though Grandma and Grandpa insisted screens would be safe enough. However, this mom is flexible on other matters, such as where the grandparents take the kids when they go out. "If you're able to let the little things go," adds Laura Mathisen, a copywriter in Spokane, Washington, "you'll find that not as many conflicts come up."

PROBLEM-SOLVE TOGETHER

When you make a rule change, let grandparents have some input. If you don't want Grandma giving the kids ice cream right before dinnertime, say something like, "Maybe we can come up with a better time to give the kids their ice cream. It's ruining their appetites to have it so close to dinner."

ALLOW GRANDPARENTS SOME SPECIAL PRIVILEGES

Give them freedom to bestow their special gifts on your children. Let them share their knowledge, recipes, hobbies, or special skills, and give them the opportunity to expose your children to new experiences. Mathisen's in-laws get to take their grandson to church. "We're not church-goers ourselves," says Mathisen, "but religion is very important to my mother-in-law, so we've decided it's important to let Grandma share her beliefs with our son." By doing so, Mathisen is showing Grandma that she plays an important role in her grandson's life.

EMERGENCY PLANS

Ten Things to Do When Your Child Care Falls Through

1. Give yourself the day off, if you can.
2. Attempt to work with the kids around.
3. Arrange a play date.
4. Ask a relative or friend to do some pinch-hit sitting.
5. See if a local teen can watch the kids for a few hours after school.
6. Call a baby-sitting service that specializes in emergency child care.
7. Use any backup child-care services provided by your spouse's company.
8. Take your children to a tot-drop center for a couple of hours.
9. See if your husband can head home a little early (or better yet, if he can take the day off altogether) so you can cram in some work time.
10. Pay your kids to take care of themselves.

SURVIVING WITHOUT CHILD CARE

In the many years that Sue Noble has been running No Problem Word Processing from her home in Tuscaloosa, Alabama, she has never once had to have a sitter come in. What's her trick? She works a lot of nights and makes sure she never takes on more work than she can handle. "I'm home to be with the kids," she says, adding that with what she earns, it wouldn't pay to have a sitter, anyway. "Everyone told me it couldn't be done," adds Debi Hamuka-Falkenham, a Connecticut graphic designer who successfully worked without child care in the early stages of her business. "But it is possible for certain people."

Of course, taking the sitter-free route is not for everyone, and it is no easy feat. You're bound to experience it eventually, though, whether it's because your sitter calls in sick, the kids are off from school, or child-care costs are simply not in your budget. These important strategies will help whenever you find yourself sitterless.

Survival Strategy #1: Have an Open-Door Policy

When you don't have someone watching the kids, you can't shut your office door on your children. Keep within earshot, and let them know that you're available anytime they need you. Jan Geleynse, from Lyden Washington, kept the playpen right next to the table where she sewed her juvenile products. "That way I could see the kids at all times," she says. Graphic designer Nancy Danahy, suggests separating your work space with a child gate so you can monitor toddlers yet keep them away from expensive and potentially dangerous office equipment.

Survival Strategy #2: Take Frequent Breaks with the Kids

Don't expect them to get by on their own for long periods. Even though her desk was just down the hall from her preschoolers' play room, Debi Hamuka-Falkenham checked on them every few minutes.

Survival Strategy #3: Squeeze Work in Whenever You Can

Of course, plan on working the nap shift, but unless your kids sleep like Rip Van Winkle, you'll need more than naptime to get business done. Prepare to spend a lot of early mornings, nights, and weekends on the job. "I grabbed time whenever I could get it," says Hamuka-Falkenham, who was often at her desk on Saturdays and Sundays. Noble types after the kids are in bed.

Survival Strategy #4: Streamline Your Work Load

Take only enough work to fit around the kids' schedules, and turn down assignments when you have to. It's tougher to meet tight deadlines when you're working without any backup. During peak times, also consider delegating tasks like housecleaning. Noble is busiest during December and April, when she's swamped with typing term papers for local college students. She gets some household help to come in two times during those months.

Survival Strategy #5: Remember Your Priorities

When work and family pressures mount, remind yourself that you're doing this to be closer to your kids. Instead of looking at all that's not getting done, suggests Hamuka-Falkenham, try to focus on the things you have already accomplished. Then make small achievable goals for yourself. "It helps the day go much better," she says. However, if you're feeling overwhelmed all the time, you've got to address whether getting a part-time caregiver makes more sense. Both your business and your children (not to mention your health and well-being) will suffer if you're constantly stressed out.

SIX SIGNS IT'S TIME TO HIRE A SITTER AFTER ALL

Have you been getting by fine without a sitter but suddenly sense that you could use some help? Here are some signals that supplemental child care may now be in order:

1. When the kids are around, you're spending more time on your work than you are with them.

2. Your children have broken the world's record for Most Videos Watched in a Day.

3. Working when the kids are sleeping is proving to be an impossible feat.

4. You're constantly working weekends.

5. Whenever your kids ask you to do something with them, you answer, "Just let me take this call first."

6. Your business is quickly growing beyond your expectations.

"SHH! MOMMY'S ON THE PHONE!"—TELEPHONE TRICKS THAT REALLY WORK

When you have no child care, your most daunting challenge is how to keep the kids quiet while you're on business calls.

✓ *Set children up with some no-mess crafts materials.* Think crayons and markers, not finger paints.

✓ *Give them some construction toys and ask them to make you a surprise.* Great attention-getters include Lego blocks, wooden blocks, jigsaw puzzles, and beads for stringing.

✓ *Pull out your telephone treasures.* Keep a box of goodies by the phone, and let the kids open it whenever you've got to be on a call. Fill it with quiet-time treats like wind-up toys, trading cards, Silly Putty, Etch-A-Sketch, stamps, stickers, and other fun stuff. Don't forget to include a few edible prizes, too, such as raisins, juice boxes, fruit roll-ups, and animals crackers.

✓ *Use a timer so kids know how long you'll be talking.* Marsha Swainston would first set her timer for fifteen minutes of playtime with her kids. Then, she set it for twenty minutes of phone time, during which the children weren't allowed to interrupt. After the call, she set the timer for another long chunk of playtime. "When I respected the timer for playtime, they quickly learned to respect it for business," she says.

✓ *Give kids their own office space.* Furnish it with all the equipment they'll need for running a business like yours. Kids will love to emulate you, so let them tap away on old keyboards and make their business calls on toy telephones (or better yet, on real phones that don't work anymore). A kiddie table and chair set makes a great desk, and file folders and old briefcases are terrific for storing children's important assignments. Deborah Lindner, a Hicksville, New York, illustrator kept two drawing boards in her office: one for herself and one for her daughter to use. Maria Chilcote, a consultant in Springfield, Virginia, created a special space in her office for her little one. "I used to try to get her to play quietly in her room while I was on the phone, but she always wound up in here with me," says Chilcote. "Then I realized that she just wanted to be with me. So I lowered one of the bookshelves in my office almost down to the floor, put a little chair there, and that was her desk. I gave her a drawer and filled it with stamps, glue sticks, paper, scissors, pictures, sparkly stuff—and that was her work. I put her play phone on her desk and gave her a pencil box with crayons, markers, and tape. And I said, 'Honey, now you have a desk just like Mommy's.' To which she replied, 'Where's my computer?' "

✓ *Pop in a video.* If you can, make it one they've been asking for but haven't seen yet. It will hold their interest for a longer time.

✓ *When all else fails, talk fast.* If you must, take the cordless phone into a closet or bathroom and close the door.

MOMPRENEUR® HALL OF FAME

SHERYL LEACH

Creator of Barney® the Dinosaur, Executive Producer of the public television series
Barney & Friends®, A Production of The Lyons Group, Richardson, Texas
Mother of One

When Sheryl Leach dreamed up a big purple dinosaur named Barney, little did she realize that he'd become an indispensable video baby-sitter for work-at-home moms everywhere. She only knew that she needed something to help hold the attention of her very active toddler for more than just five minutes. "I was sure that there must be other parents like me out there struggling with this," she says.

In her quest to occupy her two-year-old son, Leach scoured the children's television and video market. She found very few preschool programs she considered both engaging and educational, so she decided to develop a children's video series of her own, one that would entertain and teach kids in a wholesome and nonviolent way. Leach set out to create a video character who could be "a friend to all children, someone who celebrates childhood and sends the message that every child is extraordinarily special," she says.

"My original idea was that children love snugglies to carry around with them—things like blankets and teddy bears. I thought, 'Wouldn't it be neat if the snuggly that the child loved the most could actually come to life and interact with the child in a video? Then at the end of the video, it could shrink back down to size.' " That character went through a couple of incarnations in the early stages of what Leach refers to as "the Barney project." The mompreneur and former teacher started with a security blanket ("too hard to animate," she says), then tried a teddy bear, and finally settled on a dinosaur after attending a traveling dinosaur exhibition with her son. To further develop the concept, Leach enlisted video producer Dennis DeShazer and ex-teacher Kathy Parker as fellow executive producers. She also recruited a talented team of writers, early childhood education specialists, and production personnel. All worked together to bring Barney to life.

Leach was able to keep the Barney business home-based for about a year. Since money was really tight, she couldn't afford to have a nanny come to her. Instead, she managed with part-time family day care, provided by a friend of hers who looked after kids in her home. "Since he was an only child, I felt it was important for my son to be around other children," she explains. "So I'd bundle him up, pack up his stuff, and take him to my neighbor's. She was just a street away from me and we were already friends. It worked out beautifully!"

That child-care arrangement lasted through the formative years of the business, until Leach's family moved from Plano, Texas, to the countryside, about forty minutes outside of Dallas. At that point, her son was in school full-time. Leach hired a nanny/housekeeper who lived in with the family from Monday through Friday. Once Barney began to take off in 1993 and Leach's schedule became more and more stretched, her husband quit his job as president of a family-owned printing company to become a full-time stay-at-home parent. "It's been wonderful for all of us," the mompreneur says. Her son has a full-time parent around, and the role reversal has helped the couple to be more empathetic of each other's positions.

Leach stresses the importance of using child care when you're building a business, and she urges mompreneurs not to feel guilty about it. "Quality child care is such a win-win situation," the Texan points out. "The lose-lose situation is one where you feel frustration, impatience, anger, and negativity toward your children. If a mother feels trapped and is constantly struggling to finish business tasks with the kids around, her patience is going to run thin. And her children are going to pick up on that." A reliable child-care provider allows you to tend to the work at hand, so that the time you spend with your kids is relaxed and low-key, she adds. What qualities should you look for in a caregiver? Leach says it's important to have someone who's loving, kind, and compassionate, with a great sense of humor. If you can't find someone who fits the bill, we happen to know a big purple dinosaur who's available.

5

Creating Your Own Workspace

Setting up a home office today requires a bit more decision-making and money than it did when we started out. At the time Pat began freelancing, all she needed was a word processor, a painted wooden door supported by two metal filing cabinets, an answering machine, and an old-fashioned Rolodex. Her office was set up along one side of the master bedroom in her New York City apartment, with an extension phone within easy reach. By the time Ellen became a mompreneur, computers were more essential and affordable for the home office, so she bought a PC and opened for business in a spare bedroom in her house.

Today, the technological revolution demands more from home business owners, and clients expect it, too. It's almost impossible to run a twenty-first-century home business without a computer, fax machine, Internet service, and cell phone. We've both upgraded our computers several times, purchased fax machines, and installed second phone lines and Internet connections. We've also realized that our comfort and well-being should be priorities, too. Who would have thought ergonomically correct chairs were a must? But as our devotion to mompreneurship grows, we're putting in longer and longer hours in our home offices. There's no reason we shouldn't be working in surroundings that are as pleasant and comfortable as those in the outside world. That doesn't mean running out and buying everything Staples and Office Max have to offer. It's quite possible to go into business with just a few basics and a relatively small monetary investment.

MOMPRENEUR® STATISTICS: WHERE WE WORK

Most home businesses don't require a whole lot of space. This makes it relatively easy to carve out a workspace from family quarters, even if you live in an apartment. When we asked mompreneurs to tell us what room they chose as a home office, here is what they said.

Spare bedroom	25%
Basement	18%
Den/family room	9%
My own bedroom	7%
Dining room	4%
Living room	3%
Kitchen	3%
In-law apartment	1%
Other (sunroom, side porch, attic, etc.)	35%

We've even heard of setting up shop in a large walk-in closet, a hallway, or an alcove off another room. One desperate mompreneur we talked to has her computer in the dining room but makes all her phone calls in the bathroom: That's the quietest room in her house, and the door locks.

Our questionnaire also inquired, "Is this room used solely as an office?" Two-thirds of the respondents answered "yes," while one-third said "no."

A ROOM OF YOUR OWN

Once you make the decision to work from home, you should also make the commitment to set up a serious office. For both physical and psychological reasons, it's important to have a workspace you can call your own. A separate space helps form that meaningful distinction between your business and homelife and makes your work seem more significant to you, your family, and your clients. It also gives you a professional edge, providing an image boost even when you're just sitting at your desk in sweatpants, answering the phone, or composing a letter.

Of course, there are times when it's nice to take advantage of your work-from-home status and temporarily change your venue to another part of the house. For example, when the weather is especially wonderful, Pat likes to work on her laptop outside on the deck. Ellen sometimes spreads out her papers on the kitchen table so she can look in on her kids playing in the backyard or den. This freedom to move our workspace sure beats being confined to a small cubby in an office building. But don't try to wander

around your house or apartment looking for a new place to park yourself
and your work each day. It's a must to be able to return to a permanent
spot you call your office, even if it's only a desk jammed into the laundry
room or a corner of your bedroom.

Ready-Made Offices

Interior designer Gwen Nagorsky lives and works in a professional district in
Hackettstown, New Jersey, surrounded by doctors, lawyers, and insurance
agents. When she bought her Victorian home from a doctor, half of the lower
level was already converted to office space and had its own separate
entrance. Nagorsky was lucky. The transition from doctor's office to interior
design studio didn't take much effort. Since the neighborhood is amenable to
work-at-home setups, she's even allowed to hang a sign outside her office
door. Carol Guthrie, a landscape designer in Connecticut, also found the perfect spot for her home office, a winterized sunroom that overlooks her backyard. Perched at her desk and looking out her large window, she not only
gains inspiration from Mother Nature, she can also watch her children play.

Convertibles

Most mompreneurs do not find such an ideal workspace. Converting a spare
bedroom or unused part of the basement into a home office is much more
common. Deborah Lindner, a writer, illustrator, and producer of children's
educational materials, set up a computer, desk, and drawing table in a section of her full basement. When daughter Jennifer was younger, she worked
alongside Mom on a second drawing table or watched a video or listened to
music in another section of the finished basement. Marie Best, a desktop
publisher in Maryland, transformed a former guest room on the ground floor
of her home into a work space that's functional yet cozy. The subdued color
scheme, teak storage cabinets, and built-in shelving give her office a personality like the other rooms in her home instead of a sterile appearance. Nevertheless, clients comment on how professional it looks for a home office.

From Family Room to Work Room

When Betsy Johns became a consultant for Discovery Toys, she decided to
carve out office space from the huge family room in her Michigan home.
"Our house didn't have an extra room," says Johns, "so we bought office
panels to corner off a work area from our large family room." The result is a
very professional-looking and up-to-date office complete with computer,

copy machine, and other essentials. As a bonus, Johns can be in close proximity to her daughters, who love to help her stamp catalogs and hang their artwork from her office panels.

Kim Palmer, co-owner of a custom editorial and design company in Minneapolis, converted her entire playroom into an office, but not until she was given carte blanche from her kids. "Even though my children were only two and four at the time, I didn't want to take over their space without first talking to them," remembers Palmer. "So I told them that Mommy was thinking about working at home, but that she'd need a place to work. I asked them how they'd feel about letting Mommy have the playroom, if it meant I could spend more time at home and have breakfast with them every morning. My four-year-old thought for a minute and said, 'Ok, as long as I can still keep toys in there.'" During business hours, Palmer's office was off limits to her kids—in deference to her partner—but if she was trying to catch up on work in the evenings, the children were always allowed to come in and play quietly.

Space-Saving Solutions

Other moms had to be even more inventive in their search for space. Cathy Bolton, who began her specialty cookie company from her Oklahoma kitchen, soon expanded into her living room, too. "I squeezed a desk into the living room arrangement," she says, "as well as an antique cabinet to store my canned foods. (This was in accordance with a state health department regulation, which required me to remove all personal food items from the kitchen.) My home became unique." Another living room that did double duty was Joanne Walthall's. It served as an occasional showroom for her gift-importing business. Instead of seeming intrusive, the lovely picture frames and clocks that adorned the grand piano, coffee table, and bookshelves added to the ambience of her Manhattan apartment. The only time the business got in the way was right before a big trade show when the living room turned into a staging area and part-time warehouse. The family learned to just step around the cartons of samples during those hectic preshow days. Now Walthall rents a large offsite warehouse space for the ever-expanding business.

Even when there's no obvious or conventional room to transform into an office, mompreneurs can find a way. A masseuse and aromatherapist in our survey split her large bedroom down the middle to accommodate clients, while an Oregon freelance writer transformed a foyer near her living room into an inviting work space. Mud rooms, kitchens, garages, tool and garden storage areas, large walk-in closets, attics, and maid's rooms have also given up their previous identities to become home offices.

Expanding Your Frontiers

Some spirited pioneers go beyond their four walls to discover new and unusual workspaces. Lois Rogalski, a speech pathologist, added a three-room office suite onto her suburban Westchester home solely for the use of her private practice. A separate entrance allows patients to enter without interfering with household activities, but an inner door connects the space to the family's living quarters for instant access. Nancy Kalish, an enterprising Brooklyn, New York, mom, solved her space problem by renting the two-bedroom apartment next door, splitting the cost and space with a graphic designer, and transforming her half into a complete home office. This writer/editor can work undisturbed for long stretches of time, yet she's immediately accessible for a shared mommy-child lunch or a tot swimming class. Kalish started out working and living in the same apartment, but found she "couldn't get anything done. This provides just enough separation," she says.

When Lisa Ekus's successful public relations company began outgrowing her Massachusetts home, she converted a barn on her property into new headquarters. "I began my business in a spare bedroom, eventually took over a spare porch, then expanded into several other rooms of my house. When my home-based business became a business-based home I decided to renovate the barn into office space." Now Ekus and her employees comfortably share the large workspace. The barn also accommodates two desks filled with supplies for Ekus's daughters. After school and during vacations, the girls can be close at hand yet occupied as the business bustles around them.

Making a Dream Office Come True

Bonnie Tandy Leblang, a syndicated columnist, cookbook author, and national spokesperson, fantasized for years about moving from her cramped, dingy basement office to workspace upstairs, nearer to her kitchen and kids. Her dream became a reality when a major shelter magazine liked her idea of renovating the kitchen into a home office and executed the plan, reconstructing a kitchen–family room combo in her large den. Now this culinary professional has a big, beautiful workspace right where she wants it, in the heart of the home. It's filled with streamlined built-ins, including a practical and innovative wall of thirty cubby-holes to separate work projects. Leblang is convinced that her new, centrally located, well-organized office has increased her productivity, efficiency, and energy level and has added appeal to her home.

One of the features that most attracted artist and graphic designer Gail Miller to her large Tudor house was the former servants' quarters in the rear wing. "I imagined tearing down the walls between the two small rooms and hallway and forming one large, airy, sunny workspace for myself," she recalls. Several years after moving in, Miller was able to convince her family the time was right, and the walls came tumbling down. As soon as the construction was complete, Miller knew it was one of the best ideas she ever had. "The bigger space and better organization gave me the incentive and room to work," she says. "I was finally able to paint, design, and teach in one place." An unexpected fringe benefit was enough room for Miller to work side-by-side with her two boys: Mom on her design projects and the kids on their homework or a separate computer.

Planning and Personalizing Your Space

While many of us don't have the luxury of designing a home office from scratch, we can all benefit by taking a little time to plan our workspace. Before you start ripping out walls and putting up shelves, ask yourself these very basic questions.

What kind of work do I do? Certain professions, like writers, accountants, and attorneys, demand a distraction-free environment; others (craftspeople, caterers, children's entertainers) can thrive in the midst of chaos. Determine how much privacy you need to be productive.

Will I be meeting with clients? If your work involves bringing people into your home for meetings, plan this into your office space. (Your conference area can be as small and simple as two cushioned chairs surrounding a throw rug.) You also can arrange to hold meetings somewhere else in your home (dining room table, living room, etc.) or at an outside site.

Do I need to childproof my office space? This depends on the ages of your children and whether or not you will share your office with them. Even if you intend to make your workspace off-limits to your kids, a curious toddler may wander in, or a sixth-grader may need your computer for a school project.

What "perks" would I like? One of the joys of working from home is being able to make your office more homey. Do you enjoy listening to music while you work? Would you like to read your professional journals curled up in a wing chair? Why not plan these little extras into your workspace?

What is my budget? Finally, the bottom line is to figure out how much you can actually spend before you take your dreams too far. If funds are limited, invest first in quality, up-to-date equipment—computer, printer, phone, and fax—before you decorate. You can always phase in furnishings and amenities later.

How will I accommodate future growth? Success demands more space. Do you have room for expansion? What if you need to hire other employees to work out of your home office? Think about what your space needs will be five years down the road.

Tips from a Designing Mompreneur

Whether you're on a shoestring budget or the sky's the limit, you can design a home office environment that's right for you. We've enlisted the help of Julia Bayar, a work-at-home interior designer, home office specialist, and mother of three, to show us the ropes. Bayar has designed home offices for many professionals, including doctors, financial consultants, sales reps, psychotherapists, and lawyers. A good number of Bayar's clients are mompreneurs. Here are her step-by-step suggestions for a well-planned workspace:

✓ Analyze the architecture and dimensions of the potential office space.
✓ Draw up a plan that follows the existing conditions of the space. One of Bayar's recent challenges was squeezing a workspace into a tiny two-foot by four-foot niche off a hallway. She found a small but sturdy desk, equipped it with a chair and phone, and built in overhead shelving for books—all for under $1,000.

　　For an attorney who had a bigger space and budget, Bayar was able to do a bit more. "This prominent women's rights lawyer liked to keep an eye on her two children while they did their homework," recalls Bayar, "so I created a space that could be shared to some extent." To get the broadest possible work surface into the twelve-foot by fourteen-foot room, the designer had builders put up a desk that turned the corner, supported underneath by beams. She installed closed cabinets for underfoot storage and double-reinforced shelving from the ceiling down. Everything was constructed of melamite over plywood for stability and durability. Total cost of the built-ins was $3,500.

✓ Use quality materials. Bayar strongly advocates using wood and other solid materials when outfitting a home office, even though laminated particleboard built-ins and furniture are attractive, inexpensive, and widely available. Her reason comes from personal experience. "I had put up compressed particleboard shelving in my own home office when my children were little. One day, my twin daughters were playing near my desk and my baby son was crawling around the office, when all of a sudden the top shelf cracked," she remembers. "That shelf fell on the next shelf, creating a domino effect. Books and shelving came tumbling down." Luckily, Bayar's children were not nearby and everyone escaped without injury, but the designer found out the hard way that particleboard tends to absorb moisture, especially after a very snowy winter or rainy period. This causes it to expand and contract, weakening the material and increasing the danger of collapse.

✓ Go bargain hunting. "Scour flea markets, secondhand furniture shops, wholesale clubs, and tag sales for good-quality desks, well-made file cabinets, and unique storage containers," Bayar suggests. Unpainted antiques and gently used pieces can add lots of interest for less money. "Unfinished wood is also reasonable, and older kids can even help you paint or stain it." Office supply catalogs and websites can be other good ways to save money on some items.

✓ Invest in built-ins or custom furniture, if you can. When the office space is nonstandard, built-ins can be the best solution. Bayar opts for melamite over plywood if funds are limited, or solid wood for clients willing to spend more bucks.

✓ Custom furniture is also a good investment. It can pay for itself in increased productivity. If you can afford only one custom-made piece, make it your computer table or workstation. It can be designed to fit your height, left-or right-handedness, and other individual characteristics, so you won't have to contort during those long hours at the computer.

✓ Add homey touches. Select lighter woods and colors to make a female statement in your office. Other soft touches might include throw pillows on the floor or chairs, pretty bookends, an eye-catching desk set, family photos in funky frames, and whimsical accessories. "Women can take a little more leeway designing their workspace than men," Bayar feels, "and decorate with things they wouldn't put in more formal rooms."

✓ Lighten up. Illuminate all areas where tasks are routinely performed with direct light. The two most important spots are the desk/computer table and filing cabinets. Inexpensive track lighting fitted with yellow and/or white bulbs works well, as do fluorescents. (Reduce wattage if you have lots of natural daytime light.) Halogen lights tend to get very hot and are not recommended for small or overheated offices.

✓ Choose your desk chair carefully. Don't order a chair from an office catalog. It's important to try it out first. Make sure both the back and seat adjust, so your feet are flat on the floor and your pelvis tilts forward slightly. A durable cloth chair is your best bet. Leather is usually more expensive and can crack from repeated wear and tear, especially if the kids use it.

✓ Everything in its place. Women tend to be more organized than men, says Bayar, and they like offices that are functional and utilitarian as well as attractive. Include lots of containers to hold your stuff— especially those that can fit underfoot to free up other space. (For more organizational ideas, see "Clutter Control" on page 139.)

✓ Make a wish list. What would you add to your workspace if money was no object? Smaller items, such as a crystal paperweight or leather wastebasket, can be requested as gifts for a birthday or Mother's Day. Larger wishes, such as a fireplace, piped-in music, an overstuffed sofa, might have to wait a little longer.

DESIGN DO'S AND DON'TS

Do try to arrange your space in an L-shape or triangle, with a swivel-style desk chair in the middle of the configuration. With a spin of your seat or a slight roll backward or to the side, all essentials are within arm's reach.

Don't skimp on comfort, especially when it comes to your desk chair. Choose one with a cushioned seat and back, adjustable height so your feet are flat on the floor, a back that tilts and curves, and wheels on the bottom to get around easily.

Do group equipment and furnishings into different centers of operation. These might include your computer, phone/fax, mail handling area, and worktable.

Don't be stingy about storage space and lighting. Put in as many cabinets, cubbies, and shelves as you can without crowding your workspace. Illuminate individual work areas with their own direct lights.

Do plan with portability in mind. Cordless phones and laptops allow you to move your work close to your children, if necessary. Other portable conveniences are furniture on casters, baskets that can quickly be repositioned when needed, and a rolling cart to easily transport files and correspondence so you can work in the kitchen, family room, or even outside for an hour or so.

Don't set up your office where it should be; put it where you want it to be.

Do personalize the room by hanging up children's drawings and other favorite artwork, propping family photos on the desk, painting the walls your favorite color, including a knickknack or two, and adding other special touches. These not only make for a cozier space, they can also help reduce stress.

Don't do everything at once if money and/or time are tight. Start with the bare-bones basics, adding on when you can afford more. As your profits increase, you may even consider hiring a professional designer to help you make improvements. Most charge between $75 and $150 an hour for a consultation, and it wouldn't take long to toss around some design ideas.

Do plan for future growth. Architects and designers recommend that you project 25 percent more space than you currently require, especially if you're remodeling your home to accommodate an office or buying a new house with work-at-home potential.

His and Hers Offices

Julia Bayar has put her design ideas to the test on her own turf, where both she and her international attorney husband have separate home offices. Hers is in a converted second kitchen on the basement level near the family room, and his is housed in a newly enclosed sunporch off the living room. Bayar designed each space to suit the couple's different personalities and professions.

The only piece of equipment Bayar and her husband share is the copy machine, located in neutral territory. Otherwise, she's ensconced a floor below in a space that's both friendly and functional. Her office includes a drafting table, computer, and storage units, which are used both for stowing samples and files she uses on the job, as well as for her children's art projects and schoolwork. "Mothers tend to accommodate more than fathers, and their home offices often evolve into collection areas for family keepsakes and other spare things," says Bayar. Although most of her work is stored in closed cabinets, two open bookcases hold kid-related stuff.

Magazine writer Beth Levine and her lyricist-playwright husband, Bill Squier, share the *same* home office but may not "see" each other for hours on end. "We have two computers, two phone lines, and two desks, intentionally placed back-to-back so we're not looking at each other all day," jokes Levine. For the most part, this arrangement works out well—one phone line takes care of calls and faxes; the other is hooked up as a modem and acts as a default when the first line is busy. "Our main problem is office etiquette," says Levine. "I need to work in complete silence so I can stay focused, while Bill likes to listen to the radio and CDs. He also hums a lot when he's working on a lyric or taps out syllables on his desk. What really drives me crazy is his habit of reading scenes aloud to me to see how they feel! He just gets too excited by his work to stay quiet." Squier has taken to working at the local Starbucks in the mornings to give Levine a chunk of uninterrupted silence, which she much appreciates.

The two also have slightly different work schedules—a good way to prevent conflicts from arising. "Bill goes to bed later and gets up at 5:30 A.M., so he toodles around online before I get up or after I've gone to bed," says Levine. That frees up the Internet connection for Levine, who likes to do her online research and e-mail interviews during the day when their son, Levi, is in school.

EQUIPPED FOR SUCCESS

If you're just making the switch to mompreneurship or are trying to expand your home business, the biggest part of your home office budget should go toward equipment rather than furnishings. This is especially true for service-oriented endeavors such as desktop publishing, marketing, web design, law, and accounting; they must be well equipped to be competitive. Luckily, the very technology that first fed the work-at-home boom is more affordable, compact, and versatile than ever before.

What do you really need? We believe you can get by with these basic items: a computer and printer, software relevant to your business, a fax machine, a desktop telephone and/or a cordless phone, and an answering system. If you find yourself constantly using up precious work time to run out to the copy shop, a desktop copier would probably be a wise investment, too. (See our "What Every Mompreneur Needs Now" chart below.)

WHAT EVERY MOMPRENEUR NEEDS NOW

With the help of Marilyn Zelinsky Syarto, author of *Practical Home Office Solutions* (McGraw-Hill, 1999), we offer some general guidelines to help you make the wisest, most cost-effective equipment selections. Keep in mind that we couldn't possibly include all the high-tech gear out there, so we tried to zero in on the most practical and versatile basics.

ESSENTIAL EQUIPMENT	WHAT TO LOOK FOR	EXPECT TO PAY AROUND
Desktop computer	✓ Most memory you can afford ✓ Speedy microprocessor ✓ CD-ROM or CD-RW/DVD drive ✓ Quiet fan	✓ $800–$2,000
Desktop monitor	✓ 17-to 19-inch screen (to conserve eyesight!) ✓ 1,600 by 1,200 pixel images for crispness and clarity ✓ Easily adjustable in brightness and pitch ✓ As slim a profile as you can buy (most are bulky)	✓ $300–$600

ESSENTIAL EQUIPMENT	WHAT TO LOOK FOR	EXPECT TO PAY AROUND
Keyboard	✓ Under-the-desk retractable keyboard tray to reduce strain on wrists and arms while freeing up valuable workspace ✓ Space for mousing ✓ Adjustable height ✓ Wrist rests	✓ $50–$200
Everyday desktop printer	✓ High-quality color ink-jet printer ✓ 2,400 by 1,200 dpi or 2,800 by 720 dpi resolution ✓ Laser-quality black text ✓ Speedy printing time ✓ Smooth paper feeder ✓ Compatibility with both PC and Mac computers	✓ $200–$400
Freestanding plain paper fax machine	✓ Automatic document feed ✓ Automatic dial ✓ 50–100 sheet paper cassette ✓ Broadcast fax functions ✓ Speed of 6–15 seconds to transmit one page ✓ Out-of-paper storage reception capability	✓ $90–$300

ESSENTIAL EQUIPMENT	WHAT TO LOOK FOR	EXPECT TO PAY AROUND
Desktop telephone	✓ Two lines, if possible (one for business, one for personal) ✓ Cordless, if possible (900 MHz with short antenna so you can answer business calls in the yard!) ✓ Built-in digital answering machine ✓ Caller ID screen (on handset for cordless) ✓ Speakerphone for hands-free operation ✓ Distinctive ring options	✓ $50–$400 for a desktop multiline phone ✓ $80–$300 for a cordless multiline phone
Software	✓ Word processing, spreadsheet, and other programs with business form templates (These often are already installed on new computers.) ✓ Accounting software to track finances ✓ Utilities to repair damaged hard drives and prevent viruses ✓ Childproofing software to prevent children from tapping into and erasing your files	✓ $500 for word processing/ spreadsheet programs ✓ $100–$270 for accounting programs ✓ $50–$150 for utility and childproofing software

NICE IF YOU CAN AFFORD IT

If you have some money left over in your budget (or expect a big windfall and want more bells and whistles), consider these "extras." Some will help your business run much more smoothly; others are totally optional and just fun to own!

ENTICING EXTRA	WHAT TO LOOK FOR	EXPECT TO PAY AROUND
Laptop or notebook computer	✓ Slim and lightweight in size (4–6 lbs is considered good to average; over 7 lbs gives you a workout!) ✓ Long-lasting battery (3 hours average; 6 hours ideal) ✓ 13- to 15-inch screen for strain-free viewing ✓ External or internal CD-ROM/DVD drive ✓ Internal modem ✓ Ethernet connection included ✓ Mouse connection	✓ $1,500–$3,700
Desktop copier	✓ Easy-maintenance single cartridge for one-step replacement of toner, drum, and development unit ✓ Fast per-page printing (4 pages/minute is considered slow)	✓ $200–$400 (higher for optional color copy capabilities)

ENTICING EXTRA	WHAT TO LOOK FOR	EXPECT TO PAY AROUND
	✓ Ability to copy letter-and legal-size documents ✓ Large sheet input tray (250 sheets is considered plenty) ✓ Small "footprint" so it can fit onto a desk or countertop	
Scanner	✓ Slim profile ✓ One-button scanning ✓ Hinged lid to accommodate books and bulky objects ✓ Speedy scanning ✓ High resolution	✓ $130–$300
Cell phone	✓ Sound clarity ✓ Lightweight unit (3.4 ounces with battery is ideal) ✓ Long-lasting battery ✓ Dual mode (CDMA digital/analog to cover greater area) ✓ Paging function/text messaging ✓ Easy-to-read screen ✓ Easy-to-use touchpad ✓ Voicemail capability ✓ Wireless Internet access (optional)	✓ $100–$300 for phone only; service is extra (Shop around for deals—some companies offer free phones with service contracts.)

ENTICING EXTRA	WHAT TO LOOK FOR	EXPECT TO PAY AROUND
Personal digital assistant	✓ Lightweight unit (6.5 ounces is average) ✓ Large, easy-to-read screen ✓ Easy-to-use touchpad ✓ Synchronization capability ✓ Wireless e-mail option	✓ $150–$500
Internet appliance	✓ Compact size to place in kitchen, bedroom, or another area so you can check e-mail when you're not sitting at your home office computer ✓ Ability to use the same Internet provider as your computer	✓ $350–$500
Digital camera	✓ 1,600 by 1,200 pixel resolution for quality images ✓ Quick downloads to computer ✓ 3X optical zoom ✓ Multiple flash modes ✓ Large, bright screen ✓ 8 to 16 MB SmartMedia card to store images	✓ $500–$1,000 (The higher the resolution and storage capacity, the higher the price.)

Bytes of Advice

When shopping for high-tech equipment, look for brand names and reliability rather than just price. Compare warranties and extended service contracts as carefully as you compare price tags.

- ✓ Shop from companies that offer lots of service. Ask anyone who works from home: Breakdowns always happen at the worst possible times, and a quick fix can save the day.
- ✓ Don't underspend. Buy as much memory and disk space as you can. Nobody seems to complain about having too much, and it fills up very quickly.
- ✓ Try to strike a deal with the salesperson or company to install more than the basic software when you buy your computer system.
- ✓ If you don't have the funds to purchase the computer system or other office equipment you want, consider leasing. Many computer superstores and smaller outlets offer leases on name-brand merchandise, and business leasing companies have copy machines and other essentials available.
- ✓ Mail-order companies (Dell, Gateway, etc.) offer some of the best prices, selection, and customized systems. The drawback: Service is usually through a toll-free number or website, which can be frustrating.
- ✓ Don't forget to include a surge protector in your computer package. This inexpensive strip of electrical outlets guards your computer against most power disruptions. If you need more insurance, consider an uninterruptible power supply (UPS), a rechargable battery that can run a computer for several hours during a power outage, giving you a chance to save your data.
- ✓ For more protection, invest in a dependable tape backup drive. These devices automatically make a backup copy of your files and can be true lifesavers.
- ✓ Keep abreast of technological developments in home office equipment. Although the latest isn't always the greatest, it's crucial to know what's new and how it can improve your business.

SPACE MISERS

Short on space but big on equipment that can do more than one thing? Several manufacturers have developed multifunction peripherals that offer printing, faxing, copying, and scanning all in one unit. Best of all, the pricetag on these compact pieces is less than the cost of the four separate machines.

Do these multifunction wonders sound too good to be true? Some owners find they don't perform quite as well as they would as separate units. And if one function breaks down, it can put the whole piece of equipment out of commission. But these space misers can be quite a budget-wise buy for the home office; they run from around $250 to $1,000. To get the most for your money, tech expert Marilyn Zelinsky Syarto suggests looking for these key features:

✓ Compact size
✓ Crisp resolution
✓ Separate cartridges for each ink color
✓ Two-sided printing

LAPTOP LUXURIES

Perching a laptop on your lap is not always the most comfortable way to use it—especially for the long term. With so many work-at-homers using laptop or notebook computers now, savvy designers have created some innovative and ergonomically smart solutions to this problem.

✓ *Portable stands* allow you to set up a permanent spot for your laptop in your home office, but offer the flexibility of moving it and your work to another room if you choose. Most are lightweight and adjustable so you can pull up a desk chair underneath.
✓ *Lap desks* can be propped up over your legs, giving you the option of keyboarding while you're reclining on the sofa or lying in bed.
✓ *Mobile carts* are often compartmentalized with sections for the laptop, phone, paper, and even a printer.
✓ *Tray tables* may be built into easy chairs and recliners or designed to slip into place on a chair or sofa to hold a laptop.

Look for more innovations as home office design catches up with technology.

Communications Central

The technology of the last few years has created a lot of attractive options in telephones, answering systems, wireless devices, and other communications tools for home-based workers. Which products and services are best suited for work-at-home moms?

Whether you use your personal telephone line or a separate business number in your home office, you must have a basic telephone on your desk and/or a portable phone to carry around the house. Portable or cordless phones are widely preferred by mompreneurs; they allow a quick escape from noisy children or the freedom to do two things at once, such as change a diaper while taking part in a conference call. Ideally, your phone should be a two-line model so you can put one call on hold while another comes in. A less-ideal solution is to get call waiting from the phone company for an extra few dollars a month. This service can be a bit disruptive if you're in the middle of an important conversation with a client, but it's kind of essential if an emergency should arise at school.

If you can afford it, have a second line put in for a business phone. You'll soon find a business line to be worth its weight in gold; not only will it keep your kids from intercepting calls, it can help you track phone expenses. You get a free listing in the Yellow Pages to boot. Some local carriers now offer the home office line as a more economical alternative to a business line. Call your local phone company to see if this option is available.

Even if you choose to use your current personal phone line for business, you can order similar services. Cost varies regionally, but it's usually a few dollars a month for each of the following services:

Distinctive ring (a.k.a. Smart Ring, Star Ring, or Ringmate) allows you to put two numbers on one line. Each number has a different ring, so you'll know when to answer in a professional manner instead of your usual mommy voice. Jane Boyd, a work and family consultant and mother of three, finds this feature a lifesaver. "My kids now know that if the phone rings in a special way, it's time to be quiet. They also know they can't answer the phone when it rings like that."

Priority call ringing is an extension of distinctive ring. With this feature, you can program several key clients or customers into a list. Your phone will then ring in a special way when one of these priority numbers is trying to get through.

Both local and long-distance carriers provide various other services that may interest mompreneurs. *Call forwarding* shunts calls to another preprogrammed number when you're out or the line is busy. If you have two lines, it can even forward the call to your personal line's voicemail or to your cell phone when you're talking on the business line. *Call answering* is a voicemail system run by the phone company to take messages when you're out or on the phone. It can be a more professional-sounding but potentially more costly alternative to an answering machine. *Caller ID* service is another screening device; it displays the phone number of the caller so you can tell if it's a business or a personal call. *Three-way calling* allows you to set up a conference call from your home office without using any expensive or complicated equipment.

If you make a lot of long-distance calls for the same selected clients each month, you can ask your carrier to code your telephone bill. Calls will then be identified with each client's code number, making it much easier for you to figure out reimbursable long-distance expenses at the end of each month.

It's also wise to shop around for long-distance carriers. The competition is fierce, and several carriers are now offering less expensive commercial rates to home businesses. Some mompreneurs have seen their bills drop by 30 percent. Finally, if your business expands and your customer base broadens, you may want to investigate the possibility of a *toll-free number* or 1-800 number.

Answering machines have made great strides in recent years, too. Of course, you can still get your standard, inexpensive machine. But if you don't mind spending a bit more, you can fool callers into thinking they're reaching a completely staffed office rather than a one-mom operation.

Digital answering systems work like a personal office receptionist. They provide multiple voice mailboxes, so you can leave specific information for callers and they, in turn, can target messages to a certain aspect of your home business or member of your household. Some also boast fax switching, call forwarding, and paging notification, finding you wherever you may be.

Sophisticated voicemail systems are also being built into computers now. As one mompreneur told us, "Although my answering machine had better call-screening capabilities, the increase in my productivity from voicemail more than makes up for this loss."

Beepers and *cellular phones* are other communications devices many moms rely on. For mompreneurs who have to be away from their home offices for part of the day, these can be very worthwhile security blankets. You'll never miss an important call from a baby-sitter, your child, or school. Cell phones and services have become so affordable, many mompreneurs use them as their primary business number instead of having a separate line installed at home. Shop around for the best deals.

Internet service providers, commonly known as ISPs, connect you via modem or access port to e-mail service and the Internet. There are giant ISPs, such as AOL and MSN, as well as a growing number of small, local ones. At a cost of about $20 a month, communicating online can significantly cut back on phone expenses. The mompreneurs we met online through message boards, discussion forums, and other venues all value the Internet as a way to gather information quickly, exchange ideas, and network. (See chapter 7.)

DOING BUSINESS THE VIRTUAL WAY

Gandel Marketing is a full-service ad agency with three partners who hardly ever see each other in person. President Priscilla Gandel works out of her Long Branch, New Jersey, home; Creative Director of Copy Gina Bruce works from her Westchester, New York, home office; and Creative Director of Art Shelley Kawai is in Norwalk, Connecticut. The three e-mail and phone each other throughout the day and hold meetings by teleconferencing. Occasional face-to-face meetings are no sweat;

although the mompreneurs live in different states, they're all within short driving distance of each other.

"The acceptance in the work world of virtual meetings has opened many doors for me," says Bruce. "Research is done mostly through the Internet, and e-mail eliminates faxing and overnight packages for manuscripts and layouts. We even have clients in other states." But it wasn't always that easy for this single mom of one. When Bruce started her home-based advertising copywriting business, she had to take a lot of on-site meetings and assignments. Her FedEx bills were sky-high from the overnighting of diskettes, and she either had to spend hours researching in the library or lay out big bucks to purchase research materials. Now Bruce does most of her work right in her home office and is almost always available for her daughter. Clients are so impressed with the Gandel team, they rarely give a second thought to its virtual existence. One secret to their success: "Even if your business is high-tech, remember to keep that personal touch," recommends Bruce.

THE HEALTHY HOME OFFICE

Can your workspace be dangerous to your health? According to medical experts, problems as diverse as eyestrain, migraine headaches, carpal tunnel syndrome, back and neck spasms, skin rashes, and birth defects have all been linked to something in the office. Anything from the placement of your computer to the design of your desk chair to the rug on your floor can be to blame.

Home workers may be more vulnerable to these health problems because we tend to furnish our workspaces on a small budget, often relying on castoffs from other rooms of the house. While a kitchen chair might be fine for eating a meal, it's not the best seat to put in front of a monitor and keyboard. Furthermore, many of us have little or no knowledge of ergonomics, a priority among designers of commercial office space.

Ergonomics is defined as the science of designing and arranging tools to fit the user's physical and psychological requirements. In other words, making the machine fit you, instead of the other way around. With more people working from home and more time being spent at the computer, being ergonomically correct should be a major consideration when putting together a home office.

An Ounce or Two of Prevention

Your personal computer, the focus of most home-based businesses, is the crux of a number of health-related problems, including the increasingly prevalent repetitive strain disorder. This problem results from the frequent repetition of certain movements, such as tapping on a computer keyboard. Luckily, we can take steps to prevent this and other office maladies.

✓ We can't say it enough: Choose a good chair. It should adjust up and down, have proper lumbar (lower back) support, and have a backrest that tilts. These features will allow you to lean slightly backward with elbows level with or a little lower than the keyboard, wrists almost straight, and hands resting lightly on the keys. This is the most comfortable and least stressful position. Arm supports are helpful, too, for keeping upper arms roughly parallel to your trunk and comfortably bent at the elbows. The depth of the seat should suit your size; if it is too deep, use a cushion to support your back and push you forward so your knees are slightly past the end of the chair.

✓ Adjust your desk. Many of today's workstations and computer tables come equipped with knobs so you can raise, lower, and tilt the keyboard shelf or work surface to a more comfortable angle and reduce wrist fatigue and injury. Old desks can be raised with blocks or thick phone books or lowered by sawing off part of the legs. The idea is to set up your work area so it's in sync with the natural movements of your body.

✓ Use padded wrist rests, footstools, and back pillows to encourage comfortable, healthy posture.

✓ Try out an ergonomically designed keyboard. It's made to accommodate your natural movements, with keys that are arranged in left and right sections and gently curved wrist rests molded into the plastic.

✓ Ease up on your mouse. Overzealous gripping of the mouse can aggravate wrist pain and create too much tension in the fingers. Use a light touch when holding and clicking, and purchase a mouse nest to support the wrist. Better yet, replace your old mouse with an ergonomically designed touchpad that greatly reduces wrist movements and the incidence of repetitive strain disorders.

✓ Minimize monitor glare. Start by turning down the brightness and turning up the contrasts until your monitor is easy to read. If you're fortunate enough to have a window in your home office, make sure the monitor is placed so the screen doesn't reflect the natural light, and use track or recessed lights to spotlight your work areas, making sure the light doesn't bounce off the computer screen. We were surprised to learn from ergonomics experts that the monitor should be the brightest light in your workspace.

✓ Dust off your monitor screen. If that doesn't do the trick, buy a glare filter to help protect your eyes. These mesh or glass shields or hoods go over your monitor screen to increase display contrast and reduce reflection.

✓ Check your monitor height. The top of the screen should be just about level with your eyes when you look straight ahead to prevent buildup of tension in the neck.

✓ Use a document holder to place copy near your monitor at eye level.
✓ Attach a shoulder cradle to your telephone handset. This cushions the space between your head and shoulder. Two other choices are popular among mompreneurs: substituting a telephone headset for the traditional telephone or switching to a speaker phone. Both allow hands-free conversations, significantly reducing the neck and shoulder strain that results from cradling a telephone receiver.

CAN COMPUTERS HARM YOUR BABY?

Another computer-related worry is the effect of electromagnetic fields (EMFs) on the future health of users, especially pregnant women. EMFs are a type of radiation emitted by computer monitors and other electrical equipment. Some scientists feel that repeated exposure to EMFs may lead to birth defects, cancer, and other ailments. While more research into this area bears watching by work-at-home moms, most experts currently contend that the intensity of EMFs from computer monitors shouldn't cause concern. However, if the talk worries you, take these precautionary steps:

✓ Sit at least an arm's length away from your computer screen, and avoid sitting near the sides or back of your monitor. Higher levels of EMFs are emitted from these areas.
✓ If you're in the market for new equipment, choose a monitor with a larger screen. That way, you can position yourself farther away.
✓ Ask your computer dealer to show you monitors with lower EMF emission ratings. These figures are available either through the dealer or manufacturer.

Chase Away Work-at-Home Ills

These are some more steps you can take to make your home office a healthier place to work.

✓ Take frequent breaks from repetitive tasks, such as keyboarding or surfing the Net. Even if you don't think you have the time, get up and walk around every thirty to sixty minutes during your stretch at the computer.
✓ Plan short breaks into your routine, too. Take your hands off the keyboard and wiggle your fingers; take your eyes off the computer screen and focus on a favorite object in your office; or walk around

while talking on the phone. Although each of these moves takes only a few seconds, they can help relieve fatigue and muscle pressure.

✓ If you feel tension mounting, relax for a minute or two. Two techniques to try are deep breathing and head/neck rolls.

✓ Put a lot of thought into the placement of your workstation. Set up your desk and equipment so you don't have to strain or twist your neck.

✓ Stay away from synthetic paints, carpets, and fabrics, as well as toxic glues. These can be especially harmful if your home office is poorly ventilated; they tend to release gases as they age, which can cause drowsiness, headaches, itchy rashes, and more.

✓ Treat yourself to a massage. It's a surefire way to get rid of neck and shoulder tension and get some of the pampering you deserve.

CLUTTER CONTROL

Now comes the challenge: neatly and efficiently fitting all this stuff we've discussed into your workspace. Who has time to be well-organized when we barely have enough hours in the day to get our work done and care for our families? Actually, better organization can save time and earn you more money in the long run.

Start with Storage

Professional organizers almost all agree that storage should be your prime consideration. "When arranging your home office, think vertically," recommends Lisa Kanarek, author of *Organizing Your Home Office for Success* and owner of the Dallas, Texas–based company, EVERYTHING'S ORGANIZED. "Since most home offices have limited floor space, use the walls as much as possible," she goes on to say. A sturdy shelving system can house books, supplies, and equipment. Wall units that combine open shelves with closed cabinets can help conceal some of the inevitable piles of junk.

Pat salvaged some kitchen cabinets left over from a renovation and installed them in her office. If open, wall-hung shelving is the only option, stack it with baskets, plastic bins, or attractive cardboard boxes for a cleaner look. For many of us mompreneurs who have set up shop in a spare bedroom, Kanarek suggests converting the closet (or at least part of it) into a supply center. Remove the hanging rod, add interior shelves from floor to ceiling, and attach wire shelf units to the door. She's also an advocate of finding new functions for old furniture. For example, a bedroom dresser can double as storage space for office supplies and books, plus the top may be used to hold a fax, copier, or other equipment.

File Effectively

The next place to tackle is your filing system, an area that can quickly get out of control from the mountains of paper we all encounter. Stephanie Schur, the founder of SpaceOrganizers, a White Plains, New York, firm specializing in home and office organization, recommends setting up three filing categories: hot files (active), storage (on hand), and cold files (long term).

Hot files should be readily accessible, either in an upright file container or hanging rack set on your work surface, in a cascading file or rolling cart standing on the floor to one side of your desk, or in your most convenient file drawer. Filing cabinets are the most obvious choice for storage files, but don't go overboard. A four-drawer cabinet for hanging lateral or vertical file folders should suit most needs. Cabinets with more space will only encourage you to hold on to more. Schur warns us to "keep in mind that only 20 percent of all paper in files is ever retrieved." Cold files can be saved in cardboard bankers' boxes, fiberboard cubes, plastic milk crates, or stackable bins or containers. Office supply and home accessories stores and catalogs offer a great variety of colorful and practical choices. Make sure you label all your filing containers for easy retrieval, and put the most recent material near the front of each alphabetically labeled file folder. Another good way to save space is to go "paperless" as often as possible by filing important documents and forms in virtual folders in your computer's hard drive.

Clear That Desktop

If your desk looks anything like ours, it probably needs some immediate attention, too. Begin by limiting the equipment and supplies you keep on your work surface. The computer monitor and keyboard may be essential, but the printer can stand on a nearby shelf or countertop; the phone should be close at hand, but the fax needn't be. As far as supplies go, Kanarek advises keeping only those things that you use daily or weekly on top of your desk; anything else is excess clutter and will only distract you. Desk drawers and shelves above the desk are handy for keeping frequently used supplies within reach but out of the way. Schur agrees, adding, "You can use desk organizer trays and holders to help out, but don't overdo these—they, too, can create clutter." Schur also suggests using baskets or other attractive containers you already have around the house to stash desktop overflow without spending extra money.

Ten Tricks to Manage the Mess

Schur and Kanarek can straighten up the most disorganized home offices and make them (and their inhabitants) much more efficient.

1. Take every opportunity to weed out unused items. At least once or twice a year, go through material in storage files, discarding what you no longer need. Transfer the rest to your cold files.
2. Put files on the computer to keep paper accumulation down to a minimum. Don't forget to trash old computer files; otherwise your hard drive will get cluttered, too.
3. Store unread magazines in the room where they're most likely to be read. At the end of the week, clip articles you want to save and place them in a file folder. Take the folder with you to read during "dead" time (traveling on a bus, plane, or train, or while waiting for an appointment or to pick up your kids).
4. Store supplies and materials near where you will use them. For example, keep computer manuals near the computer; stationery near your printer; fax paper and cover sheets near your fax machine.
5. Keep extra supplies in a compact storage space as close to your home office as possible instead of stowing them all over the house. This gives you a better idea of what you own and will help prevent stockpiling too many unnecessary supplies.
6. Straighten out your supplies on a regular basis, keeping a list of those items that are running low.
7. Order or buy supplies in bulk, but don't overbuy. When you shop in a store, bring a sample of your fax paper, printer cartridge, etc. with you to avoid a mistake.
8. Group telephone cords and other wires together and tuck them out of sight whenever possible.
9. Replace stacking trays with stacking bins. Bins hold more and can stack on the floor, clearing your desktop for work.
10. Replace message slips with a phone log that you keep next to your phone and/or answering machine. When retrieving messages, record the date, name of caller, his or her company, the phone message, and the number.

Cheap Frills

Add one or more of these fun extras to your home office to inspire you to get down to serious work each day:

✓ Envelope-style file folders that keep papers from slipping out. They come in an array of hues so you can color-code your filing system for easier retrieval.
✓ Brightly colored, heavy-gauge cardboard upright files to hold magazines, catalogs, and phone directories.
✓ Plastic-coated wire letter trays and/or wall rack to help sort mail, paperwork, and reading material.
✓ Computer monitor screen-savers, mouse pads, and wrist rests in whimsical, colorful designs. There's something for everyone, from celestial-patterned mouse pads to screen-savers picturing your favorite cartoon characters or family members to wrist rests in neon shades.
✓ Corkboard computer monitor frame that doubles as a mini–bulletin board for posting notes, messages, and small photos.
✓ Tiny furry animals or miniature leather jackets for storing an idle computer mouse.
✓ Mini vacuum set to clean computer keyboard. Attaches to hose of regular vacuum cleaner.
✓ CD or Zip disk case made of sturdy cardboard covered in an attractive print. Two slide-out drawers hold disks.

Where to find these accessories? Mail-order catalogs and websites like Lillian Vernon, The Container Store, Target, and Hold Everything are devoting more room to the home office market. Check out the office supply stores such as Staples or Office Max and the less-expensive home furnishings chains such as Pier 1, Crate and Barrel, and Bed, Bath and Beyond too.

STOCKING UP

Here's a checklist of supplies to have on hand so you're not caught short in a pinch:

✓ Stationery (letterhead) and envelopes
✓ Business cards
✓ Large manila envelopes (at least 9" × 12" in size)
✓ Printer paper
✓ Fax paper
✓ Extra printer cartridge
✓ Rolodex (If you prefer a nonelectronic address book!)
✓ Ruled legal or writing pads
✓ File folders
✓ Computer disks
✓ Pens
✓ Pencils

- ✓ Pencil sharpener
- ✓ Hi-Liter markers
- ✓ Heavy-duty stapler and staples
- ✓ Paper clips
- ✓ Rubber bands
- ✓ Scotch tape
- ✓ Scissors
- ✓ Push pins
- ✓ Post-it notes
- ✓ Calculator
- ✓ Postage stamps
- ✓ An updated copy of your résumé

MAKING YOUR SPACE KID-FRIENDLY

When we asked the mompreneurs in our survey, "How have you made your workspace kid-friendly?" fifty-five percent answered, "It's not." Even so, our statistics show that a good percentage of work-at-home moms do try to accommodate their children in some way—maybe not during the bulk of their workday, but at least for a small part of the time.

MOMPRENEUR STATISTIC

Kid-Friendly Home Offices

Child has his or her own desk/supplies	32%
Office is also used as a family room	7%
Kids play games on the office computer	5%
Homework is done in the office	1%

Where to Draw the Line

Setting up a kid-friendly home office does have its benefits, but beware of your space becoming overly chummy. Too much interaction between your children and your business can hinder productivity, and in some cases, even cause major setbacks (like the time Pat's son accidentally deleted an assigned article she had not yet printed or backed up from her hard drive). How to prevent these crises? By physically and psychologically safeguarding your space.

✓ If your children are young, invest in a desktop shell for your computer. These software packages provide a colorful overlay to the traditional Windows or Mac desktop, allowing you to shield your hard drive and separate your children's software from your own. Another alternative is partitioning your disk drive. This allows your work to be in one portion of the drive; your childrens' in another. A computer consultant can help you work out this arrangement.

✓ Keep little ones from jamming Play-Doh, American cheese, paper clips, and other foreign objects into your disk drive by attaching a piece of cardboard or duct tape across the opening.

✓ Protect your hardware (printer, keyboard, and monitor) with inexpensive plastic covers. Other options are keyboard skins and mouse houses.

✓ Purchase a cord-housing unit to contain the tangle of wires from your computer and printer.

✓ Keep magnets out of your office. They can wipe out computer files in a flash.

✓ Supervise your child's first trips into cyberspace. Venture out together and identify those locations that are acceptable and those that are off-limits. Many chat areas and clubs are specifically geared to children; others are appropriate for both youngsters and grownups; but some are for adult eyes and ears only.

✓ Install parental controls on your Web browser or through your ISP to keep youngsters off inappropriate sites.

✓ Reinforce the message that kids should not give out their last names, addresses, or phone numbers online, and never agree to meet any online friends in person.

Childproofing Your Office

Fredda Kwitman, a therapist in Westchester, New York, started with the obvious when she set up her home-based practice: no sharp corners on furniture, stain-resistant upholstery fabrics, and no breakable objects. Now that her children are older and she can be a little more lenient, Kwitman still puts safety first in her home office that doubles as a family room. Leslee Feiwus, who runs a pen pal subscription service in her Texas home, puts everything that's important or potentially dangerous on high shelves. Nancy Coleman, a California personal trainer and owner of a children's mail-order company, does the same, but balances it by filling bottom drawers and baskets with toys that her son can easily reach. She also keeps the trash basket perched in an out-of-the-way spot.

Childproofing is a must for mompreneurs with children under age six and a smart idea even if the kids are a little older. There are plenty of potential danger spots in the home office, according to Robert Mendelson, M.D., F.A.A.P., a pediatrician in Portland, Oregon. Below are several of his suggestions to make your workspace safer, especially when your kids are near you as you work.

- ✓ Never put your child in an infant seat that's set on top of your desk or a countertop. Even if your baby seems pretty placid and inactive, she may suddenly tip over the infant seat by moving in a new or different way.
- ✓ Never use a walker! Walkers have resulted in countless serious infant and toddler accidents, and they're strongly discouraged by the American Academy of Pediatrics. Dr. Mendelson suggests using a device without wheels that holds an infant upright, allowing him to stand up, rock back and forth, and play without the danger of falling down a flight of stairs or scooting into a heavy piece of furniture.
- ✓ Crawl around on your hands and knees at your child's level looking for sharp corners, drawers that can be pulled out, electrical outlets, etc., then childproof. Plug up exposed outlets with plastic covers, shield sharp corners with rubber or soft plastic protectors, and lock drawers and cabinets that should be off-limits with safety latches or other closures. One work-at-home mom found file cabinets with velcro locks; she can easily open the drawers, but her toddler can't.
- ✓ Juice up your computer, fax, answering machine, and other electrical equipment with safety plugs that can't be removed from outlets by little hands. Another idea from Dr. Mendelson is a locking device that screws into the outlet plate to keep the plugs firmly in place.
- ✓ Enclose or arrange electric cords from your computer and other equipment so they don't hang over the edge of your workstation. The last thing you want is for a child to tug on a dangling cord and pull a piece of equipment onto his head.
- ✓ Keep small objects out of your kids' reach. Paper clips, rubber bands, thumbtacks or pushpins, staples, etc. can easily be swallowed by a curious toddler. Sharp points on pencils, tacks, staples, and scissors can puncture the skin.
- ✓ Store harmful office chemicals in an inaccessible spot. The liquid or powdered toner used for copy machines and ink cartridges for your printer are poisonous if swallowed.
- ✓ Avoid upholstered furniture with buttons.
- ✓ Be careful of cords hanging from window shades, miniblinds, or curtains. These have been the cause of accidental strangulations. A device called a cord divider, sold in hardware stores, can prevent this tragedy. (If the cord forms a loop, another easy safety measure is to cut the cord at the bottom of the loop and knot each end.)

✓ Keep a small, portable fire extinguisher handy near your workspace,
especially if it's in an area of the house that's fairly removed from the
living quarters.

✓ Cover the knob on your office door with a doorknob slip so children
can't enter when you're not there.

✓ If you're fortunate enough to be renovating a portion of your home
into an office, hire a licensed contractor to do any demolition or
sanding, and keep your children away from the area. In older houses
especially, particles escaping from lead-based paint can pose a
possible health risk, so lead-based paint must be removed by a
professional.

TAKING THE HOME OFFICE OUT OF THE HOME

Susan Rietano-Davey and her partner, Sue Glasspiegel, run their company,
Flexible Resources, from their Connecticut homes. Being in the recruitment
business, they often must make presentations or meet with groups of clients.
Since the partners live some distance apart, they rent a conference room for
the day to hold these meetings. Located halfway between their two home
offices, it's convenient, spacious, and one of a growing number of auxiliary
services now being offered to home-based workers.

✓ Real estate companies, office supply stores, and private businesses
providing everything from voice mailboxes to messenger services are
capitalizing on the work-at-home boom.

✓ A number of business centers provide an address and conference room
for as little as $50 to $100 a month, depending on how often you use
the meeting space. Many now offer rentals by the hour (as well as per
day or per week) to accommodate the growing short-term demand by
home workers. It's a smart investment if you need a businesslike
atmosphere for a group meeting.

✓ Copy centers that used to only provide copying services now offer
hookups for laptop computers, free customer service phones for local
calls, fax machines, and video conferencing.

✓ Rent a virtual office from a growing number of communications-
oriented companies, starting at about $10 a month. Depending on the
supplier and how much you want to spend, this service will provide a
voice mailbox; take messages in a businesslike tone; automatically fax
out catalog pages, price lists, or any other prearranged material; accept
your fax mail; and supply you with beeper or pager service.

✓ Hook up with an answering service. These are the most professional-
sounding and personal of all your options for taking phone calls and
messages. It may be worth the extra price if you want to give the

impression that you have a secretary or receptionist. It's an especially valuable service for mompreneurs who are relocating to a new home and/or town and don't want to lose business in the move.

✓ Compare rates of the different express shipping services before using the best-known or traditional one—overnight and two-day delivery of documents has become much more competitive. For larger packages, check out the post office and Amtrak, as well as the usual carriers, to find the best deal.

✓ Messenger services are the most convenient, speedy, and sometimes even the most economical way to send packages to local addresses. Not only do they offer same-day service, they always pick up at your home office.

✓ Hotel lobbies are becoming popular meeting places for professionals with home offices. Restaurants, parks, and even the public library are some other alternatives.

MOMPRENUER® HALL OF FAME

LYN PETERSON
President and Founder of Motif Designs, New Rochelle, New York
Mother of Four

With four children, a business, and at times, various other family members and pets occupying her household, Lyn Peterson knows how important it is to decorate for comfort, flexibility, and economy—in short, real life. Along with her husband, Karl Friberg, Peterson owns and operates Motif Designs, a multimillion-dollar interior design, fabric, and wall-coverings firm with dealings around the world. (She's in the design end; he takes care of production and sales.) What began as a retail fabric and wallpaper store catapulted into the big leagues when Peterson's own designs drew the interest of stylish companies like Marimekko. Now the company has numerous employees and is growing at an annual rate of 20 percent.

Whether she's overseeing the licensing of a new home furnishings collection or recycling a battered but well-loved sofa for a client with young children, this real-life decorator has the same goal: to make the places people live as beautiful and functional as possible so the true meaning of the word *home* rings through. Her fifteen-room house in suburban New York reflects this down-to-earth philosophy. It's often used as a Motif showcase and think tank, addressing such problems as

(continued)

how to factor the kids into every decorating equation and how to change things around in response to new situations.

"Once upon a time, the whole design studio was out of my house—stat cameras, computers, three employees—the works," Peterson says. "But it put too much strain on my home—too much mess and activity." Now she divides her portion of the business between home and Motif headquarters via a combination design library and home office hooked up by computer to the main office. This allows her to do some design work and writing at home, as well as supervise photo shoots for catalogues, magazines, and ads using the rooms in her house as a backdrop.

"Home offices are coming out of the closet and taking front center in family life," comments this mompreneur, and hers is a case in point. She chose a room in the front of the house for her workspace so she originally could see FedEx arriving and the kids coming home from school. The office is paneled in dark wood, with both closed and open cabinetry. Computer games nestle next to fabric swatches and children's stories share shelf space with design reference books. Peterson works from a high, secretarial-style desk. A cozy reading chair with an ottoman, good lighting, and plenty of underneath storage to minimize clutter add to the efficiency and ambience. Her recommendation to other work-at-home moms: "Buy the best office furniture you can afford. Heavy-duty pieces last, and you won't outgrow them as your family and success grow." She also stresses the necessity of "making the space attractive with flattering lighting. Your home office should not look like a laboratory—it should be a place to reflect, think, be inspired."

How does Peterson manage to keep all her balls in the air? "I run my life on a triage basis," she remarks. "The most seriously wounded gets treated first." This usually works, whether it's a child, big account, or employee who gets her immediate attention. She has also learned to prioritize on a need-to-know basis. "I may not know my kids' homerooms at middle school, but I coach the tennis team." Peterson goes on to say, "I work some very long days, some nights, and even some weekends. But then I take time off for intramural sports, school plays, outings, family adventures, and fun." Motif's employees benefit from her balancing strategies, too. It's a flexible, parent-friendly workplace where, in Peterson's words, "we believe people should have a successful life, not just a job or career."

6

Planning and Organizing Your Time

Even though we're both writers with similar assignments and deadlines, our workdays have very different rhythms. Over the years, the pace we each keep has been set by the age of our kids and the demands of their activities. Because Ellen's kids are younger, she's constantly working in shorter spurts, often interrupting business to shuttle the kids to school and extracurricular activities. Pat, whose kids are older, and finally able to drive, has longer stretches in which to do business every day. We've discovered that it isn't so much the number of hours you put in that affects your productivity. Rather, it's how disciplined and organized you are when that work time arrives. Whether you're able to work for just one hour or full eight-hour shifts, you've got to set your schedule and your priorities, then stick to them as best you can—through chicken pox, baby-sitting crises, and school commitments.

WHAT'S THE BEST SCHEDULE FOR YOU?

Should you work half days or full days? During the day or at night? There are numerous work options available to mompreneurs, and they'll change as your children grow. No doubt you'll sample several and even combine a few of them at once during your work-at-home tenure. Here are the arrangements most popular with the moms in our survey:

The Part-Day Plan

You put in a half day or so at work and then spend the rest of the time with your kids. Lisa Rothstein, of the Creative Brownie Company in Ohio, devoted every morning to business, but saved the afternoons for outings with her toddler. Technical writer Lisa Dillon prefered working 9 A.M. to 2 P.M. Mondays through Thursdays while a nanny watched her baby. That gave the Oregon mom and her daughter four afternoons plus all day Friday together. Some moms work around the nursery school schedule, logging in time on the mornings or afternoons that their children are in class.

Time On/Time Off

In this part-time schedule, mompreneurs work a few full days a week, with some days off in between. When Ellen's kids were babies, she got a sitter and worked all day Mondays, Wednesdays, and Fridays, saving Tuesdays and Thursdays for kid stuff. Some moms put their kids in preschool or day care two or three half days, then extend those days with supplemental child care. Others opt for a full-day preschool or day-care program a few times a week. Whichever way you do it, mom and children get some uninterrupted days off each week to spend together.

The Sleep Shift

You work while the kids are in bed: early mornings, late nights, and naptimes. If your kids are long and reliable nappers, you can get a lot done. Otherwise, it'll be necessary to supplement naptimes with child care of some sort. Because her baby Natalie rarely dozed for long, Idaho writer Julie Fanselow got a sitter for two additional hours in the afternoons. When she was really busy, Fanselow worked after Natalie went to bed at night and before she got up in the morning. The sleep shift is a handy fallback option when you're on a tight deadline or your sitter has canceled. Lots of moms also routinely rely on the early-morning and late-night hours (when the business phone and household are quietest) for catching up on less demanding tasks, like paperwork and e-mail. New York marketing consultant Andrea Disario often returns to her desk between the hours of 9 and 11 P.M. to do clerical work, billing, mailings, cutting and pasting, and other chores that "don't require a brain." Before her business outgrew her home, Connecticut landscape designer Carol Guthrie frequently rose at 4 or 5 A.M. because she found it "a peaceful and productive time to work." She compensated by scheduling in a short 40-minute nap while her kids were at school—"Quite easy to do when your bed is right upstairs," she points out.

We do know many mompreneurs who are so successful at fitting business around their kids' sleep schedules that they do it all the time—and don't use any child care at all. A word of caution before you try this, however: You'll get a lot less shut-eye when you pull this shift on a regular basis, and if you're not careful, this demanding schedule can result in a severe case of burnout. Before you attempt working this way, make sure you're the kind of person who can survive on very little sleep.

We've found that the mompreneurs who consistently work the sleep shift are likely to refer to themselves as "morning people" or "night owls." "I love writing late at night and faxing the stories off at all hours," says Mary Gillett, a Michigan-based freelancer. In addition, these women tend to be in professions that don't require a lot of phone contact or client interaction, such as writing, proofreading, copyediting, secretarial services, desktop publishing, and graphic design. If this doesn't sound like you, shoot for daytime hours and save the sleep shift as a backup.

The Fragmented Format

An offshoot of the sleep shift, this plan requires you to work through kids' naps, plus grab whatever other business time you can get. Instead of having long blocks to count on each week, you'll always be working in short shifts planned around children's attention spans and preschool schedules and your short-term child care availability.

To do this effectively day after day, you've got to say good-bye to the nine-to-five mentality. If you've got young children, you'll rarely get more than an hour or two at a time to work. "I learned to adjust," says writer Julie Fanselow. "Even though I worked in a fairly fragmented fashion, everything got done." "Compartmentalize your time," suggests Andrea Disario, by working frequent short time slots around your kids' schedules. For example, you might work 9:30 to 11:30 A.M., while they're in nursery school; 4 to 6 P.M., while they're at a play date; and 9 to 11 P.M., after they're in bed, she explains. You'll learn to gauge just how much business you can realistically expect to finish while the kids are underfoot. "Both my children are very good at playing by themselves and can do so for an hour or more before needing a little guidance," says Elise Ravenscroft, a desktop publisher from Gaithersburg, Maryland. You'll be surprised at how much you can accomplish in so little time.

The School Schedule

When your kids are in school full-time, you can work almost all day every day, yet still be there for homework, snacks, car pools, and other after-school activities. Before she moved her Pennsylvania graphic design firm out of the home, Marilyn Vaughn worked straight through from 8:30 A.M. to 3:30 P.M. every day. Everything else was kid time, she says.

Though most mompreneurs yearn for the day when their kids are finally in school, working according to the academic calendar does have its draw-backs. There's no child-care alternative when kids are home sick. Since few of us have the luxury of totally closing down our business during winter, spring, and summer breaks, we often wind up enrolling our children in camps and other vacation child-care programs. "I had no idea how many holidays and school vacations kids had until I tried to work from home," notes Disario.

Still, if you plan far enough in advance, you can enjoy some of those long-term school vacations yourself. One summer, writer Theresa Kump found out that her husband, an attorney, would have to spend the entire summer working in Paris. She was able to adjust her workload so the whole family could join him—something she never could have pulled off in a traditional job.

Full-Timing It

Though the majority of the mompreneurs we polled keep part-time hours, a healthy sampling have discovered that a full-time schedule suits their business best. Karen McCloud's home-based graphic design firm in Vermont became so successful that this energetic mom put in forty- to fifty-hour work weeks. McCloud is often back at her desk again after she's tucked her boys into bed.

Full-time work-at-homers don't have to do all their business from their home offices, though. They might be telecommuters, like Maria Tomsic, a senior automotive designer in Michigan who was the first person in her company to try out a flexible work schedule. She worked three full days from home and went into the office at company headquarters the other two days a week. It wasn't easy at first, and Tomsic found herself working all hours of the night trying to meet deadlines, finish the housework, and care for her infant. "It was terrible for me physically and emotionally, she says. But once she reassessed the situation and decided to get more help with the child care and the household chores, "I felt very much in control of things," Tomsic says.

What's Your Best Trick for Juggling Work and Family?

Be organized and disciplined	31%
Work after all are in bed or before they're up	23%
Stop working when kids get home	13%
Supportive spouse	10%
Flexibility	6%
Sense of humor	5%

Mompreneur Time Tricks

Mompreneurs "don't need a time-management program. They need a change-management program," says work-at-home mom Maria Chilcote, a business training consultant in Virginia who runs workshops on home businesses. You might know exactly what you want to get done on a certain day, she explains, but then your kids get up and one of them's sick. Or your neighbor has an emergency and drops off two of her kids while she rushes the other one to the hospital. On those days, "you can take your time management list, put it in the blender, and turn it on puree," Chilcote says.

With that in mind, we've come up with some preventive time tricks. They won't free you of frustrating setbacks, but they will help you be better prepared for them so that you can easily regroup when surprises happen. These preventive time tricks will also help you avoid or deal with common mompreneur problems, such as taking on too much, doing business round-the-clock, allowing work to invade family life, and having constant interruptions from family, friends, neighbors, repair people, and telephone solicitors.

Set a Work Schedule

Put aside consistent hours to work every week, but know that they could change at a moment's notice. All it takes is a few snowflakes or strep germs to turn a mompreneur's day upside down.

There's no foolproof formula for selecting office hours, and yours will be influenced by your work habits, the kind of business you're in, and the age of your kids. Sometimes it takes a while to find the arrangement that fits your family. "The best solution is the one that feels right for you and your children," points out Elizabeth Goldsmith, a public relations consultant from Pepper Pike, Ohio. Your work schedule will change as your kids grow. The routine that seems perfect when they're babies may no longer be appropriate when your little ones reach the preschool and grade school years, so expect to reevaluate and adjust your business hours as time goes on.

Have Loads of Backups

A mompreneur can never have too many contingency plans. "I have backups for everything: baby-sitters, vendors, computer files, even business clothes," says Loraine Goodenough, a desktop publisher from Lorton, Virginia. (You never know when a child might throw up on your one and only suit on the day you have a big meeting.) The most important backup is an alternative work schedule for those times when your regular working hours are thrown off by unexpected circumstances. Always have some solutions in place ahead of time so you'll be prepared when problems inevitably occur.

Build a Safety Cushion into Your Work Schedule

Veteran mompreneurs learn to expect the unexpected: snowstorms, sick kids, no-show baby-sitters, nightmare home remodelings. With surprises like these, consistently working down to the wire can be downright dangerous. To stay ahead of the game, work-at-home moms need to build a safety net into their schedules. "I always aim to get projects finished a week or two before the real deadline," says Connie Lagan, a small business consultant from New York. That way, if something derails her plan, she can still meet her deadline in plenty of time. "Someone was astonished recently when I turned in a project over a month early," recalls Loraine Goodenough. "I tried to explain that if I didn't do it then, my kids would find a way to make me miss the deadline. By working so far in advance, I fooled my kids' deadline radar."

Another way to childproof your schedule is to work before the kids get up. Joanne DeMarchi, a California nutritionist, regularly does business in the early mornings so her workday won't be a total loss if one of her kids wakes up with the flu or there's an emergency school closing. If you can, keep your nights open for those crunch times when working the nine-to-midnight shift is unavoidable. Everyone goes through different prime time swings, notes Ronni Eisenberg, a mompreneur who's a professional organizer in Westport, Connecticut, and also co-author of *Organize Yourself!* and several other organizational books. "You may go through short periods where you're working every night," she says. Then things calm down again and you're likely to find yourself falling asleep shortly after the kids.

Plan Ahead for Holidays and Vacations

Prepare far in advance for vacation and holiday time so that you can adjust your work schedule to accommodate any upcoming changes in the routine. Mark these periods clearly on your calendar, add any other special family or school events that you'll want to be free for, then plan your workload around these dates. "When I know about things far enough in advance, I can block myself out and allow for some time off," says Debbie Mumford, a New York naturalist. Another mompreneur, who's a land use consultant in Oregon, always strives to tie up major projects by the end of the school year so she can enjoy lots of summertime activities with her children. "There were weeks one summer that I didn't work at all," she says. Even if you'll be working the whole summer through, advance planning will pay off when it's time to register for camp or line up a mother's helper for two months.

Snatch Windows of Opportunity

Figure out what you can and can't do with the children around. Save complex projects for the times you'll be able to work without the young ones underfoot. Then keep smaller, simpler jobs on hand that you can easily pick up and put down again when you're all together. As a manager of four non-profit associations, Cathy DeVito Fink spends an incredible amount of time on the phone planning events, juggling calendars, coordinating volunteers, and servicing members. She schedules all her phone work for when her son is in school and fits in other, less complicated production work when he is home. "It's amazing how many envelopes you can stuff or how many financial statements you can review when the kids are around," says this mompreneur from Falls Church, Virginia.

Running business errands on family time is another fairly painless way to get work done with the kids in tow. "I am often able to combine a job drop-off with a special trip to the zoo or park," notes Elise Ravenscroft, a desktop publisher. Cathy DeVito Fink groups errands around the time school gets out. "If you buy the kids a Slurpee every once in a while, they really don't mind going to the post office, bank, or printer," she says.

Don't overlook the spare five minutes here or ten minutes there. These small parcels of time are perfect for completing tiny tasks such as returning a call, sending a fax, addressing an envelope, or printing out a job. When she's headed to the pediatrician or anywhere else where she's bound to have a wait, Loraine Goodenough brings along newsletters to scan or cards for jotting quick notes to clients.

What else can you fit in when you have just a few minutes? How about going through the business cards that are piling up in your pocketbook or scribbling some notes to yourself about an upcoming job? Other quickie ideas include checking your e-mail, listening to answering machine messages, addressing note cards, stamping envelopes, and sorting and opening your mail. We're sure you'll find lots more little things to keep you busy when you've got a spare second.

Make Short To-Do Lists

"I've finally learned that putting more things on my to-do list does not mean I'm going to get more done," says Loraine Goodenough. In fact, if you put too many things on your list, you'll only be sabotaging your productivity, and you'll never feel like you're getting anything accomplished. So hold the list to two or three important goals for that day.

"Goal-setting is very important," emphasizes Cathy DeVito Fink. "Before I close up my office every evening, I go through my list of things to do and update it. Every morning I have a nice prioritized list for the day. (Of course, by noon the list is shot to hell.) But at least I start my day organized."

Adds Debbie Mumford, who runs The Nature of Things, an environmental education program in Purdys, New York, "Be honest with yourself and realistic about what you can accomplish." Sometimes we have unreasonable expectations and then end up feeling let down and disappointed when we can't fulfill them, she explains. But a short to-do list will set you up for success.

Plan your list the night before, advises organizing expert Ronni Eisenberg. Think about the most important things you must get done and set your priorities, she says. "Is it the proposal that needs your attention? The filing that's piled high? Your insurance papers?" With your priorities identified, you'll be ready to go when work time begins.

Know the Value of Your Time

Family and work tend to consume every hour, leaving little time for anything else. Even though it's tough to do at first, you've got to become selective about the professional and personal projects you take on. Decide which ones are most worth your effort and will reap the biggest rewards in dollars, future opportunities, and satisfaction. As Julie Fanselow puts it, "Time is a precious commodity for work-at-home women. We simply can't take twenty hours to do a project we could do in ten. I will still give clients an outstanding piece of work (better than most writers can do in the same amount of time), but I will not make three phone calls when two will do. And I will not write away for still more information when what's in my files will suffice." When Fanselow feels she can't do the project justice in such a short amount of time, however, she will turn it down altogether, although that's easier said than done, she adds.

It might be tempting to take any job you can get, but think hard before you grab rush assignments or long-term projects that preclude you from taking other work. A job with a too-quick turnaround might be impossible to complete if you're hit with a family crisis, and long-term assignments can sometimes snowball to unpredictable proportions, leaving you little freedom for anything else. Remember the flexibility factor when evaluating business projects.

The same goes for volunteer work, whether it's serving on the PTA or coaching the local Little League. Because we have more leeway in our work schedules, mompreneurs tend to book up any free time by helping out at church, school, and sports events. That's good, as long as these don't eat up too much of your family hours. If the activity gives you more hands-on time with your own kids or benefits them directly, it's worth it. If it's the kind of commitment that requires lots of evening meetings away from your family, you may want to reconsider. Pat wanted to stay involved with her children's PTAs, but she knew the frequent board meetings would cut into her evening time with the boys. Instead, she produced the newsletter, which fit more easily around her family and business routines. Before you say yes to any time-consuming task—whether business or personal—make sure it's something you really want to do.

Learn to Say No

It's a workday and you're at your desk reading a Post-it note that your husband stuck to the lamp. It says, "Hi honey—How's work? Could you pick up my shirts from the cleaner's?" Then the phone rings and it's your daughter's class mother asking you to bake cupcakes for the Halloween party tomorrow. You no sooner hang up when your preschooler, who has momentarily snuck away from the baby-sitter, knocks on your door wanting to play Candyland. Before you run out to the cleaner's, drag out the mixer, or plop on the floor with your three-year-old, how about mouthing the following letters: N-O. If that's too strong for you, smile and try the more polite version. "I'd really like to, but I'm working right now." For more ways to say no, see "More Ways to Say No When a Simple No Won't Do," on page 158.

You've got to unleash the power of saying no. It's the key to guarding your work and family time. A calm, polite refusal is essential when you're on a deadline and that old friend calls to chat or when the stay-at-home mom down the block drops by for coffee. You'll need to say no to running for the school board or to keep play dates out of your house on your workdays. You'll also have to say no to yourself sometimes when your discipline falters and you're tempted to raid the fridge or drive to the mall on deadline day.

Saying no is especially necessary for those times you'll have to turn down work assignments. Word processor Julie Pophal says, "My kids come first, and I've learned I can't be supermom, so sometimes I say no to work. Life's too short to just always go for the money."

MORE WAYS TO SAY NO WHEN A SIMPLE NO WON'T DO

WHEN . . .	STAY FRIENDLY, CALM, AND CONFIDENT, AND TRY SAYING . . .
A new client offers you a ridiculously low fee for your services.	"That's well below my usual rate. We'd need to negotiate a higher fee before I could accept the job."
Your best client asks you to do a job, but you're just too busy to take it on at this moment.	"I wish I could help out this time, but my schedule is so jammed up that I can't take anything else on right now. If you like, I can refer you to a great person who might be available."
You're working and your children want to demonstrate the new toy that Grandma just bought them.	"I really want to see it, but I've got to finish up this work right now. Save it for me, and as soon as I'm done, we can play."
A client wants to meet with you at the time you're usually driving the afternoon car pool.	"My afternoons are booked up with other appointments, but my mornings are open. Can we do something then?"
A neighbor drops by to chat on one of your work days.	"Today's a work day for me, and I must get back to my desk. Let's talk another time when I'm not working."
A client wants to meet in your office, and you're not crazy about conducting business amid the clutter and the clatter of your kids.	"My office is quite small, and it isn't very comfortable for meetings, but I do know a quiet little coffee shop down the street that would be perfect."

WHEN . . .	STAY FRIENDLY, CALM, AND CONFIDENT, AND TRY SAYING . . .
Your husband asks you to do personal errands on your work time.	"Honey, I really get thrown off my work schedule if I have to leave my desk during the day. Is there any way you can do it on your way home? If not, let's try to figure out a solution that's fair for both of us."
Telephone solicitors monopolize your work time with their pitches.	"Thank you, but I'm not interested. Oops, I have another business call coming in. Bye, and thanks for calling."
Your toddler wails when the baby-sitter arrives.	After a warm good-bye hug and kiss, "Mommy's going to work now. I'll see you later and we'll have some fun together."
It's snowing, the schools are closed, and the working mom next door asks you to watch her kids so she can get to the office.	"I have to work today, too. Maybe we can come up with a plan that's good for both of us. I'll take the kids for the morning if you can get home early and take mine for the afternoon."

Delegate

Once you're proficient at saying no, you've got to learn another important word: *delegate*. You'll have more time and less pressure if you recruit people to help you with certain household and business tasks. For example, you can cut the hours you spend cleaning and cooking by assigning parts of those jobs to family members. "We all share household chores and duties," says mompreneur Marjoree Fougere, a Canadian interior decorator. Pat used to hang a work wheel in the kitchen indicating each family member's job for the week—when Josh had to take out the garbage or Matt was responsible for cleaning the cat's litter box, for example. Ellen's two children are responsible for clearing their dinner plates, making their beds, and separating the family's recyclables. Other good jobs for younger kids include emptying the dishwasher, setting the table, sorting the laundry, and helping with meal preparations.

If you're fortunate—and a good number of the mompreneurs we talked to were—your spouse will lend a helping hand, too. Pat's husband, Elliott, is a gourmet cook who doesn't mind alternating as the family chef. Ellen's husband, Bob, does the weekly food shopping and is so good at it that Ellen's embarrassed to admit she can't remember the last time she was in a supermarket! He's a pro at laundry and doing dishes, too.

Expert delegators are always on the lookout for clever ways to cut corners and gain time. Stephani Perlmutter, a Chicago public relations consultant and mom of twins, realized she'd be less stressed in the mornings and evenings if she didn't have to rush around making breakfast and dinner. She had her baby-sitter come earlier and feed the boys breakfast, and by arranging to have the sitter stay a little longer at the end of the day, Perlmutter was able to get supper started and still have time to play with the kids as it cooked. Tammy Youngman, a Florida marketing and advertising consultant, had the foresight to hire a full-time nanny with great office skills. When Youngman's daughter was napping or at preschool, the nanny helped with the telephones and the billing and also ran personal and business errands for her boss. We know mompreneurs who've even hired professional organizers to help them streamline business tasks and identify the best ones to farm out.

Determine the areas of your business that make sense to delegate, whether you do it on a regular basis or just when you're in a pinch. You might consider contracting out your mailing lists, your bookkeeping, or your filing. Laura Mathisen, a promotions and public relations consultant in Washington State hired an assistant to come in twice a week to process her mail. She sorted and opened all the business mail and put any personal mail into a separate file for Mathisen to read later. On occasion, Loraine Goodenough hires friends to stuff envelopes for her. "You have to know when it's worth it to hire people to help you, just to save time," says Maria Chilcote, who often hires an outside contractor to do her desktop publishing.

Involve Your Kids in Your Business

Lighten your load by giving your children office jobs to do. You'll benefit by having little assistants, and the kids will feel pride and accomplishment in knowing they're helping you out. You'll also be cultivating a better understanding of your business and its contribution to the family's finances. Here's how some moms get their kids involved. (For more ideas, see "Twenty-Five Office Jobs Kids Can Do," on page 161.)

Loraine Goodenough got some of her best desktop design advice from what she called her "Committee of Eight," a team of eight-year-olds that included her daughter and some neighborhood friends. "I'd say, 'What do you think?' and they'd inevitably respond 'Make it fuschia,' " says Goodenough. Tracia Ledford, a crafts columnist, designer, and artist in Orlando,

Florida, valued the artistic input of her daughter, Katelyn, so much that she made her a partner in her business. The mother and daughter team now design crafts together under the catchy moniker of Mom and Me.

TWENTY-FIVE OFFICE JOBS KIDS CAN DO

Find the tasks best-suited to your children's ages and responsibility levels. You'll get more cooperation, and you will help increase their understanding of the work ethic if you pay them a small salary for their services.

1. Collect the mail and deliver it to your office.
2. Separate the family and the business mail.
3. Open your mail.
4. Make photocopies.
5. Collect your faxes.
6. Stuff envelopes.
7. Seal and stamp envelopes.
8. Put labels on packages.
9. Staple things.
10. Sharpen pencils.
11. Add columns of figures on a calculator.
12. Help collate materials.
13. Make new file folders for projects.
14. File things away.
15. Put letters through the postage meter.
16. Mail letters.
17. Critique and test products.
18. Hand out flyers and brochures.
19. Promote your business to their friends and their friends' parents.
20. Alphabetize the business cards you've collected.
21. Copy addresses onto your Rolodex cards.
22. Put away office supplies.

23. Collect paper destined for the garbage and recycle it for drawings or stories on the unused side.

24. Help decorate your office walls with their artwork.

25. Help with web research and other Internet-related challenges.

Let Some Stuff Go

Get out of the supermom mind-set. You can't do everything, so don't even try. Instead, determine which household and business tasks you can comfortably skimp on or let go of altogether. By facing the fact that it's truly impossible to do it all, you'll free yourself of a lot of guilt and feelings of incompetence.

Cleaning is often the first thing to fall by the wayside in most mompreneurs' households. We're not suggesting that you abandon cleaning completely, but you might consider doing it differently—and a lot less frequently. Stop worrying about the things that people outside the family rarely see (closets, drawers, the interior and top of the fridge), and focus on the stuff that has to get done (laundry, bathrooms, dishes). "I do the least cleaning one can do and not be on the Health Department's hit list," comments Loraine Goodenough. You can slash cleaning time by catching messes before they get out of hand. For example, dust-bust the Cheerio under the kitchen chair now, before it gets dragged into the living room on your toddler's sneaker and ground into the carpet. As for major cleanings, "do one thing each day and keep to that schedule every week," suggests Joy Sacramone, a mom from Everett, Massachusetts, who runs a home-based cleaning service called Joy of Cleaning. If you can afford it, consider hiring a cleaning service, even if it's only once a month. The cost is well worth it when you look at the time and effort it will save you.

On the business side, weed out the jobs that no longer make the most sensible use of your time or talents. It's fine to grab whatever work you can get at the beginning of your home-based career, but many of us continue to take on small, unprofitable projects simply because we have an allegiance to the client. For example, until recently, Ellen frequently accepted low-paying assignments from former employers. Now that she's established, she realizes that working for rock-bottom prices only undermines her worth and her efforts. It was hard, but she's learned to pass on the jobs that won't bring her the market rate or higher.

The price tag isn't the only essential factor when weighing whether a job's worthwhile. Even if the project is profitable, you've got to think about the kind of work it requires. Is it something challenging and rewarding? Does it help you hone new skills? Does it further your career and lead to fresh opportunities? If the answer is no and you've got plenty of other work to fall back on, decline such projects from now on. In the past, Pat readily accepted recipe-editing jobs. She figured they paid fairly well and were easy to squeeze in around her writing assignments. She's begun turning them down lately because she'd rather devote her efforts to more personally fulfilling and creative projects.

As you become more experienced as a mompreneur, you'll find it easier to separate the household and business duties that are worthwhile from the ones that are a waste of your time.

Make Time for Yourself

"Don't get so busy that you forget about yourself," cautions Lisa Marie Nelson, a children's music producer in California. It may seem impossible to fit personal time into the work/family equation, but you can do it. You've got to do it, for the sake of your sanity, your well-being, and your self-confidence. As Nelson says, "If your priority is your health and peace of mind, you will be able to handle all the juggling." Maureen LaMarca, a public relations consultant in New Jersey, agrees. "If you feel good, it all works."

Pick something you like to do, whether it's a walk, a workout, or a manicure, and write it on your calendar along with your family and business obligations. Daria Price Bowman, a marketing consultant from New Hope, Pennsylvania, and Maureen LaMarca's business partner, takes time out every day to ride her exercise bike, although she's still trying to train herself not to answer the phone while she's pedaling. Lisa Marie Nelson always schedules a lunch break for herself and makes sure she keeps the appointment. Writer Cathy Wald forces herself out for a walk a few times a week for brainstorming and a breath of fresh air. Just a little bit of private time each week will help you feel energized and more in control of things. The break can be spur of the moment, too. "Sometimes my husband watches Natalie while I go to a movie," says Julie Fanselow. "It makes all the difference in the world. I'm ready to face the new work week with enthusiasm and energy."

ARE YOU DOING TOO MUCH?

Are you always feeling frazzled and unable to balance work and family? If so, you need to reassess your priorities and figure out what you can drop and what you can delegate. With some self-management tricks (we offer lots in this chapter) it is possible to step off the treadmill and regain control of your work-at-home life. If you answer yes to many of the following questions, it's time for you to slow down.

✓ Are you always running for the business phone during your off hours?

✓ Is your family constantly complaining that you never have time for them?

✓ Are you too tired to talk to your husband at the end of the day, let alone do anything else with him?

✓ Do you constantly think about work, even when you're playing games with the kids or reading them stories?

✓ Would you rather be in your office than with your family?

✓ Do your evenings always seem to be monopolized by meetings for business and volunteer organizations?

✓ Have you stopped enjoying your work?

✓ Do you always seem to have more work than you can handle?

✓ Do you have difficulty making the time for family vacations?

✓ Do you take office paperwork and equipment on family vacations and then spend an inordinate amount of time working on them?

✓ Do you constantly feel as if you're spinning out of control?

PREVENTING BUSINESS FROM TAKING OVER FAMILY LIFE

To be a successful work-at-homer, you've got to be a self-starter, but being a self-stopper is equally important. Just as you have to motivate yourself to turn the work mode switch on, you also have to force yourself to turn it off sometimes. Turning work off is one of the biggest challenges facing mompreneurs. "I'm up at 5:30, and where do I go? Straight downstairs to my office," says Joy Sacramone. "After supper I'll remember that I didn't do something, and I'll go back downstairs. You never have a lot of time to spend not thinking about your business, because it's right here."

While keeping work and family time separate is certainly tough to do, it isn't impossible. You just need to harness the same discipline that keeps your business running and use it to keep work from running out of control. "If you're smart enough to have your own business, then you're smart enough to figure out how to keep it out of your hair," advises Pepper Schwartz, Ph.D., a columnist and a professor of sociology at the University of Washington in Seattle and author of the book *Peer Marriage: How Love Between Equals Really Works.*

Give Yourself a Quitting Time

When you're employed in an office outside the home, you leave work behind at the end of the day. Mompreneurs deserve that same privilege. Decide on the office hours that make the most sense and stick to them. "You have to give yourself rules and regulations and look at them as something you're breaking if you don't follow through on them," says Dr. Schwartz. Of course, at times, certain unexpected circumstances will force you to work during family time, but if you save this as your emergency option, it won't be so upsetting for everyone when it happens. To keep yourself from burning out on those inevitable occasions you do find yourself working nights and weekends, give yourself a time limit and make sure you stop when you reach it.

Announce Your Office Hours to Your Family

"Make it a public declaration," says Dr. Schwartz. "It's like saying that you're going on a diet and telling everyone. It's more embarrassing when they see you're not doing it." It's also important to let your family know that you've factored in their needs when setting up your business schedule. Explain why this system works for you, and listen to what they have to say about it. "Negotiate and talk to your family about what they want and what they don't like about the way you're doing things," says Dr. Schwartz. Figure out a solution that takes into consideration everyone's desires, she adds. Once you're in agreement, consider it a deal. "Unless you renegotiate, you have to go with that deal," Dr. Schwartz says.

Activate Your Answering Machine or Voicemail During Off Hours

Don't keep interrupting your family time to go listen to your messages. Lower the volume on the machine, if that's what it takes to keep yourself from eavesdropping on incoming messages while you're at the dinner table or doing homework with the kids, suggests Dr. Schwartz. Little tricks like these help you set clearer work boundaries for yourself and your clients.

Clients who call desktop publisher Cecille Hansen after hours get a message that says, "Thank you for calling HCW. Our normal hours are from nine to five. Please call back during these hours, and we'll be happy to assist you." This is a professional way to let clients know when they can and cannot get in touch with you. Hansen is meticulous about returning any missed calls promptly during her business time.

When Gwen Nagorsky first began her interior design business in Hackettstown, New Jersey, she'd always run to answer the business phone, even if it rang late in the evening. "I finally realized how ridiculous this was," she says. "If I had a studio outside the house, I would never have known about the call until the next morning." Now Nagorsky knows that she can't be on call twenty-four hours and keeps her machine on after she's done for the day. But her husband sometimes worries about the calls she's ignoring, she says. Nagorsky remembers one Sunday night when the phone rang at about 10:00, and she didn't answer it. "My husband went nuts, thinking that this could be the million-dollar client I've been waiting for," she explains. "I figured that it was a client calling to inform me that her wall covering came in damaged. I did not want to deal with it in any case. Whatever it was, it could wait till Monday morning."

Don't Open Business Mail on Weekends

You wouldn't see that mail if you worked nine to five in a traditional office.

Limit Answering E-Mail and Conversing Online

Lots of mompreneurs fit this in on nights and weekends, and that's okay, as long as you limit yourself to a half hour or so at a time. This keeps online costs down, too.

Close the Door on Work When the Day Is Done

Find physical and psychological ways to keep yourself from focusing on business when it's time to pay attention to your family. If your office has a door, shut it. Better yet, lock it, advises Dr. Schwartz. If it doesn't, consider screening off your work space with some sort of partition. Symbolic acts such as these help reinforce your separation from the work, she adds. When a physical barrier isn't possible, you'll have to build a mental one. Play little mind games like the one Loraine Goodenough has devised. "Sometimes I just have to throw a mental blanket across my desk, and say, 'This is not here right now. My kids need the next half hour, or they'll never leave me alone again.' "

Carve Out Couple Time

Don't let your relationship with your spouse or significant other fall to the bottom of your priority list. Together, find rituals that will help keep you connected, advises Dr. Schwartz. Talk with your partner about the physical and emotional needs you share, and be clever about setting aside time for them, she says—whether that means making dates to go out, sending each other love letters by fax or e-mail, or simply "going at it like gangbusters twice a week."

Couple time is a rare but treasured commodity in the Mumford household. Debbie Mumford spends much of her day on the road, driving to her next nature presentation, while her husband, Allan, who works nights, is home helping out with the child care and chores. The two meet for lunch regularly, even if it means brown-bagging it on the side of the highway. "If we didn't do that, we'd never see each other," Mumford says. When lunch dates aren't possible, they keep in touch by cell phone.

It's important to allow yourselves time every day (however brief) to communicate and to talk about more than just the kids and the business. It's very easy to allow conversations to become utilitarian, Dr. Schwartz says, but you have to slow down and key into each other's feelings as well. Ask caring questions like "How are you feeling?" and "What are you worrying about?" Dr. Schwartz suggests, or make plans together to take up a hobby or to go away for a few days without the kids. Little gestures like these help you focus on your life as a couple and prevent your relationship from getting lost in the chaos of the work week.

Don't Take Your Laptop or Cellular Phone to Family Events

If you're calling back clients from the sidelines of the soccer field or tabulating your expenses before the curtain goes up on the school play, you're projecting the message that your job is more important than your kids. Work-related tasks might be handy to have around during downtime—while waiting for the kids to finish after-school activities or on the train to a lunch date—but at family functions, these are downright intrusive. If you often bring your laptop into bed with you at night so you can finish up some work, get it out of there, urges Dr. Schwartz. If you live in tight quarters and absolutely must have office equipment in your bedroom, she suggests you don't allow yourself to go near it after a certain time in the evening. "The bed is a place where you go to sleep or you make love or you talk." If you're bringing a laptop or other work stuff in too, you're "confusing what's supposed to happen there," Dr. Schwartz explains.

Remember, You're the Boss

You are in charge of your time, and only you can keep your hours from spinning out of control. When they do, get quickly back on track by enforcing your work-at-home guidelines and by reminding yourself why you chose this job option in the first place—for family flexibility.

HOUSE RULES

Review these rules with your family, then post them in a prominent place so everyone learns to respect your work time.

1. Mommy can't play games or run errands during work time.

2. Everyone needs to help out with household chores.

3. No noise while Mom's on a business call. Absolutely no interruptions, unless it's an emergency. (We will discuss as a family what constitutes an emergency. Screaming that you need juice immediately or you're going to die doesn't qualify.)

4. Don't enter Mom's work space without her permission.

5. Hands off Mom's business equipment, unless she gives permission first.

6. Talk to Mom when there's anything bothering you about her work schedule, and feel free to offer your suggestions on how things could operate more smoothly. (But please bring them up during Mommy time, not business hours.)

KEEPING TRACK OF IT ALL

You've got a client meeting at 10, a pediatrician's appointment at 11:30, and a deadline to meet by the end of the day. How do you make sure none of your family or business obligations fall through the cracks? Here are our favorite organizational strategies:

Mark Family and Business Events on the Same Calendar

"Schedule children's needs like real business meetings on your calendar," advises Andrea Disario, so that you won't inadvertently set a lunch date for the same day you're going on your son's class trip. Organization expert and author Ronni Eisenberg hangs a family calendar in the kitchen and lists each child's activities in a different color. She also writes in any major work events that will impact the family, such as business trips. This system makes it easy for the whole family and the sitter to know at a glance what's going on, Eisenberg says. Loraine Goodenough works from a color-coded day planner. "Early in the month I pencil in gray all the networking events I'm supposed to go to. Then I put in red pencil somebody else's problem that I have to work around, such as no school, husband's day off, or school events I need to attend. These are in red because I need to see them more clearly, and they could affect what work I'll get done that day."

Give Yourself Reminders of Things You Must Do

"If a project is due by the twenty-fifth of the month, I make a note days or even weeks ahead of time and input it in my schedule book," says desktop publisher Cecille Hansen. "This way, there are no missed deadlines and you do feel organized." The margins of Loraine Goodenough's desk calendar are filled with phone numbers and little notes to herself. "I'll write things like, 'Does so and so need a brochure yet?' or 'Mail draft now.' " She also writes in when she completes assignments. "In case someone calls me and asks, 'Weren't you going to mail me a draft?' I can say, 'Yes, I mailed it last Tuesday. Isn't it there yet?' "

Keep Kid-Related Phone Numbers in Your Office

The numbers for your children's schools, sitters, play dates, pediatricians, after-school activities, and so forth should all be close at hand while you work. Ronni Eisenberg prefers keeping these in a separate kids' telephone book, but you could also put them on your business Rolodex or Personal Digital Assistant.

Use an Electronic Organizer

Do your scheduling on a handheld Personal Digital Assistant, such as a Palm Pilot. This way you can take it with you to review when you're sitting in the pediatrician's office or waiting for the Girl Scouts meeting to let out.

File What You Need, Toss What You Don't

Set aside a few minutes at the end of each workday to go through the papers on your desk, suggests Ronni Eisenberg. "Have a place for everything," she says, so that you can file things away promptly to avoid mountains of paper all over your office. Get rid of documents, mail, or other paper that isn't relevant to your business. "I have two garbage cans in my office," Eisenberg says. That way she can get rid of any junk the moment it comes in. This reduces the amount of clutter on your desk and helps you feel more in control.

STAYING ON THE WORK TRACK

It happens to all of us. A huge deadline is looming, and suddenly we're hit with the urge to wash the floors, raid the fridge, bake cookies, take the kids to the beach—anything but complete the job at hand. How do you stick with it when you'd really rather slack off? Try these self discipline strategies:

Get Dressed in Business Clothes

Dress as if you're working outside the home. You'll be surprised at how your pace picks up once you've got to wear panty hose and heels again. Tell yourself the faster you work, the quicker you'll get to take them off.

Hang "Not Now, I'm Working" Signs

If you often daydream about those tulip bulbs you need to plant, post a sign on the back door or tack one to your gardening gloves. Just have to take a spin in the car? Stick one on your steering wheel. Is your problem area the refrigerator, the laundry room, the exercise bike? Hang a sign there, or any-where else you might need to be nudged back to your desk.

Bring Healthy Snacks and Beverages into Your Workspace

Discourage frequent (and fattening) trips to the kitchen. Crunchy crudités, whole-grain crackers, dried fruits, and a bottle of sparkling water or thermos of coffee or hot tea will satisfy cravings when you're in the mood to munch.

Break Big Tasks into Smaller, More Manageable Pieces

Give yourself a deadline for finishing each smaller task. For example, at 9 you might pledge, "I'm going to finish typing these five pages by 11." When you reach that goal, promise yourself, "I'm going to have all ten pages done by 1," and so on.

Keep Offline

Unless you're waiting for an important e-mail message, stay out of your online mailbox or bulletin board forums. This is not the time for chatting with your friends in cyberspace. Promise yourself that you'll log on later, once the important work is done.

Give Yourself Incentives for Finishing

Offer yourself little rewards so that you have something to look forward to at the end of the project. We're thinking of inexpensive luxuries like a bubble bath, a bouquet of flowers, a new novel, or an afternoon movie, not M&Ms.

Don't Attempt Any Housework

On days when your self-discipline is shaky, even throwing a load of wash in the machine can send you spinning into the goof-off cycle.

Let Your Machine Screen Phone Calls

This gives you a quiet chunk of time to work without interruptions, yet you can still grab the important calls you're waiting for.

Calculate Your Child-Care Costs

Nothing jolts you back to reality faster than a quick reminder of how much you're paying someone to entertain your kids while you work. So hop to it. Someone's got to pay those baby-sitter bills. You would like to make more than your sitter, wouldn't you?

PRODUCTIVITY BOOSTERS

- ✓ Wake up before the kids so you get a head start on your day.
- ✓ Get a cordless phone for taking business calls from anywhere in the house.
- ✓ Keep pens and paper in every room (and in the car, too) for jotting down ideas and phone messages.
- ✓ Group similar activities, such as appointments, calls, and errands.
- ✓ Have a good office filing system to avoid paper pileup.
- ✓ Arrange for child care so you can work without interruptions.
- ✓ Carry a cellular phone or beeper so you don't miss important business calls when you're away from your desk.
- ✓ Work on a laptop computer during waiting or commuting time.

✓ Work out faithfully.
✓ List your top three business goals for the year and hang them over your desk.
✓ Save shopping time by ordering stamps, business equipment, and other office essentials online.
✓ Eat high-energy foods and don't skip meals.
✓ Ignore the doorbell, especially if pesty drop-in neighbors are a problem.
✓ Get a good night's sleep. Everyone has to work late nights from time to time, but don't make it a habit. If you do, you'll quickly burn out, and so will your business.

MOMPRENEUR® HALL OF FAME

JUDITH VIORST
Poet, Novelist, and Children's Book Author, Washington, D.C.
Mother of Three

In the 1960s and '70s, Judith Viorst was a work-at-home writer, authoring children's books, columns for *Redbook* magazine, and humorous poetry anthologies such as *It's Hard to Be Hip over Thirty and Other Tragedies of Married Life*. She was also busy raising three sons. The boys—Anthony, Nicholas, and Alexander—provided their mom with plenty of material and even became the central characters in stories such as *I'll Fix Anthony* and *Alexander, Who Used to Be Rich Last Sunday*. They also presented her with lots of work-at-home challenges. Viorst quickly discovered that mothering and meeting deadlines required more than organization and self-discipline, so she developed a few survival strategies to help her get her books and columns in on time.

First of all, "I wrote whenever I could," she says. "I required no writing atmosphere, no writing location or inspiration or mood. I wasn't able to wait for the ideal moment. I had to write whenever it was humanly possible." She worked on assignments while her boys were at nursery school, while they were napping, and while they were in the care of her housekeeper or other young moms from the neighborhood. Sometimes Viorst even managed to pen a few paragraphs while sitting in the pediatrician's waiting room.

The author was always careful to build crisis time into her writing schedule. "I gave myself very generous deadlines, well aware that there would be many trips to the emergency room and times that the boys might need my help with an essay they were stuck on. So I never had to choose between getting something in on time and doing something that my kids needed."

Shortcuts were essential, too, particularly those that helped streamline the household chores. One of Viorst's favorite tricks was something she called the "same sock solution." She bought each son ten pairs of socks in one color. "I didn't go nuts matching up socks," she says. She also simplified bed-making for the boys by eliminating the top sheets and using only a fitted sheet and a quilt that doubled as a bedspread. "Everyone could get a neat-looking bed with minimum effort," she points out. In addition, she taught her sons to make their own school lunches early on. "The learning process was torture, because I could have made lunch a million times faster," without a mess, she recalls. But it encouraged their independence and saved time in the long run.

Viorst says she was lucky to have lots of hands-on help from her husband, Milton, a home-based political writer. "I was the primary caregiver, but he was very, very important," she says. In the '60s and early '70s, when it wasn't yet fashionable to share parenting responsibilities, Milton Viorst changed diapers, made breakfast, and did middle-of-the-night feedings. "He was absolutely ahead of his time," his wife says. "Before there was even a woman's movement, he pitched in, just on the simple basis of fairness." She adds that he was a wonderful role model for the Viorst boys, who are now grown men who can cook, clean up a kitchen, and even iron. "They have a completely nonsexist attitude about pitching in."

Her sons have been out of the house for some time now, but Viorst has fond memories of her years as a work-at-home mother. "I could always go to the school plays and the field days and the Halloween parades. And I could be in the kitchen when they came home from school. You can have your best conversations when they're having a snack. You just hang out and learn a lot about them, and slip in a lot of messages to them under very casual circumstances."

That's not to say that the author of *Alexander and the Terrible, Horrible, No Good, Very Bad Day* hasn't had a few terrible, horrible, no good, very bad days as a mompreneur. She'll never forget the time when the kids were ten, eight, and five, and the family had just moved from an apartment to their very first house in Washington, D.C. "I was sitting in my office writing, thinking that the boys were quietly occupied upstairs. The phone rang and this very elegant voice said, 'Hello, Mrs. Viorst. I don't mean to be a nosy neighbor, but do you want your three sons on the roof?' " Viorst dropped the phone and raced off to

(continued)

discover that the kids had climbed out of a third-floor window and were cavorting on top of the house.

Exciting events like these no longer happen in the Viorst household, and the writer admits that it took her a while to adjust to working in a kid-free environment. She wasn't used to writing in silence, without a single trip to the emergency room. "I felt a tremendous amount of pressure," she says. "I felt I should be writing *War and Peace,* at least, because up to then my whole writing career had been a juggling act and now I had all this freedom, all this time."

7

Your Personal and Professional Image

All working mothers have trouble balancing their dual roles, but mompreneurs seem to go through more frequent identity crises. There are days when we see ourselves as productive wage earners, capable of writing astute, influential material and negotiating tough business deals. Then there are other days when that professional veneer suddenly cracks as we try to supervise an out-of-control play date for a preschooler or tell the second-grade teacher (once again) why we're not available to serve refreshments for the holiday party. Since we work primarily from home, we often go from being mothers to businesswomen to mothers and back again, all in the course of a few hours. We don't always know which hat we're wearing when, and many times the people around us don't know, either.

When Pat's son Josh was in kindergarten, he often drew pictures of his family members. One of Pat's favorites was a drawing of her sitting at her desk writing an article. It so captured the essence of mompreneurship, she hung it on her office wall for inspiration. Several months later, Josh's teacher had the class dictate stories about their families, which she compiled into a book for each student. When Josh was asked the occupations of his parents, he forgot all about his artistic impression and told the teacher his mom was a homemaker. As Josh got older, he grew to better understand the concept of working at home (with a little help from Pat). Now, both he and his younger brother Matt can be found boasting about the magazine pieces and books their mom has written.

Ellen's kids have never been the source of her identity issues. It's with other adults that she feels she could use a little image-boosting. Everyone from house painters to plumbers to PTA presidents have a tough time believing she has a real job. Ellen really can't blame them. After all, she's always home to answer the door or the phone, and when she does, she's usually wearing a sweatsuit instead of a power suit.

YOU CAN'T BE SERIOUS!

Why do work-at-home moms have such difficulty convincing relatives, friends, teachers, neighbors, contractors, repairmen, mothers who work outside the home, clients—in short, the world at large—that we have real jobs even though our offices are in our homes? Is it because we dress casually and are available to drive the car pool and go on class trips? Or is it because we don't always consider ourselves as committed or earnest about our work as those with jobs in the traditional workplace?

The answer probably encompasses a little bit of both, plus all the other factors that go into forming a working mother's self-concept. It's time we changed our image for the better. After all, there are plenty of us around now to make our message heard. We are a viable, productive part of the workforce and want to be recognized as such. To begin, we have to persuade those closest to home: our husbands, children, parents, and friends. Then it's necessary to work on ourselves, polishing up a businesslike veneer so clients, teachers, employees, and other unrelated adults see us in a professional light. The last step is to reach out and network—both formally and informally. Whether you're standing on the sidelines at your son's soccer game, attending a neighborhood block party, or eating at an industry luncheon, get the word out that you're a mompreneur. The more visible we are and the more contacts we have, the more seriously we'll be taken.

FAMILY TIES

Family flexibility is one of the prime reasons many of us have chosen to work at home, but sometimes being flexible can work against you. When you're readily available to your children, husband, or other relatives, they tend to get confused about whether you're a mother or businesswoman first. And they may take advantage of you.

Children

"My kids didn't even realize I had a job, since I only worked when they were in school or asleep," says Marilyn Vaughn, a single mom who ran a graphic design firm from a spare bedroom in her apartment before she expanded to an outside office. "It's funny," she continues, "because sometimes we were out and the kids saw a poster and said 'That's neat.' I'd say 'I made that,' and they would be shocked." Surprisingly, Vaughn is not alone. A number of mompreneurs report that their biggest image problem occurs with their own children, who are often blissfully ignorant of the fact that mom works.

How can you change this impression? Make them aware of what you do from the time they are little. Ellen certainly did, with great results. One day, five-year-old Amy was on a play date at a buddy's house. She saw a PC in the kitchen and asked her friend's mom if she was planning to work while they played. Maria Tomsic was also successful with this strategy. Every morning, this Michigan mother used to don a power suit and commute to her corporate job at United Technologies Automotive. After the birth of her second baby, she negotiated a part-time telecommuting arrangement, working from home three days a week. To get her young boys used to the idea that mom was working even though she wasn't rushing out the door to a job, Tomsic talked to them frequently about her business. "Early on, my work was part of our daily conversations," she recalls, "so they think it is all very normal."

As a work-at-home mother, it's easier and more natural to involve your children in your business. When they're young, it can be a simple explanation of what you do and the office hours you keep. The offspring of toy distributors, children's book authors, or birthday party entertainers catch on quickest; a picture is worth a thousand words. As kids reach school age, they can be given small, helpful chores to do, like licking stamps, packing boxes, even sending faxes and filing. (See chapters 4 and 6 for more ideas.) Older children are also better able to appreciate the fruits of your labor. Show them some tangible evidence of what you're actually doing behind your office door—a brochure, a published magazine piece, a dance tape, a T-shirt design, etc.—and ask for their input.

It's okay to show off a little, too. A low-key way to start is by volunteering to talk in your children's classes about being a mompreneur. Many schools hold career days or weekly lunch meetings at which different parents discuss their businesses or jobs. This is a perfect opportunity to fully explain the work-at-home option to your child and his or her classmates.

The next step is to venture forth into the business world. Susan Kippur, a management consultant who runs in-house training sessions for executives at large corporations, was booked at Prudential on Take Your Daughter to Work Day one year. After Kippur got the okay from her client (who was also a parent), her twelve-year-old daughter came along and shadowed her mom around the human resources department. Communication and hands-on interaction can work wonders for your self-esteem; your kids will soon be bragging about you.

If all else fails, bring up the bottom line. A sure way to reinforce the value of your work is to show how it's contributing to the family's lifestyle. Your income is helping to buy those Rollerblades, computer games, designer sneakers, Disney World vacations, and other goodies your kids and husbands crave.

MIRROR IMAGE

Many times in the course of writing this book, we've seen how involvement and interaction can help turn a mompreneur into a very positive role model for her kids. Virginian Cathy DeVito Fink, a home-based manager of nonprofit associations, started small. She asked her son to help stuff envelopes, paste labels on packages, and do other minor tasks connected with her business. Soon he asked to be set up with a home business, too. With a computer and a modest stockpile of supplies, he began creating his own business cards, letterhead, flyers, posters, etc. Now he loves telling his friends that he and his mom work at home. "It's such a great feeling that he's proud of being part of the business," says Fink. "Both of my adult stepsons are also inspired to be entrepreneurs and work for themselves some day. It's a nice trait to pass along."

Husbands

Spouses generally seem to come in two varieties: "very supportive" and "needs enlightenment." With a little training, the latter type eventually becomes more like the former. Usually, it's the little things that need work. "My husband and I recently had a blowup because we were out of milk," reports the owner of a thriving graphic design business. "He couldn't understand how I could let that happen when I'm home all day. I said to him, 'Do you really think I'm paying attention to how much milk is in the house when I'm trying to run a business and be available for the kids?' "

She is not alone; other mompreneurs get into domestic spats over equally petty matters. There are plenty of husbands who assume we should pick up the dry cleaning, take the dog to the vet, or deal with the roofers just because we're home and they're not. If they should happen to take a day off from work, watch out. Anne Kyle, a freelance writer in Ossining, New York, gripes that her husband uses the phone and other equipment she needs for her work when he stays home from the office. "It's taken a long time to get him to respect my need for privacy and the fact that I have first dibs on the house because it's my office," she says.

But these same husbands are often full of pride and admiration for their wives' accomplishments, even if they don't always show it. Other mates are a bit more demonstrative. Mary Beth Neblett works out of her North Carolina home as director of field operations for a consulting firm that holds focus groups and brainstorming sessions. It's an exciting job that occasionally takes her on the road for two to three days at a time—a difficult feat for a mother with two small children and limited child care. But Mr. Neblett saw it as a possibility before she did. "I couldn't have done it without the support of a husband who believes I have just as much right as he does to leave my family behind at times in order to be successful," she says. "As he told another husband one day (who couldn't believe that John would let me leave him at home with the kids for more than a few hours at a time), 'If I didn't let her do this, she would not be a whole person, and she would not be happy. And if she's not happy, she can't be a good wife and mother. And then none of us is happy.'" We could all learn a thing or two from the Nebletts.

Mothers and Others

Since they generally don't witness our home businesses on a day-to-day basis, parents, in-laws, and siblings can have an even tougher time understanding mompreneurship. It's not unusual to be asked, "Why can't you be the one who drives Grandma to her doctor's appointment at 10 A.M.?" and "Why don't you offer to take care of your nephew when the nursery school has a day off and your sister has to go to work?" In some families, it can take years of explanation before the message finally sinks in: "I work, too."

Rebecca Bostick, an architect based in Alexandria, Virginia, told us it took three years before her mother actually realized hers was a real business, not just something she was playing at. It wasn't because Bostick failed to establish a professional image right from the beginning. It just didn't always work out the way she planned. "Soon after I started my business, I decided to get my own copy machine," she remembers. "Instead of buying a copier from Staples, which I could carry home, I bought a larger one from a big company. Part of the price included two guys setting up the equipment and giving a quick training session."

Bostick's first image problem arose when she was showing the men where to put the copier—in a room that doubled as her husband's study/storage area. "As they carried it in, I was kicking his underwear and shirt into the closet and closing dresser drawers," she recalls. "I was a bit embarrassed but determined not to show it." That wasn't the worst of it. "After they had installed the copier and were explaining the special features, my mother walked in unexpectedly," says Bostick. "In the loudest, sweetest voice, she said, 'Oh, princess, I'm so proud of you—your first big machine.' When the installers looked at each other and mouthed 'princess,' I knew my professional image was shot for good." In retrospect, Bostick finds this story amusing, but at the time, she was ready to scream. The motto: You have to promote yourself and educate your extended family just as you would clients and customers—and don't give up.

INSTANT IMAGE BOOSTERS

Want to feel more like a professional while you're working from home? Try these tips:

- ✓ Don't let the kids pick up the phone unless they're extremely well trained.
- ✓ Answer the phone with your business name.
- ✓ Practice speaking with a voice that's businesslike yet friendly.
- ✓ Stand during phone conversations.
- ✓ Record an appropriate message for your answering system or voice-mail—without childish giggles in the background.
- ✓ Establish set business hours and stick to them.
- ✓ Substitute slacks or a comfy skirt for your usual jeans or sweats every now and then.
- ✓ Add a fashionable accessory to your work-at-home outfit.
- ✓ Put on makeup.
- ✓ Read an article in a professional journal or trade paper.
- ✓ Straighten up your desk.
- ✓ Call, write, or e-mail an old or new colleague.
- ✓ Make a cold call to drum up new business.
- ✓ Brag discreetly about your work.

YOUR PUBLIC PERSONA

Friends, neighbors, and teachers sometimes need a bit of enlightenment, too, judging from our own experiences and those of other mompreneurs. Knowing you're home, they often feel free to ask you to watch their kids, sub in the car pool at a moment's notice, come over for coffee, yak on the phone, or sign up for class mother. Don't get us wrong—these things are fine, in moderation. In fact, we've found that meeting a friend at the local coffee bar or going to the nature center with a group of first-graders are just two of the bonuses of working from home. But it is important to make sure everyone is clear about your work schedule and time constraints so they don't take advantage of you.

Sarah Edwards has a surefire but cordial way of accomplishing this: Tell anyone (current and potential business contacts excluded, of course) who calls or drops in, "These are my business hours; I'll catch up with you later." She also suggests clearly stating these hours on your answering machine or voicemail message so friends, mothers, telephone solicitors, etc. know exactly when you're working and won't bother you.

Friends and Neighbors

One of Pat's friends, a mother who works outside the home, had some trouble with this until Pat's son, Matt, set her straight. Matt had a half-day off from school and was playing with this friend's son at her house. After a couple of hours, she asked the boys if they wanted to switch houses and go over to Pat's. Matt immediately piped up, "But my mom's working today to meet a deadline." Everyone was very impressed, and the boys stayed where they were.

To make sure friends and neighbors don't feel resentful, it's important to reciprocate. Pat arranged to have her son's friend over for a play date on the next half-day, and she often hosts group activities for her children's pals, building them into her schedule ahead of time. Neighbors whom you might have brushed off when you're too busy to chat can be invited over for a barbecue or holiday open house at a later time.

It's also important to be supportive of each other. Work-at-home mothers often feel caught in the middle of what the media has labeled the *Mommy Wars*. It sometimes seems that neither mothers who work outside the home nor full-time, stay-at-home moms completely understand mompreneurship. At various times, both sides have experienced resentment, jealousy, superiority, inadequacy, or empathy toward us and toward each other. Meanwhile, we have feelings of competitiveness, self-doubt, and conflict, just as they probably do.

Even so, we think it's possible for all of us to come out feeling like winners. Mompreneurs can act as mediators of a sort on this battleground. To begin, it's important to validate the choices other mothers have made. Much of a mom's self-worth rests on knowing she's made the right choice for herself and her family. After all, we don't like it when they diminish our choice as something less than a real job. Next, discreetly promote mompreneurship as a workable plan of action. All kinds of mothers will appreciate knowing more about this option, and you'll feel good publicizing it. Last of all, let's ban the term *Mommy Wars* from our vocabulary. It's time to accept the idea that we're all in this together, and we're all doing the best we can.

Teachers

There's a good chance that many of your children's teachers will be working mothers, too. This can work both ways: Some may consider you a full-fledged working mother like themselves, and others may feel free to call on you to help with any number of activities, knowing that you're home. Then there's the added conflict mompreneurs may feel about volunteering in school. Carin Rubenstein, a freelance journalist from North Tarrytown, New

York, summed up these feelings well. She responded to our two questions, "What do you like best about working at home?" and "What do you like least about working at home?" with the same answer: "Can go on school trips." Being available for our kids is one of the reasons we choose to work from home, but we don't want to be too available. The smartest solution for us has been to pick and choose our school commitments to best suit our work schedules, sticking to those we enjoy most. (See "Learn to Say No" in chapter 6 on page 157). We've found most teachers, PTA committee heads, and other parent recruiters to be pretty receptive of our solution, although some may have to be reminded several times before they understand.

BUSINESS SPEAK

Sometimes the truth sounds very unprofessional. Here's how to fool phone callers into thinking everything's under control.

INSTEAD OF SAYING . . .	SAY . . .
"I have to take my son to the pediatrician."	"I can't make it, I have a meeting."
"That's my car pool day."	"Wednesday is better for me."
"I can't, I'll be in Disney World."	"I'll be out of town that week."
"Hold on, my toddler is about to give the cat a haircut."	"My other line is ringing."
"Pipe down kids, I'm on the phone."	"This is a bad connection. Let me call you back." Or quietly push the mute button and continue your conversation.
"I'm in the middle of dinner."	"I'm on a conference call right now. May I get back to you in the morning?"

Clients, Customers, and Business Associates

As home-based companies continue to flourish, clients and other business associates are acknowledging their value and professionalism. Others are finally realizing what we all know: It's foolish to overlook some of the most dedicated workers and innovative, competitive businesses just because they don't have a fancy address. Once they've experienced a job well done, their image of us often becomes even more positive. Beverley Williams, founder of the American Association of Home Based Businesses and owner of a successful desktop publishing company, still likes to feel new people out before she takes on a job. This Maryland businesswoman half-jokingly asks prospective clients two questions: "Does it really matter what I'm wearing when I'm talking to you on the phone?" and "Aren't you jealous that I'm working from home?" Their answers immediately help her gauge how professional an image she needs to maintain in this relationship and how much fun she'll have working with this person.

If you're not sure of a client's sense of humor or you're trying to negotiate an intricate financing deal for your business, it's wiser to start off by being as professional as possible. Susan Kippur, a management consultant who works with large corporations, tries to answer her business line far away from her barking dog, and she has instructed her daughters to be extra quiet during phone calls. "New clients don't always know they're calling a home business," she says, "and I sometimes camouflage the fact at first." Once a business relationship is established, however, many work-at-homers feel comfortable enough to be more up front.

Since you never know exactly how child-friendly a client or caller will be, play it safe until you can be sure. In Kippur's area of expertise, a polished, professional image is a big selling point. Generally, however, home businesses that are more consumer- or family-oriented are a little more relaxed. Ellen, who writes about toys and parenting topics, says that having kids is a professional plus. A customer calling Betsy Polivy for a baby gift basket wouldn't think twice about hearing a toddler crying in the background, nor would a teacher asking Debbie Mumford to come in with her animals for a nature lesson. Many of our mompreneurs are totally surprised how the tide seems to be turning in more conservative lines of work.

Susan Belkin, a home-based attorney in Westchester County, New York, felt that a law practice demanded a certain level of professionalism, and she worked hard to measure up. In exchange for the flexible hours she worked, Belkin allowed her clients to call at odd times, if necessary. One evening several years ago, her husband wasn't home, she was busy putting her son to sleep, and her young daughter was watching one of her favorite videos, *The Music Man*. The phone rang, and the little girl preempted the answering machine and picked it up on the first ring. "My client told my daughter that he needed to speak to her mommy, so she placed the receiver on the television and started the three-story climb upstairs to give me the message," Belkin recalls. "All the while, Robert Preston, in all his music-man glory, extolled the virtues of '76 Trombones.' This was not the image of professional competence that I was trying to convey to all my hard-won clients." Belkin raced to the telephone, picked up the receiver, and heard her client on the other end singing, "Dum de de dum dum dum dum de dum de dum!" It turned out his favorite musical in the whole world was *The Music Man,* and he loved listening to it for over five minutes. In the most businesslike tone she could muster, Belkin answered his question about an upcoming real estate closing. "He then thanked me and remarked about the convenience of my legal services, my responsiveness, my child secretary, and the glories of *The Music Man.* I don't recall ever receiving such praise when I worked for a corporation."

Sometimes the volume of business you do will gain you professional respect no matter what's going on at your house or how you're dressed. Texan Sharon Meehan had recently started her specialty food company, Ham I Am!, when she landed the Neiman Marcus catalog as an account. "Neiman's has a special packing system for the products they feature, and we had to learn it," she recalls. The merchandising giant sent a group of managers over to Meehan's house to show her the ropes. "I answered the door in my bathrobe, holding a coffee cup in one hand, my hair soaking wet from the shower," remembers Meehan. "The women who worked with me were all moms who brought their kids along so they could play with my kids. And here are the execs in nice suits and driving big Lincolns. I'm sure they drove off thinking 'what a colossal waste of time that was!' " Five years later, Ham I Am! was doing so much business with FedEx that its drivers were loading up big, empty trucks with Meehan's products three times a day! Nevertheless, there are still those who are a bit resentful and impatient when they see you dressed in a bathrobe or hear a child's voice in the background. Mompreneurs soon learn how to assess each situation individually and put their best professional foot forward.

WHEN ALL SYSTEMS FAIL, SHOULD YOU?

Occasionally, that professional image you've worked so hard to achieve can be instantly shattered by the cancellation of a baby-sitter or the illness of a child. This happened to Deborah Finch, a mompreneur who runs an administrative/paralegal support services firm from her Maryland home. She had to present an extremely important proposal to three men she had never met—with her five-year-old daughter in tow.

"I arrived at the meeting and sat Sarah down with her coloring books, crayons, and picture books on one side of an enormous conference table," Finch remembers. "I had explained to her previously how important this meeting was, and that I could not be interrupted unless it was an emergency." Finch could tell that not one of the men was impressed with the idea that she had brought Sarah or worked from home. However, Sarah remained perfectly quiet throughout the meeting, and gradually their mistrust seemed to ease. "Just as we were about to conclude," Finch continues, "Sarah said in a stage whisper, 'Mom!' 'Sarah, shush,' I whispered." This went on several times until Sarah whispered in a louder voice once again. "Sarah, please," her mom pleaded quietly. "She just looked at me. I sighed. 'Is it important?' 'Yes,' she replied. 'What is it?' I was barely able to keep the impatience out of my voice. Sarah got up from her seat, walked around to my side, and whispered, 'I love you!' I got the contract."

Ourselves

Once we've tackled relatives, friends, and business associates, many of us have to do a pretty persuasive selling job on ourselves. Mompreneurs are famous for capitulating to everyone's wishes and demands before attending to their own. Constance Hallinan Lagan learned early on as a home-based craftswoman to take her business seriously and prioritize her professional activities. Even with four daughters to distract her, she became so successful at enhancing her own self-image, she began giving workshops on the subject to professionally employed and entrepreneurial women. In the process, she built a second home business. Lagan believes "perception is everything. Your view of yourself determines how others perceive you. You must think well of yourself before anyone else will." Her Entrepreneurial Center for Small Business Development offers programs in goal-setting, stress-reduction, public speaking, networking, and marketing—all designed to increase self-esteem and personal and professional happiness.

How can the rest of us become so self-assured? The secret seems to lie in building up a strong identity as both a mother and a businesswoman. Mompreneurship is a conscious decision to do just that. Be patient—it can take some time and effort.

THE MOMPRENEUR MAKEOVER

Faster than a speeding bullet, several times a day, we're called on to make that switch from mom to professional and back again, and most of us don't even have a telephone booth to change in. Instead of Superman, we have Lynn Heritage to the rescue, armed with advice on making that psychological change easier by enhancing your physical appearance. "Women always feel better being dressed, with their hair combed and some makeup in place, even during a phone conversation," believes Heritage, a sales director for Mary Kay Cosmetics. "By taking care of yourself, you treat what you're doing with respect, and others will respect it, too."

How can a harried, bedraggled mom be quickly transformed into a businesswoman who looks like she really is the head of her own company? All it takes is Heritage's inspirational little bag of tricks:

✓ Start with a good haircut. It should be neat, fashionably shaped, easy-care, and have a price tag higher than $15. You're worth more than that.

✓ Brighten up your new do with a little color. Highlights not only add pizzazz, they can lift your spirits and make you feel more upbeat.

✓ Take good care of your skin, cleansing and moisturizing every day. If you start with good skin, you won't have to cover up as much.

✓ Use a foundation with built-in sunscreen to protect and even out your skin color. A lighter foundation helps you look younger.

✓ Choose classic, natural-looking makeup for every day. It shouldn't change the way you look, just the way people look at you.

✓ Put together a personalized makeup kit geared to your hair and skin color. Include these five basics: mascara, subtle eye color (shadow), foundation, cheek color (blusher), and lipstick.

✓ Keep a spare kit of the basics in your car, briefcase, or diaper bag so you can freshen up on the go.

✓ Use soft colors to emphasize your best features, usually your mouth and/or eyes.

✓ On a dull day, apply a brighter lipstick.

✓ Match your makeup to your wardrobe. Choose a warm color palette for warm tones (oranges, browns, etc.); a cool palette for cool tones (blues, pinks, purples). Color-coordinated compacts make it simple.

✓ Save more complicated makeup (facial highlighter, eyebrow pencil, eyeliner, and lipliner) for those occasions when you want to make a more dramatic statement.

✓ Wear earrings to draw attention to your eyes and give a lift to your face. For a professional look, choose a pair that's medium in size, not tiny studs or the large, dangling type.

✓ Pamper yourself occasionally with a salon manicure and/or pedicure.

All of these tips are easy to follow, but some may be difficult to put into practice in certain lines of work. (A personal trainer, for example, may find bold earrings a bit cumbersome.) By making an effort to pay attention to the details, you're saying a lot about yourself and your business. The more pulled-together you look, the more positive your attitude and self-image will be.

DRESSING THE PART

When asked, "What do you like best about working at home?" many of our respondents' answers had to do with the dress code—or lack thereof. "No panty hose" was a popular one, as was "a more casual wardrobe." And "spending less money on clothes" was seen as a real attraction.

Those of us who are holed up in home offices most days tend to favor sweats, jeans, shorts, and a T-shirt, or similar sloppy clothing. One work-at-home mom we know opts for just underwear during heat waves. There are also times when we want to be just a tad more professional. After all, looking good on the outside can make you feel better and more secure on the inside. And what about those days when we have to venture forth to make a presentation, meet with clients, or attend networking events? We've found that mompreneurs can dress for success without loading up on conventional business suits or spending a bundle.

Mary Lou Andre, mother of twin boys and founder of Organization by Design, a Massachusetts-based fashion consulting business, suggests starting by looking in your closet. "Chances are you already own several of the items you need," she says. "And while you're there, toss out the clothes that you're not wearing anymore. A well-organized closet goes a long way toward helping you quickly change roles from mom to businesswoman." Andre shows us how to go from a Mommy and Me class to a lunch with colleagues, a sales conference, and PTA meeting with a few wardrobe basics and a couple of current pieces.

- ✓ Start with at least one good suit in a dark neutral color, such as black, navy, brown, or gray. (These are best at hiding spit-up and grubby handprints!) Pantsuits are the most practical choice for women these days and are universally acceptable at client meetings and conferences. Opt for a classic look that won't go out of style next season and is comfortable to wear.
- ✓ Have at least one pair of black pants—they can be dressed up or down to match the occasion. Well-fitting black jeans are even a workable option. Coordinate them with a black T-shirt and pastel or bright-colored blazer, and you have a great outfit.
- ✓ Stock up on different tops to give your suits, pants, and skirts versatility. Crisp cotton shirts in white and flattering colors instantly add pizazz to dark bottoms. Cardigan twin sweater sets are a smart choice for a softer way to set a business tone.
- ✓ Treat tops like accessories! You can wear the same pair of black pants for several years, updating them with a stylish top or two in this season's hottest color and fabric.
- ✓ Search for a simple skirt (in whatever length looks best on you) or a sheath-style dress to wear with a blazer or the jacket from your pantsuit. This will give you a totally new look that can take you into an evening event with ease. For a less formal statement, choose a denim or black skirt.
- ✓ The best shoe color to incorporate into your wardrobe is black. A dress pump and loafer in this color are good starters. An ankle boot with pants and long skirts is a fun alternative. Match your panty hose or hosiery to your shoe color.

✓ Jewelry, scarves, and other accessories add a personal touch and can give one outfit many different looks. Less is often more in terms of accessorizing in a professional setting. Simple gold or silver jewelry—costume or the real thing—and pearls are always good bets.

✓ Donate—don't discard—the clothing you no longer want. Women's shelters, charities, and consignment shops are always on the lookout for recycled items.

Andre leaves us with these words of advice: "Don't confuse casual dress with sloppy dress. If you want others to view you as a genuine working mother—even though you work from home—you can't look like you just rolled out of bed." Occasionally, when you're sitting at your desk and no one but your two-year-old can see what you look like, you may want to put on nicely tailored, clean clothes instead of your smelly sweats . . . just to give yourself the right mind-set.

WHEN ONLY A POWER SUIT WILL DO

Every mompreneur should have at least one classic, tailored suit or outfit in her closet for those occasions that demand a more conservative, high-powered look. Buy a suit or dress-and-jacket combo that makes you feel like a million dollars when you wear it—even if your income is in the low five figures! It should be well-made, comfortable, versatile, and stylish but not too trendy—and it should be flattering. It's not a bad idea to have a personal shopper help you choose and accessorize your power suit, adding the right shoes, panty hose, costume jewelry, and a couple of blouses to change the overall look. Since this is a wardrobe item you will wear again and again, it's okay to splurge a little.

MANAGING THE STRESS IN YOUR LIFE

If you had the choice, would you want to be totally free of stress? Probably not. As mompreneur and psychotherapist Fredda Clemens Kwitman points out, "Stress can motivate and mobilize us to accomplish things we might never have thought possible." Although a little stress is good, too much can make us cranky, ill-tempered, and unproductive. Haven't we all had those overloaded days when we've screamed at our kids, argued with our husbands, and blown a short fuse with a client? Kwitman adds, "When stress is not handled and experienced positively, it leaves us anxious and depleted—emotionally and physically."

Nancy Coleman found that out the hard way. She was working from home as a personal trainer after the birth of her son, Davis, managing to maintain just the right motherhood/business balance. Then she invented Cool Drool,™ a bandanna-type bib, and found herself suddenly spinning out of control. Her invention took off, and this California mompreneur was overwhelmed with having so many new things happening at once. "I had so much expected of me, and I thought I should be able to do it all," says Coleman. "A few months later, the stress got so bad that my jaw locked up with temporomandibular joint syndrome. I decided that I had to relax, take it slow, and enjoy my baby and family." She started going on long walks, watching her diet, and doing body work.

Although we can't completely eliminate stress from our hectic lives, we can learn how to resist and reduce it. Kwitman, who has taught several workshops on the subject, begins by showing participants how to make their bodies less prone to stress:

Get adequate sleep and rest. You'll be more in control and productive in the long run if you take time to recharge your body.

Slow down. Take the time to deliberately slow down when you notice yourself continuously rushing and tensing up.

Utilize deep breathing. Sit or lie down, close your eyes, and breathe deeply and quietly for a few minutes. Five minutes is actually a long time for this exercise.

Relax. Moms know this is easier said than done, but downtime can be squeezed in if it's a priority. Even fifteen minutes a day helps. Some techniques to try include creative visualization, yoga, tai chi, meditation, and progressive muscle relaxation. See more suggestions in "Stress Busters" below.

Don't neglect nutrition and exercise. A well-balanced diet and regular physical activity work hand-in-hand to build up resistance and energize and refresh your body.

STRESS BUSTERS

Taking a few moments to unwind can help you control everyday pressures and present a more pleasant, polished image to the world. Here are some simple ways to reduce stress:

- ✓ Go for a walk.
- ✓ Hug and kiss your kids.
- ✓ Stroke your dog or cat.
- ✓ Take a bubble bath.
- ✓ Do neck rolls and shoulder squeezes.
- ✓ Turn on relaxation music and listen quietly.
- ✓ Work out as regularly as you can.

✓ Take a long look at your kids' artwork hanging on your office walls.

✓ Plan a lunch break, even it's only for fifteen minutes. Don't eat at your desk—at least not too often.

✓ Keep herbal tea, a mug, and a carafe of hot water at your desk for soothing, caffeine-free sips.

✓ Treat yourself to a relaxing facial or massage.

✓ Put your feet up and read a book or magazine—nonbusiness publications only, please.

✓ Take your cordless phone and laptop out on the deck or into the garden and work there. The change of pace can be liberating.

✓ See a movie with a girlfriend.

✓ Vent your work-at-home frustrations in online chat rooms for quick, cheap therapy. (See "Networking Online, page 195.)

✓ Learn to laugh when crises strike. At the very least, be able to laugh when they're over.

✓ Write yourself inspirational messages such as "Don't Give Up" and "You're Doing a Great Job," and tack them to your bulletin board.

✓ Play hookey. If you can't spare a whole day off, how about quitting early and taking the kids to the park or planning another impromptu escape?

✓ Think of all you've accomplished, not of what's gone wrong. When you feel overwhelmed or your schedule's fallen apart, it helps to take a few deep breaths and think about your successes. After all, running a business while tending sick kids, tracking down replacement baby-sitters, or standing knee-deep in flood water is quite a feat.

MAKING CONNECTIONS

Can you guess the number-one answer to our question, "What do you like least about working from home?" If you chose loneliness or isolation, you have lots of companions. The majority of our respondents felt the same way. "I miss the idle chatter and free flow of ideas over the coffee station," writer Donna Haupt noted on the questionnaire we sent out. Many of us feel this is the biggest drawback of working from home. What can we do to rekindle that sense of camaraderie we felt in the workplace? How can we network to generate new leads and referrals?

Ellen and Pat actually met Haupt through a writers' group in their area. A few moms who were members of the Westchester/Fairfield chapter of The National Writer's Union felt the need for an offshoot, a smaller group targeted more precisely to our needs. We rounded up about eight people, arranged to meet for lunch, and discussed everything from toilet training to baby-sitters to agents to magazine editors we've known and loved. That first meeting was such a hit, we all decided to give our group a name—Westchester Mothers Who Write (WMWW)—and get together on a regular basis. We've been exchanging information, tips, and yes, gossip, monthly for many years now. When we eat out, our only criteria for choosing a restaurant is that it doesn't serve chicken nuggets and fries.

Although WMWW began as an informal support group, it's grown larger and more focused through the years. We now hold evening meetings as well, themed to different topics of interest—complete with handouts prepared by the host. Occasionally, we invite magazine editors, agents, and other professionals to share their expertise. Valuable contacts have been made and freelance pieces assigned as a result of our networking efforts.

Networking in the twenty-first century doesn't have to mean power lunches or racing to hand out business cards faster than the next guy at a big corporate function, conference, or trade show. Sure, this can be a good way to make prestigious contacts and land more clients and customers, but it's not the only way, especially for mompreneurs who have limited time and child care.

MOMPRENEUR STATISTIC

What Have You Found Are the Best Ways to Network?

Memberships/workshops/professional organizations	84%
Just talking	20%
Referrals/references	16%
Online	15%
Fliers/advertising	3%
Volunteering in community	3%

Informal Networking

Mompreneurs sometimes make their best connections where they least expect to: in the playground, on a school or church committee, or at a social gathering. Kids and work are often the main topics of conversation during these casual encounters, offering plenty of openings for you to subtly plug your business. One home-based publicist we know got her first client by patronizing a local children's bookstore, browsing the shelves with her son in tow. She mentioned to the owners that she had a background in public relations, and they asked her to handle their promotions. She did, and they turned into one of her biggest clients.

Daria Price Bowman, a marketing communications consultant, talks to everyone she meets—at airports, children's sporting events, school commit-tees, and parties. Then she tries to follow up whenever someone gives her a tip, and she is generous about sharing leads, too. "I like to get others together even when there's no direct benefit to me," she says. "It's good karma." It's also good business; the more people you tell, the more prospects you'll have, even if they don't pan out right away.

Pat found this out when she and a graphic artist friend were asked to put together a PTA brochure. Both mompreneurs had served as volunteers on var-ious PTA committees and chatted about their work-at-home lives. When the brochure project came up, the president immediately tapped them to do it. Ellen discovered a great support system at her gym that may eventually lead to a job or two. She joined during the writing of our first book to keep her stress level (and weight) down. In the process, she met some wonderful workout friends and found the camaraderie energizing. Her fellow exercisers were always there when she needed a boost of confidence or words of encouragement. Not only that, their excitement in her book kept Ellen moti-vated to stay on deadline. A couple of them even turned out to be sources for some of our work-at-home stories.

Formal Networking

Word of mouth seems to be the way mompreneurs get a good chunk of their business, but according to our survey, that word is more often spread through a professional network than a personal one. We join all kinds of organizations—some geared especially to business owners (Chambers of Commerce, women business owners associations), some to our particular specialty (fashion, law, advertising, food, graphic arts, public speaking), and some unrelated to work (alumni groups, philanthropic organizations). There's a professional affiliation, industry group, or trade association for almost every interest.

Time and child-care limits make it necessary for mompreneurs to pick and choose their formal face-to-face networking commitments carefully. Money is a limitation, too; dues and meeting costs can add up to hundreds of dollars a year. Kellee K. Harris, owner of MarketSpark, has learned how to draw the line when it comes to joining groups. She used to belong to five or six orga-nizations but has whittled it down to two or three of the most helpful and interesting ones. She also tries to avoid evening and weekend meetings. Becoming an active participant is also key. "Most of the networking takes place on the committee level," says Harris, "not at the big luncheons or din-ners." The conferences, conventions, and large meal functions are better for gathering information, exchanging ideas, and socializing rather than gaining new clients.

HOW WE MAKE FRIENDS AND INFLUENCE PEOPLE

Most mompreneurs use a combination plan of personal (free) and professional (dues paying) contacts to get business. Some of us have even found ways to include our children in our networking arrangements.

Paula Mielke Public Relations Consultant St. Paul, Minnesota	Served on the board of Women in Communications; sets goal of one networking lunch per week; does pro bono work for children's literature group
Michelle Murphy Freelance Writer/Editor Madison, Connecticut	Started Connecticut chapter of American Association of Home Based Businesses; belongs to grad school alumni group and writers' group
Gail Klotz Tape Transcription and Word Processing Rockville, Maryland	Chamber of Commerce and women's business group; all her family and friends send referrals
Linda Karesh Sales Consultant for The Worth Collection Scarsdale, New York	Westchester Association of Women Business Owners; Women in Sales; board of directors of YWCA; Junior League; friends who are working women
Judy Fisher Screen Printer Weleetka, Oklahoma	Craft shows; prints business phone number on all her T-shirts
Marsha Swainston Sales Consultant for Discovery Toys Lenexa, Kansas	Everywhere she goes as a mom, she networks as the toy lady; the more time she spends with her kids, the bigger the business grows
Dolores Maes Uniform Business Peralta, New Mexico	Trade shows, women's organizations, Chamber of Commerce events; wears her work

Joanne Walthall
   Gift Importer
   New York, New York
	Trade shows (i.e., gift show in Atlanta, stationery show in New York); develops close ties with other vendors; Women's Commission on Refugee Children

Mindy Hermann
   Food and Nutrition
   Writer/Agent
   Mt. Kisco, New York
	New York Women's Culinary Alliance, American Dietetic Association; press events

Katherine Holstrom
   Event Planner/
   Newspaper Publisher
   Merrifield, Virginia
	MATCH (a networking organization in metro D.C. for work-at-home moms); children's schools and activities

Gwen Nagorsky
   Interior Designer
   Hackettstown, New Jersey
	Volunteer work in fundraising for local hospital, town, and school; entertaining attorney husband's clients

Joanna K. Hayes
   Accountant
   Tustin, California
	Online discussion groups, stays in touch with CPAs she met while employed at her former firm; co-op preschool

Home-Based Groups

In 1991, there were plenty of professional organizations Beverley Williams could join, but no one was addressing her needs as a home-based business-woman. As the owner of a desktop publishing company, she had lots of questions about running a business from home but no good source of answers. So this Maryland grandmompreneur founded the American Association of Home Based Businesses (AAHBB) and immediately drew a following of independent business owners and telecommuters. There are now numerous chapters around the country to offer support, information, and job referrals to members. The organization also raises public awareness about the viability of home businesses through media interviews, government lobbying efforts, workshops, and its website, www.aahbb.org.

As Williams was igniting interest on the national level, other homebound moms were starting local support groups of their own. One of the most successful is a metro D.C.–based association called MATCH, an acronym for Mothers' Access to Careers at Home. According to the brochure (designed and written by two members), MATCH is made up of moms who have chosen to balance their families and careers by working from home. The organization not only offers peer support, image-building, and great networking opportunities, it promotes the work-at-home alternative to the business community and corporate world. We can attest to MATCH's networking skills; many members from northern Virginia and Maryland heard about our book at their meetings and participated in our survey.

While MATCH has a clearly professional bent, other groups were founded by mothers looking for another kind of support. Mothers and More is a national, nonprofit group for women who have put their careers on hold to raise their children. American Mothers at Home is a similar group for stay-at-home mothers who want to feel better about their choice. Most of the moms who join are looking for ways to forge strong new identities, combat loneliness, and meet other women in the same boat. Both organizations also work to bring work/family issues to the forefront and encourage respect and recognition for at-home mothering.

There are a number of other associations catering to the special needs of mothers, parents, the self-employed, home-based executives and lawyers, entrepreneurs, small business owners, and others who spend much of their lives at home. All provide various benefits with membership. These may include newsletters or publications, insurance packages, discounts on products and services, home office equipment deals, databases, mailing lists, etc. For a complete guide to these organizations and what they offer, see the networking resources, pages 294 and 295 in chapter 11.

NETWORKING ONLINE

We believe that face-to-face contact is a very valuable way to beat the isolation of working from home and boost your business. But we've also come to embrace the Internet for its amazing networking powers. The solid friendships and business connections you forge in the virtual world can be just as strong or stronger than the ones you form in the real world. Without leaving the comfort of your home, you can communicate with other work-from-home moms in countless chat rooms and message boards; exchange leads and referrals through discussion groups, e-mail lists, and online communities; "test" out a business idea in a nonthreatening, supportive group of like-minded people; and discover new markets for your product or service.

As the work-from-home experts on iVillage.com's Work Channel, we know firsthand how beneficial online networking can be. Our chats and boards are energized by inspirational mompreneurs sharing strategies and building relationships with other mompreneurs. Sometimes it's enough to just have a "virtual shoulder" to cry on; other times, we help each other get a home business off the ground, juggle the demands of work and family, recruit other moms, share resources, or land a big client or customer. In cyberspace, anything is possible!

CREATIVE BONDING

When Cabot, Pennsylvania, artist Lynn Korff first took her Korff Ceramic Originals business on the web in 1999, she was clueless. "I was lucky to find several online women's communities where I could go for the support and information I needed to create Korfforiginals.com," she remembers. "Once I realized my business was going to succeed, I wanted to pay back all the moms who took the time to help me get started." So this enterprising mompreneur decided to include an information packet about other mom-owned businesses every time she sent out an order of her hand-crafted, hand-painted ceramic giftware. She named the packet "The Mom Pack," and by fall 2000, was distributing business cards, brochures, and other materials from over 125 participants.

The moms involved in The Mom Pack found the cross-promotion so professionally and personally rewarding, they began exchanging website links as well. And soon they started an e-mail exchange through www.eGroups.com, where they share tips about building online businesses. In just a short time, www.mompack.com has grown into a large network of moms helping moms, nurtured by virtual camaraderie and common business goals.

THE MOM-TO-MOM NETWORK

iVillage and The Mom Pack are just two of many support sites for work-at-home moms. Many other active communities thrive on the web, a number of which were started by mothers for mothers. Here's where to go to nurture your personal and professional growth—and connect with other mompreneurs.

- ✓ Bizy Moms; www.bizymoms.com
- ✓ Club Mom; www.clubmom.com
- ✓ Entrepreneurial Parent; www.en-parent.com
- ✓ Home Based Working Moms; www.hbwm.com
- ✓ Main Street Mom; www.mainstreetmom.com
- ✓ Mompreneurs Online; www.mompreneursonline.com

✓ Moms Help Moms; www.momshelpmoms.com
✓ Moms Network Exchange; www.momsnetwork.com
✓ Mother's Home Business Network; www.homeworkingmom.com
✓ Mothers & More, www.mothersandmore.org
✓ National Association of At-Home Mothers;
www.athomemothers.com
✓ ParentPreneur Club; www.parentpreneurclub.com
✓ WAHM; www.wahm.com

The connections you make online can sometimes lead to "real" networking groups offline. We know moms who have initiated these groups themselves after meeting in chat rooms or through message boards. In other cases, virtual community leaders direct interested work-at-homers to a group that has formed in their locale. Susan Scheid, a Columbus, Ohio, web designer, had been an enthusiastic participant in online communities for several years but desperately wanted to do some in-person networking. After much searching, she couldn't find an organization for home business owners in her area, so with encouragement from her online pals, she decided to start one herself. The result is MommyCo (www.mommyco.com), a website that helps work-at-home moms who live near each other form real-time networking groups.

The response was immediate and overwhelming. "I hadn't even set a date for my own local meeting when I began training leaders and organizing meeting schedules for other moms," reports Scheid. "In just a few days, fifteen different groups formed in thirteen states!" The concept behind all the MommyCo groups is to get home business owners together about once a month to share tips and resources and offer support. "It's meant to be very laid-back and relaxed, much like gathering with your co-workers around the water cooler in a traditional office," Scheid says. She offers group leaders business cards, letterhead, press releases, marketing ideas, and meeting suggestions to get the ball rolling. But there are no membership dues or rule books.

Network Like a Pro

"The main aim of networking is to give and to get information and to establish relationships with a variety of people," stresses Donna Fisher, a professional who conducts seminars on the subject. These ten tips will get you going:

1. Tell all friends, family members, and neighbors about your business. They're often the best source of referrals.
2. Send out short notes describing your business to everyone you know or knew in the outside work world.

3. Fill up your Rolodex and e-mail address book. Collect names and business cards wherever you go for future contact.
4. Maximize business card exchanges by noting something memorable about the person or their business on the card.
5. Follow up on leads. After a trade show or networking event, call or drop a note or e-mail to the best prospects.
6. Return calls promptly. When people make the effort to call you, get back to them as soon as possible.
7. Make cold calls to businesses or other professionals you would like to work for or with. Find names in association or Internet directories or your local Yellow Pages.
8. Thank people for their help or business. Send out thank-you notes for leads and referrals; show gratitude to new or steady clients with small tokens of appreciation.
9. Ask for advice from experts in your information network. Don't be shy; most people are very receptive. Offer your expertise in return.
10. Enjoy a friendly relationship with other mompreneurs in your line of work. When they have a job offer they can't accept, they may pass it along to you.

Reaching Out to the Community

One of the best ways to network is through community involvement. Not only does it increase your visibility and contacts, you'll be providing valuable expertise where it may be needed most. The positive feedback you receive can only bolster your self-esteem. It all adds up to a more serious image for your business and a more favorable impression of you.

Mompreneurs can reach out to their communities in a number of ways:

✓ Offer to speak to members of the Junior League, PTA, a church or synagogue group, a civic club, or other organization of women. The topic of mompreneurship is sure to spark interest among these audiences.
✓ Band together with other work-at-home moms and hold job option workshops, explaining the many paths mompreneurs can take.
✓ Hire helpers from local shelters, retirement homes, or community houses when you need some extra pairs of hands.
✓ Use high school and college interns to help out in your home office and learn the ropes of a home-based business.
✓ Submit your name to a community or district career database to network and be called on for your expertise.
✓ Offer to do pro bono work for a nonprofit agency, local hospital, or other needy institution. Designing a brochure, balancing the books,

tutoring disadvantaged children, or writing a press release for free now may lead to monetary rewards later on.

MARKETING YOURSELF AND YOUR BUSINESS

Establishing a positive image and networking effectively are just two of the parts to a much larger whole: marketing. In simplest terms, marketing means selling your business to the public. For mompreneurs, whose business and personal lives are so closely entwined, it also means selling yourself.

Kellee K. Harris, founder and owner of MarketSpark, a home-based company specializing in sports and fitness marketing, uses her well-honed business skills to promote her clients, company, and mompreneurship. Case in point: Soon after the birth of her third daughter, she sent out a clever four-color brochure announcing the event to clients and the media. Pictured on the front was Harris's "Management Advisory Board": her two older daughters and the family dog. Daughter Kira was captioned "Creative Advisor," sister Kelsey was "Conflict Resolution Advisor," and Sherman Tank, the St. Bernard, was "Collections Advisor." Inside the brochure was a photo of a crying baby Kareena, listed as "Scheduling Advisor." "I got more positive response from this announcement than any other marketing piece I ever sent out," says Harris. "People really remember it."

Instead of hiding the fact that she's a mother, Harris capitalizes on her human side, an approach that endears her to clients, especially those who are working parents themselves. At the same time, she's projecting a totally professional image and attracting more and more business. How does this Portland, Oregon, mompreneur do it? She starts by putting her basic marketing philosophy to work each day: "You can't promote your business by sitting in your office." Then she explores every avenue she can to get out into the public eye. These are just some of her cost-effective, winning strategies:

- ✓ Put a lot of thought into your company name. Harris chose MarketSpark because it's an energetic word that immediately tells the world what she's about. It's also more creative and catchy than using your own name, a practice Harris discourages unless you're well-known in your field.
- ✓ *Spark* is the hook that draws people in and unifies the company's image. Harris uses a sparkler graphic on her business cards, letterhead, and all the materials that come out of her office. She has also given the name *Sparkler* to her newsletter, audiotape series, and her website.
- ✓ Business cards are a very important marketing tool. If possible, spend a little more for a sturdy card that will get noticed and won't fall apart in a prospect's pocket. Harris's own card is hot pink and black with— you guessed it!—a sparkler printed on it.

✓ Don't market yourself like a product. Since her job experience was in product management, Harris made this mistake at first, sending out brochures, direct mail pieces, and similar promotional materials about her company. But she didn't get much response. "I finally realized that in a service business, people are buying *you*. Clients have to be convinced that you're knowledgeable about your business."

✓ Educate the public about your expertise. For Harris, public speaking has been a powerful way to prove herself, push her company to the forefront, and get business. She holds seminars and gives speeches at conferences, Chamber of Commerce meetings, and other public forums. For a service-type business, public speaking can be more effective and much less expensive than advertising.

✓ Position yourself as an expert in the media. Offer to write a newspaper column or publish a newsletter that will reach potential clients and others in your network. Harris does a marketing column for *Home-Based Business News,* a newspaper for the work-from-home community in the Northwestern states. E-zines and websites are also good outlets for columns, articles, and related content.

✓ Exhibit at trade shows. Although this may seem like a major expense, you can reach lots of people in a short amount of time if you target your niche and choose the shows geared toward your industry or service. Harris attends the major show in her specialty—sports marketing—as well as those organized for the growing small- and home-business audience.

✓ Become actively involved in a professional or business association. *Active* is the operative word for seeking out clients in your business. And getting involved is very important. Harris became an officer of one organization and a committee member of another to maximize her networking potential.

✓ Publicly express your thanks to clients. Every year, Harris buys a table at the Chamber of Commerce Thanksgiving Breakfast and invites her top clients. Set at each place is a beautiful gift basket (made by another home-based businesswoman) for everyone at the breakfast to see. This gesture gets a lot of attention from the hundreds of attendees, and it's a gracious way for Harris to tell her clients, "Thank you for a great year."

MAKING THE MOST OF A TRADE SHOW

In Kellee K. Harris's words, "Trade shows offer home-based businesses one of the most cost-effective, immediate-response methods today for marketing and sales." In fact, this marketing expert grew so fond of trade shows as a way of selling her services, she decided to go into the business herself. To give cost-conscious mompreneurs and other small business owners a chance to look bigger and better, she now rents out portable trade booths—which normally sell for $4,000 to $5,000 each—for $150 a day or $350 a week. Sometimes, moms with compatible businesses team up to share a booth, slashing the cost further. Once you have your booth in place, here are five winning trade show tactics to try:

✓ Give a seminar. Most shows offer programs with featured speakers; volunteer to participate as a leader or panelist.
✓ Be available to dispense information and advice to potential clients and customers. If you're out giving your seminar or grabbing a bite, have someone cover for you.
✓ Stock up on business cards, brochures, and other handouts. The last thing you want to do is run short.
✓ Network. This is a good opportunity to meet new information sources and discover hot leads.
✓ Sell yourself. The vast amount of traffic that flows through a typical trade show provides the chance to reach many key buyers. Don't forget to market your product or services to other exhibitors, too.

THE FRUGAL ENTREPRENEUR

Shiela Zia founded Transition Resources for Women, a home-based Oregon company specializing in career counseling and work/family options. She developed these low- and no-cost ideas for promoting your business, even if you're short on funds:

✓ Sponsor a local sports team (baseball, bowling, etc.). Provide them with T-shirts printed with both the team name and your business name.
✓ Donate your services or products to a local fund-raising drive as an auction or raffle item.
✓ Contact a nearby radio or cable station and offer to do a free program on your area of expertise.
✓ Create a recognition award for community members (who may also be current or potential customers or clients). When your company presents the award, alert the local media.
✓ Get involved with your town or county Chamber of Commerce by chairing a committee.
✓ If your Yellow Pages or newspaper ad is several sizes larger than the competition, consider reducing its size. Discontinue other ads that aren't generating clients.

✓ Imprint fancy foil labels with your company name. Affix them to the front of inexpensive folders to deliver work to clients.

✓ Hand out your business card freely, but distribute more costly brochures only as needed.

✓ Use the web to exchange links, join discussion lists, contribute content, and send out e-mail newsletters—all for free.

✓ In your eagerness to save money, don't forget that the more successful and busy you become, the more your time is worth.

MOMPRENEUR® HALL OF FAME

KATHY SMITH

President, Kathy Smith Lifestyles, a Fitness and Lifestyle Company, Los Angeles, California
Mother of Two

For over twenty years, Kathy Smith has not only helped tone American bodies but has shaped our attitudes toward health, fitness, and nutrition. Fans across the country have worked out with Smith through her numerous best-selling exercise videos, which cover everything from step aerobics to body sculpting to aeroboxing to yoga. Others have benefited from her Walkfit Weight Loss System and her fitness equipment, audiotapes, books, TV broadcasts, interactive CD-ROM programs, and line of vitamins. In her rise from fitness instructor to head of a hugely successful company, selling over $250 million into the consumer marketplace, Smith has always believed in an integrated approach to exercise and business. She advocates a combination of exercise with stress reduction, weight maintenance, and emotional well-being to obtain a totally healthy lifestyle. When she became a work-from-home mom, she found this mind-body approach more important than ever.

Having children in the middle of her ascent to fame and fortune didn't throw Smith off track. In fact, motherhood helped her achieve more focus and balance in her life. Soon after daughter Katie was born, Smith brought the infant to company headquarters every day. She'd work while Katie hung out in a bassinet or playpen. By the time the baby was four months old, Smith decided it would be more productive to work out of her house. She set up a full office in an extra room, hired a nanny, and "became very comfortable with it, enjoying it immensely." When daughter Perrie came along two and a half years later, Smith continued the arrangement, always being very involved in her children's lives.

Since she is totally hooked up to the main office via computer, fax, and a phone system, Smith works from home most of the time and has

a flexible routine. When she does go out, it's to visit the recording studio, meet with a distributor, or consult on packaging or copy. Her workspace is right in the center of the house, so the girls have easy access to
Mom. They've always been included in the business, too, appearing in
some of the videos and on the pages of several magazines. With the
help of a housekeeper and a very involved husband, 90 percent of the
time it all works out, even through conference calls and staff meetings.
"As soon as they were old enough, I sat down with my daughters to
explain my work-at-home situation and why working is important to
me," recalls Smith. "Occasionally I've had to use the high sign to tell
them to lower their voices while I'm on the phone, but they've learned
well."

This mompreneur has learned from her children, too. The patience
she has developed as a mother makes her less judgmental and critical of
employees. This, in turn, has resulted in more positive relationships and
an increase in productivity. Smith also finds she's making decisions with
a gentler approach and bringing a more compassionate side to her business. "These changes have made my company grow as my children
grow," says Smith. Her strong emphasis on marketing and public relations has helped a lot as well. "I'm very proud of my products and what
I'm handing down to my daughters," she adds.

With all this going for her, Smith still has a bit of an image problem. "I
don't like to come across like I'm bragging, so I try not to talk about my
work much. But one of my biggest frustrations is other women not
understanding what I do." This became apparent when Smith and her
husband co-chaired an auction at Katie's school, an activity she volunteered for because she wanted to be more involved in her kids' school.
One of the other mothers on the committee asked her if she was retired
now. "I had to laugh. 'No, not retired, just adding this to everything else
on my plate.' Plus, I had to explain that I don't just do one exercise
video a year and that's it," Smith remembers. "Just for a video, I have to
research it, choreograph, shoot, market it, etc., not to mention all the
other things we do, and I do, to run my company."

On the other hand, she's been an inspirational role model to many
women with her balanced, sensible approach to exercise. Once Smith
became a work-at-home mom, her priorities shifted and her attitude
toward fitness became a bit more relaxed, a change that many mompreneurs will welcome. "Why should you have to make the choice between
snuggling with your one-year-old or clocking minutes in the gym on the
StairMaster?" she says. "It's important to find physical activities you enjoy

(continued)

doing that fit into your lifestyle." To meet this goal, we first have to look at fitness differently, thinking in terms of movement rather than exercise. Thirty minutes a day of walking, swimming, playing freeze tag with the kids, working out to a tape, or biking can help you attain a good fitness level. "There's no need to have the perfect body; what you need to be healthy requires less time and energy than you think," Smith says. Besides, being fit can do wonders for any mom's self-esteem and confidence.

8

Protecting Yourself and Your Business

We'll be the first to admit that when it comes to the legal aspects of running a home business, we were a little behind the times. As freelance writers, we never thought it necessary to incorporate, purchase additional liability insurance, investigate zoning laws, or look into guarding against computer theft. After all, we work in almost complete obscurity, our most frequent visits are from UPS or FedEx, we very rarely have clients coming to our home offices, and our businesses don't require any large or specialized equipment.

Eventually, however, we realized the wisdom of learning more about the legalities of working from home. The phenomenal growth and increased status and visibility of home-based businesses means we can no longer ignore these details. Today, there is more to consider in starting a business and setting up a home office. With new laws, regulations, and options constantly developing, we can't promise it will get any easier in the near future, either. What we can promise is this: a clear and detailed picture of what you need to know now to protect yourself and your home business so both will thrive and prosper. Our information is based on 2001 rules, regulations, and choices. We recommend that you read up on current zoning laws in your community, IRS deductions, insurance plans, local, state, and national licensing agreements, etc., and stay alert to changes in these areas and all other matters that can affect home workers, especially mothers. Chapter 11 offers a comprehensive listing of helpful resources.

TAKING CARE OF BUSINESS

These are the legal points to consider before you open up shop:

1. Structure

Are you going to operate your business as a sole proprietorship, a partnership, or a corporation? Most mompreneurs start out as sole proprietors; it's the least complicated way to go. If you decide on a partnership or corporation, you will probably need an attorney to draw up papers.

2. Name

What is your business going to be called? If you're a sole proprietor who plans on using a name for your business other than your own name, you must register a *fictitious name statement* with the county clerk or state tax office. This statement is also known as a *d/b/a* or *doing business as,* and forms are available from the above offices. Filing fees range from $10 to $100, depending on locale. If you decide to incorporate under a particular corporate or trade name, filing with the state is a bit more complicated and may require the services of an attorney. Keep in mind that if you use a name other than your own, you should purchase a business owner's policy for liability coverage (see pages 227–228).

3. Trademark

Do you wish to protect your business name from use by others? Two sole proprietors operating in the same geographic area cannot legally use the same name. Filing your fictitious name statement will therefore protect your name to a certain extent, but some home businesses wish to safeguard their rights on the national level. This can be done by obtaining a *federal service mark registration* or *trademark* through the Patent and Trademark Office in Washington, D.C. (see chapter 11). Be forewarned: The registration process can be time-consuming and fairly expensive.

4. Domain Name

Do you want to use your business name as your domain name on the web? Don't assume that just because you established a d/b/a or even trademarked your name, you will automatically be able to use it as a domain name. In the frenzied dot-com rush of the past few years, huge quantities of names were snapped up—some by unscrupulous cybersquatters who never intend to use them. Go on the web immediately—to any of the domain registration sites—and see if your name is available. If it is, reserve it now; it costs about $35 per year through NetworkSolutions.com and other sites. If it's not available, come up with a domain name as close to your business name as possible and reserve that. Even if you're not planning to build a site right away, almost every home business should eventually have a web presence, and you must register your name before someone else does!

5. Licensing

Does your home business require a license, permit, or certificate to operate? We recommend that all home businesses file a business certificate with their town to play it safe, but going beyond that depends on what state, county, or municipality you live in and what type of work you're doing. Businesses such as day care and catering have more stringent health and safety regulations than architecture or public relations. Some professions are regulated by the state and require an occupational license to operate. Since permits and licenses vary by location, the best approach is to check with other mompreneurs working in your field as well as municipal, county, and state government offices. Or visit www.sba.gov, to find links to the business licensing departments in each state. The cost of a business license will either be based on your annual gross income or be a flat fee, depending on where you are doing business.

6. Employee ID Number

Do you intend to hire employees or use independent contractors? If so, you'll need to obtain a *federal employee identification number (EIN)* from your local IRS office. If you plan to operate solo, you can use your Social Security number as your EIN on tax documents and similar forms. Even so, some sole proprietors find it useful to have a bona fide EIN (along with their d/b/a) to open a business bank account, apply for resale certificates, and get trade discounts.

7. Zoning

What are the zoning ordinances for home-based businesses in your neighborhood? These laws are written and enforced by local boards, not the state or federal government. To get the scoop on restrictions, look up city or town ordinances, call your municipal zoning department or city planning commission (anonymously if necessary), or speak to other home workers. Check out homeowner associations, co-op boards, and condominium complexes, too; they may have their own work-at-home restrictions, particularly for nuisance businesses that can annoy neighbors. Generally, rural areas have fewer limitations than more populated suburbs and cities. Keep in mind that most zoning laws are pretty antiquated (some date back to the sweatshop era or the early days of suburbia) and are currently being revised to keep pace with the boom in home-based businesses.

8. Insurance

Will operating your home business increase your insurance needs? Most likely it will, but this also varies according to your type of business. Since most standard homeowner's or renter's policies usually don't cover the cost of all your business-related equipment, you should probably get a rider to protect your expensive investment from fire, theft, lightning, and other damage. Liability for injuries is another area to look into. Anyone coming into your home office or onto your property in a business-related visit (even the UPS delivery person) can file suit if hurt. Other types of insurance purchased by home workers include product liability, professional liability, health, and additional automobile coverage (details on pages 227–231).

HANGING UP YOUR SHINGLE

While most mompreneurs don't literally hang up a shingle, they do want to be up front about doing business at home. That's why zoning laws should be one of the first areas to investigate, especially if you're moving to a new neighborhood.

"Although they may not even know it, many home-based businesses are in flagrant violation of the law," says Sarah Edwards, co-author of several books on working from home. "But the current laws are archaic and undergoing radical change . . . mostly for the better." In the past, zoning boards usually did not enforce these outdated ordinances unless a neighbor complained. These days, however, communities are becoming aware of the advantages home businesses can provide in terms of revenues from property and income taxes, neighborhood safety, and increased real estate value.

Portland, Oregon, is one municipality that instituted more supportive zoning regulations and now has a 40 percent compliance rate among home-based workers and more dollars coming into its tax base. Through a surge in telecommuting and pressure from a growing work-at-home constituency, Chicago, Illinois, liberalized its ordinance to allow a wider variety of home businesses within certain limitations. Not only is the city profiting, home workers no longer have to hide like outlaws.

As technology continues to feed the home office boom, other communities are following suit and updating their laws. Right in our own backyards, the traditionally conservative village of Scarsdale, New York, proposed zoning changes that were "at the cutting edge of this kind of legislation," according to former mayor Walter Handelman. Instead of limiting home offices and studios to a few listed professions as in the past, the law now characterizes home businesses as either *visible* or *invisible*. Visible businesses, those considered to have an impact on the neighborhood (i.e., doctors and music teachers), continue to be regulated through a special permit and variance granted by the local board. Invisible businesses, those high-tech operations that rely primarily on computer, fax, and phone, are required to register but do not need a permit. For both visible and invisible businesses, home office space is limited to one-fourth the living space or 350 square feet. Restrictions were also placed on storage facilities, signs, retail sales from the home, client visits, and the number of outside employees.

Not surprisingly, some home workers think this legislation falls far short of "cutting edge." First of all, how can you classify some of the more creative home-based businesses? Would a strategic planner who runs focus groups from home be considered visible or invisible? How about an image consultant who displays clothing and accessories in her family room? There was also a significant outcry against limiting employees and business visitors to home offices, especially if off-street parking is available. As one work-at-home attorney pointed out, the IRS requires documentation of client visits in order to take the home office deduction. Nearby communities are revamping their ordinances to allow one to two outside employees and one customer or client visit at a time, and Scarsdale is paying attention.

What's happening in our neck of the woods is happening in other locales across the country; as outdated zoning laws are being amended, home workers are speaking up and being heard. In Stillwater, Oklahoma, for example, the local Chamber of Commerce teamed up with home-based business owners to create a broad new ordinance based on these simple points: The principal use of the home must remain residential; the average casual observer must not be able to tell there's a business in the home; and the neighborhood must suffer no adverse impact from noise, traffic, or anything else. This is close to the goal of the American Planning Association, which suggests that the "ideal ordinance be flexible enough to allow an owner to incubate a small home business, but firm enough to push a full-fledged enterprise into a commercial zone."

Other communities presently go by a similar "see no evil, hear no evil, smell no evil" zoning rule. In other words, as long as a home-based business does not interfere with the residential character of the neighborhood, create parking problems, generate excessive noise, emit unpleasant odors, or elicit complaints from neighbors, zoning officials will turn a blind eye. In fact, a model regulation to this effect was written up by a Georgia attorney and was adopted by 400 condominium associations in the Atlanta area. A number of forward-thinking locales are now constructing new homes specifically designed to accommodate both living and working space. In Lynwood, Illinois, houses built on one-acre lots are zoned residential in the front and commercial in the rear, so the home business does not affect the character of the neighborhood at all. Here and in other parts of the country, working at home is viewed as an asset to the community.

Although the majority of local governments are relaxing their regulations on home offices, some townships are proposing zoning ordinances that can make working from home difficult or even impossible. Their feeling is that a proliferation of home businesses can hurt the worth of their homes, even though other communities have seen real estate values go up. The bottom line: Take advantage of the zoning revolution going on right now. As a home worker, this is the best time to speak up, join forces with other mompreneurs, and advocate positive changes at local zoning board meetings. Until the laws are revamped, do your best to be in compliance. If you get slapped with a violation, don't ignore it. You can run up fines for each additional day your business operates illegally. The best way to stay out of trouble is to be a considerate neighbor.

Be a Good Neighbor

It's smart to let your neighbors know what you're doing and seek out their support. A little cooperation and courtesy can help avoid many zoning hassles. Here are some other tips:

- ✓ Consider getting a post office box at an outside location, especially if you receive a lot of mail and packages. Your letter carrier and your neighbors will be appreciative and more accepting of your home business.
- ✓ Provide parking on your premises that won't block your neighbors' homes, driveways, or garages.
- ✓ Keep traffic to a minimum, trying to schedule clients, visitors, and even deliveries so neighbors aren't bothered by lots of cars and trucks converging on the street at once.
- ✓ Store all business-related materials and products inside your home.

An unsightly outdoor storage shed or even a messy, packed-to-the-gills garage may irritate neighbors.

✓ Neatness counts when it comes to garbage, too. Put out bulky discards only on the designated days, be conscientious about recycling, and have enough trash cans to prevent unsightly overflows.

✓ Make sure your block can handle the extra phone cables and electrical lines you may need to run your computer, fax, telephone, Internet connection, etc. The last thing you want to do is cause a major blackout in your neighborhood.

✓ If you can afford to, volunteer or barter your professional services to neighbors. You'll get a lot of goodwill and cooperation in return.

Two Zoning Horror Stories

Although these are the exceptions to the rule, picky neighbors and tight interpretation of zoning laws have caused trouble for home businesses in places as diverse as suburban New Rochelle, New York, and rural Jefferson, Maryland.

Evelyne Simon, a home-based businesswoman from New Rochelle, New York, ran into problems because her work didn't fall into the short list of occupations allowed by the city. According to a provision in the 1955 zoning ordinance (updated from the 1920s), architects, doctors, dentists, lawyers, dance instructors, and milliners were permitted to have home offices, but management consultants like Simon were not. (No doubt there weren't very many around back then.) When disgruntled neighbors complained about the use of her garage as a home office, she applied for a permit to convert her family room into a work space. Not only was the building permit denied, the zoning board forced Simon to shut down her business. She appealed her case but lost, ran up fines and legal fees, and was forced to move her consulting business out of her home, even though she considers herself as much a professional as a lawyer or architect and more relevant to life today than a milliner.

Tom and Georgia Patrick, a work-at-home couple operating two small businesses from their Maryland farm, were also cited for zoning violations. As consultants running a research and marketing firm and an agricultural and conservation organization, their work was low-key and unobtrusive. Even so, two neighbors complained, and the Patricks were charged as criminals in violation of the zoning laws!

WORKING YOUR WAY THROUGH THE ZONING MAZE

Even if your local zoning laws are outdated, you may be able to operate totally aboveboard. Here's what to check out:

1. Get a list of the home businesses that are prohibited and permitted in your neighborhood, and see where yours fits in.

2. Find out if you can be legit simply by registering your business with the town and paying a nominal fee.

3. If your home office violates the current zoning code, request a variance or exception for your business. As long as neighbors don't object, it will probably be granted.

4. Arrange for a home inspection by the zoning board, if necessary.

5. Apply for a permit or license to operate your business, if required.

6. Look into restrictions on outdoor signs, structural alterations, percent of home office space, use of outside buildings for storage and/or work space, business visitors, and employees. These vary greatly from place to place.

Licenses and Permits

Counties and states have different laws regarding licenses or permits for home business. Sometimes it depends on where you live; other times, it depends on what you do. In general, the government is stricter about regulating businesses that deal with public health and safety. These include the following:

Catering/food production
Day care
Lodging
Cosmetology
Haircutting
Marriage counseling
Employment services
Animal care
Auto repair

In some states, labor laws require that all home-based businesses conducting any type of commercial activity be licensed. In others, a license is mandatory for certain occupations or professions, such as CPAs, physicians, engineers, and hairstylists. Again, do your homework: Check with other mompreneurs and local government offices to see if your business must have a special permit or license to operate.

Dealing with authorities who regulate permits and licenses can be a lot like dealing with neighbors: Courtesy and cooperation go a long way. Cathy

Bolton, a mompreneur from Oklahoma who started a baking business from her home kitchen, found the health department to be very supportive when she worked with them. "I always tell home-based business owners that they have a commitment to shell out what it might take to conform to regulations," she says. "In my case, it meant redoing my kitchen." Bolton also struck up a clever deal with the local health inspector. "I had an infant at the time I began my business, and I could get a lot of work done when he took naps. The health inspector tended to pop in without warning, and inevitably he would come while my baby was napping and wake him up," she remembers. "So I created this system with him. If the shades were open, he could come right in; if they were closed, he should come back later." To Bolton's delight, the health inspector agreed, and they developed a wonderful working relationship.

STRUCTURING YOUR HOME BUSINESS

We didn't think much about the structure of our businesses when we started out. Like many mompreneurs in our survey, we ended up as sole proprietors, mostly by default. Terri Lonier, author of *Working Solo, 2nd Edition* (John Wiley & Sons, 1998) explains a sole proprietorship as a venture in which "you and your business are one and the same—you *are* the business." That means you receive all the profits but are responsible for all the liabilities, too. The gains and losses from your home business are filed on your personal tax return (IRS Schedule C, Form 1040).

A sole proprietorship is the easiest way to go and the choice of many work-at-home mothers. Most of us run service-oriented businesses without too much risk involved. It is also much simpler to start out as a sole proprietor and incorporate later, rather than do it the other way around. The major drawback of a sole proprietorship is that creditors can come after your personal assets (home, car, bank accounts, investments, etc.) if your business is subject to financial problems or lawsuits.

Home workers who offer goods or services that can incur liability or large debt may want to incorporate. Susan Kippur, a New York City–based management consultant, formed an S corporation to protect herself against clients who felt they could sue if her techniques or advice didn't produce the desired results. It also made sense for Beth Hilson to incorporate her mail-order food business for extra protection. According to Lonier, a corporation is "a business established as a distinct legal entity, separate from the individuals who own it." Incorporating doesn't come cheap. It costs between $500 and $1,500 to set up a corporation and almost $1,000 in annual fees to keep it going. If liability is your main concern, you may be fine with a sole proprietorship protected by extra liability insurance (see pages 227–228). So before you decide on this route, weigh the pros and cons of the different types of corporate structures (see the chart on pages 216–217), and consult an accountant and attorney.

Standard or Subchapter C Corporations

This is the type in which taxes are paid at a corporate rate by the business itself. Profits can be taxed twice: once on corporate earnings and a second time on dividends paid to you and other shareholders. However, as the employer of the corporation, you can fully deduct health insurance premiums and all medical expenses for you and your family—a real plus in these days of rising health care costs.

A Personal Services Corporation or Professional Corporation

These are C corporations designed for professional people such as doctors, lawyers, accountants, engineers, architects, and certain consultants. This group is taxed at the highest rate: 35 percent. CPA/CIA (Certified Internal Auditor) Betty Kohls Stehman tells clients to "avoid this corporate classification if you possibly can."

Even though mompreneur Stehman is an accountant, she formed her own company, Entrepreneurial Financial Services, Inc., as an S corporation by issuing a certain percentage of her stock to shareholders. If your profession falls into one of the above categories, check with your accountant or financial planner to see if you can do the same.

Subchapter S Corporations

You will pay tax on your business once on a personal level, much the same as a sole proprietorship or partnership. This type offers most of the advantages of incorporation without the tax complexities of a C corporation, but you don't get the health benefits. Since earnings are taxed according to an individual's tax rate, a high-income mompreneur may be better off paying the maximum 35 percent corporate tax rate of a C corporation.

Partnerships

Another kind of business structure, partnerships are defined by Lonier as "an association of two or more persons who serve as co-owners of a business." When mompreneurs become partners, they usually form a general partnership, or an LLC (see page 215) giving each an agreed-upon portion of the business and an active role in running it. This is how it works:

- ✓ A written partnership agreement, preferably drawn up by a lawyer, should spell out the exact terms of the joint business venture. Verbal agreements are sometimes used among friends or married couples, but keep in mind that these are not binding.
- ✓ The business is inseparable from the partners. If one co-owner gets into legal or financial trouble, the other must accept half the blame.
- ✓ Taxes are paid individually, based on the percentage of the company each partner owns. This is usually fifty-fifty but can be any other split worked out in the original partnership agreement.
- ✓ Partners file two tax returns: IRS Form 1065 to show how much money each partner gained and lost during the year, and Form 1040 (personal tax return), documenting the income earned from the business.
- ✓ The partnership automatically dissolves if one partner dies, unless otherwise stated in the partnership agreement.

A limited partnership, on the other hand, has one or more silent partners who invest money in the business but have no say in its management and no liability. The general partner in this arrangement—usually the person with the entrepreneurial spirit—has full legal and financial responsibility.

Limited Liability Companies (LLCs)

Although LLCs were created to meet the needs of joint venture between large corporations, they are often used by small business partners seeking an alternative to S corporations or limited partnerships. This relatively new business structure is not yet legal in every state, so check before you decide to go this route. Like a corporation, an LLC limits your liability, but as in a partnership, you pay no corporate income taxes—you're taxed on an individual level.

PAIRING UP

Partnerships are popular among mompreneurs. Sharing a business can take some of the anxiety out of ownership, increase flexibility and family time, and decrease the loneliness of working from home. But according to Bonnie Tandy Leblang, a Connecticut mom who wears several different hats, "Partnerships are like marriages. They require constant work." She should know. She writes a syndicated newspaper column with one partner, co-authors cookbooks with another, and runs a speakers' bureau with yet another.

A successful partnership begins by teaming up with someone who shares your vision and complements your skills. Ann Herman and Carol Coleman are a good example. These two Larchmont, New York, moms pooled their talents and resources to invent Ballwall, a collection of sports targets to help kids practice baseball pitching, football passing, and scoring goals in street hockey and soccer. Coleman is a former banker, and Herman was a teacher. The idea for Ballwall was hatched in the Coleman backyard, when mother and son were working on pitching skills together. Coleman bought a large canvas tarp at a hardware store, drew a target on it, and the idea became a reality. Herman came up with the name Ballwall, and with the help of an artist, they all worked out the design problems. Several incarnations later, it was patented, copyrighted, and marketed.

"The partnership was informal at first," remembers Coleman, "but then we had to incorporate for liability reasons. When we drew up the articles of incorporation, we split our company's shares fifty-fifty, giving the artist 4 percent sweat equity." Many mompreneur partnerships start out with verbal or casually written agreements, then become more formalized as they grow. "Get something in writing," the experts advise, and we tend to agree. No matter how close your relationship with your partner is today, it could change quickly. That also includes the ever-growing numbers of husband-wife teams running businesses together from home. Right from the beginning, figure out the division of labor, expenses, and profit and have an agreement drawn up and notarized.

YOUR BUSINESS STRUCTURE

TYPE	ADVANTAGES	DISADVANTAGES
C corporation	Limited personal liability for business-related lawsuits and debts Can transfer ownership and sell shares Health insurance and other benefits deductible Instant status for raising capital	Risk of paying double income tax Expensive to form and maintain Complicated paperwork

TYPE	ADVANTAGES	DISADVANTAGES
S corporation	Income taxed on personal level Limited personal liability Can transfer ownership and sell shares Maintenance costs can be less than C corporation	Restricted to ten or fewer shareholders No deductions for health insurance
Sole proprietor	Simple to set up and maintain All profits and control go to owner Earnings taxed at personal level Potential tax benefits for business losses	Resources for expansion limited Personal responsibility for all business-related lawsuits and debt Business dissolves upon death or retirement
Partnership	Relatively simple to set up and maintain Income taxed at personal level Sharing of resources, talents, and responsibility	Partners are liable for each other's actions Possible end of business upon death or retirement of one partner Must share profits
LLC	Income taxed on personal level Limited personal liability Income and deductions flow through the partners	Not available in all states Not available to sole proprietors Dissolves upon death or withdrawal of any member

WHEN SHOULD YOU CALL AN ATTORNEY?

Most home-based businesses don't face legal dilemmas on a regular basis. Besides, some of the day-to-day matters can be resolved with a little research, common sense, and networking with other mompreneurs. But there are times when the services of a bona fide attorney can prove invaluable, especially if you don't want minor problems to turn into major (and expensive) crises. We suggest hiring a lawyer familiar with small and home business issues if you plan to:

✓ Form a partnership or corporation
✓ Change the structure of your business
✓ Draw up or look over a complicated contract
✓ Initiate or settle a lawsuit
✓ Mediate a zoning dispute or appeal a violation
✓ Trademark a name or patent a product
✓ Sell or buy a company
✓ File for protection from creditors

SCAMS AND SWINDLES

Beware: The lure of earning money at home may draw you into some shady deals. You've probably seen print ads offering big bucks for stuffing envelopes, assembling jewelry or crafts, selling products or services by telephone, computer consulting, or writing children's books. Lately, television infomercials and the Internet have joined the fray, peddling "business opportunities" and costly job training seminars to impressionable viewers and surfers. While some of these come-ons are legitimate, many are too good to be true.

Before you sign up, read all the fine print and check out the company carefully. The Mother's Home Business Network of East Meadow, New York, released a "fraud detector" to help expose work-at-home scams. Some of its suggestions and others are included in the questions below. If any of your answers are yes, we suggest you proceed with extreme caution or forget about following through altogether.

✓ Is the business opportunity available for only a limited time?
✓ Are you being asked to send money for information or materials?
✓ Does the company promote "hidden" opportunities?
✓ Does the company have an unlisted phone number?
✓ Is the company promising to set you up with an 800 or 900 phone number?

✓ Does the Better Business Bureau, the Department of Consumer Affairs, the FTC, or the Postal Inspector have a record of complaints against the company?

If the company seems legitimate, it's still essential to run a credit check and ask for and investigate references of their other home-based employees. One of the respondents in our survey alerted us to the low pay and poor quality of one product assembly business. The unassembled products had to be paid for up front, then marketed and resold by the work-at-home mom herself. There's no profit in unsold merchandise.

Keep on your toes. As more and more people seek the opportunity to work from home, there will be more and more get-rich-quick scams attracting them—especially online. But you can use the web to do a little sleuthing. Chat rooms and message boards on the work-at-home mom sites are particularly helpful for scoping out an opportunity (see page 296 for sites).

TAX TIME

Tax laws have become more favorable to home-based workers since we wrote the first edition of *Mompreneurs*. During the 1990s, the IRS was particularly strict about who could take the home office deduction. Many self-employed work-from-homers did not file for this deduction because they were afraid it would raise a "red flag" and a possible audit. But new office-in-home rules went into effect in January 1999, loosening IRS standards and increasing eligibility.

We're going to explain the new tax guidelines in the next few pages. Even so, it doesn't hurt to go over your own tax return with an accountant or tax advisor, especially if you're just starting up. One of the first things these experts will tell you to do is report ALL the income from your home business. Undeclared earnings can get you into big trouble with the IRS. Since taxes are paid only on profits, it's much smarter to take the maximum deductions off the top to reduce your income.

The Home Office Deduction

If you are self-employed and work from home in a space that is used regularly and exclusively for your business, you can take the home office deduction. Even interior decorators, event planners, salespeople, and consultants who spend a lot of time on-site now qualify *if* they have no other location where they conduct a substantial amount of administrative work. Accountant and tax expert Jan Zobel adds that your home office doesn't necessarily have to be in a separate room, but it must be a clearly defined workspace where no personal activities take place. If you have a sofa bed in the room for overnight guests or a TV the whole family gathers to watch, you may be suspect.

The home office deduction can take a significant bite out of your tax bill. Here's how it adds up:

Calculating the deduction:

✓ Figure out the approximate percentage of your home used for business. For example, if you have an eight room house and your office occupies one room, your percentage would be approximately 12.5 percent. You can also add up the total square footage of your home and the square footage of your workspace to figure out the percentage.
✓ Add together your rent or mortgage interest, utilities, maintenance, real estate taxes, and insurance and multiply the total by the percentage you use for your business. (If you own your home, you can also factor in the depreciation on the room or space you work in.) Your final figure is your allowable home office deduction.

Besides reducing your taxes right off the top, Zobel points out three additional benefits to taking the office-in-home deduction:

✓ When you deduct personal expenses (mortgage and real estate tax, for instance) as business expenses, they not only reduce your income tax, but also your self-employment tax.
✓ By claiming a home office, you're able to deduct rent, utilities, insurance, and depreciation that you can't otherwise take as expenses.
✓ Taking the home office deduction allows you to deduct more car expenses. Without a deductible office-in-home, you generally cannot claim the miles you drive from home to your first business stop of the day and from your last stop of the day back home.

Business Expenses

Even if you don't take the home office deduction, there are many other expenses you can deduct to shrink your tax bill. Pat's accountant, Dan Heilig of Heilig and Andreotti, Ltd., makes sure she keeps all her receipts throughout the year and a running log of expenses to prove her deductions are legitimate. Heilig advises that business expenses can cover many items and services, including office supplies, printing, postage and shipping, phone and Internet service used for your business, memberships in professional organizations, subscriptions to journals and magazines needed in your work, advertising fees, business insurance, seminars, courses, and services by other professionals (accountants, attorneys, etc.). Major improvements, such as a new computer system or a suite of office furniture, can either be immediately deducted up to $25,000 in the year they are purchased or depreciated over several years. (Five years is the typical depreciation period for most equipment.) It's worth it to deduct large equipment purchases right away if your business is showing a profit.

Travel and Entertainment

Deductions for travel and entertainment expenses are limited to 50 percent of expenses. While it's important to keep receipts, the IRS has increased the expense limit allowed without a receipt to $75 per business meal. Dan Heilig adds a note of caution, however: "It's highly recommended that mompreneurs maintain a diary or log for every calendar year. If you make entries for all your meetings, meals, purchases, and other expenses, the IRS will consider the diary a valid record even if you don't have all your receipts."

Car leasing or purchase costs can be deductible if they fall within certain guidelines. Unincorporated work-at-home moms have to prove the amount of time the car is used for business and deduct only that cost, while a mompreneur who is incorporated can deduct the entire lease payment, then pay back to her company the personal-use dollar amount. Be sure to look over the provisions of the lease carefully, especially the "option to buy" section. If you purchase a car for business, you can file by the "actual expense" method (tracking gas, mileage, insurance, maintenance, and depreciation) or by the IRS standard (32.5 cents/mile), calculating the approximate percentage used for business.

Health Care Costs

Home businesses can deduct health care costs. Sole proprietors, partnerships, and S corporations can deduct 60 percent of their health insurance premiums as of 2001.

As far as medical expenses go, today's laws are not too generous. You are allowed to deduct medical expenses only to the extent that they exceed 7.5 percent of your adjusted gross income. Thankfully, most relatively healthy families don't reach that amount. But the IRS considers more than doctor visits in its calculations, and things can add up in bad years.

Here's what can be figured in:

✓ Prescription drugs
✓ Artificial teeth and limbs
✓ Eyeglasses and hearing aids

✓ Special schools for the handicapped
✓ Transportation and lodging
✓ Modifications to a residence to accommodate a medical condition

Child Care

The cost of child care is deductible, varying according to your income level. You can write off between 20 and 30 percent of your expenses—up to $2,400 for one child or $4,800 for two or more—and receive a tax credit of $720 for one child or $1,440 for two or more. Don't forget to factor in more than just baby-sitting costs; nursery school tuition, summer camp, and after-school day care count, too. To qualify for the credit, both parents have to work or be looking for work, and it can only be applied to children age thirteen and under. (See page 225 for more on taxes and children.)

Retirement Plans

One of the best tax shelters for the self-employed, retirement plans allow you to set aside a portion of your annual earnings in a tax-deferred savings plan, then deduct this contribution from your income tax for that year. The type of plan you choose has a lot to do with how much you can afford to put away. Self-employed mompreneurs can choose any of three types of retirement plans.

In a *Keogh Plan*, you can invest anywhere from 13 to 20 percent of your net income for that tax year. The maximum amount of your income that can be used in computing this contribution is $150,000; if you earn a higher yearly salary, you may want to look into starting more than one Keogh account. The drawback of a Keogh is that some plans require you to contribute the same amount each year—a difficult feat if your income varies a lot.

An *IRA* (*Individual Retirement Account*) is another way to go. You can start these plans with a small sum of money and contribute different amounts every year. As of this writing, there's a $2,000 annual cap on IRA contributions.

In a *SEP* (*Simplified Employee Pension Plan*), on the other hand, you can contribute up to 15 percent or $30,000 of your income. If you're the head of a small company that employs others, you can set up SEPs for yourself and your workers.

Keogh, IRA, and SEP plans can be established through banks, life insurance companies, mutual funds, and other institutions. An investment counselor can help evaluate your situation and point you toward the best option.

Are you leaving an outside job to start a home-based business? If so, check with your accountant or tax advisor about rolling over any retirement benefits you may have accrued into your own plan. At the present time, the government gives you sixty days to roll over without a penalty.

Note: If your spouse is an active participant in a retirement plan at his workplace, your IRA, SEP, or Keogh deduction may be limited; check this out with your accountant. But everyone is able to contribute to a Roth IRA even if they are covered by a retirement plan at work. Check with your tax advisor about income limits.

Self-Employment Taxes

These support such federal programs as Social Security and Medicare. As of 2001, a 15.3 percent tax is imposed on the first $80,400 of your net income; earnings over that are subject to a 2.9 percent tax. If business is booming, S corporation status can help you take out some of your profits as corporate distributions rather than salary. This can help reduce the amount you pay in self-employment taxes for the time being, but the IRS is considering changing this favorable tax treatment.

Social Security

Withholding Social Security for child-care providers and household help was brought to the forefront by the plights of several female presidential appointees. Since then, working mothers have had to be more careful about paying Social Security taxes, and in some cases, unemployment and workers' compensation or disability for their employees. The taxes apply to all hired help eighteen years of age and older who earn over $1,200 annually, whether they're keeping the books for your business or baby-sitting your children. Payment is usually made with a quarterly employment tax return; you're required to submit W-2 forms at the end of the year and give each employee a 1099. (See page 107 for more on the Nanny Tax.)

Estimated Taxes

The federal government and some states and municipalities require estimated taxes from self-employed business people who expect to pay at least $1,000 in annual taxes. You're obligated to keep track of approximately how much you'll owe in income tax and self-employment tax for the coming year, based on your previous year's earnings. (You're actually expected to pay at least 90 percent of your current tax bill or 100 percent of last year's bill.) Payments are due on a quarterly basis: April 15, June 15, September 15, and January 15 of the following year. If you're late or don't pay enough you may receive a penalty; if you overpay you'll receive a refund.

A mompreneur who files a joint tax return with a husband who works outside the home technically should pay estimated taxes on her home business. However, the IRS tends to look the other way if enough is witheld from the husband's paycheck to cover both. But if you suddenly find your home business taking off and profits skyrocketing, speak to your tax advisor about estimated taxes.

Sales Tax

Sales tax varies from state to state. If you're selling any product at retail, you have to collect sales tax from your customers. You are then responsible for sending in the collected tax in quarterly payments, which may be due on different dates than your estimated taxes. Sound complicated? It can get even more tricky. If you're in the mail-order business, states can charge tax according to the point of delivery of your product. With customers all over the country, paying sales tax can become a nightmare. Turn to your accountant or specially designed computer software for help.

STATUS SEEKING

In the eyes of the IRS, the technical title you go by can affect how much you pay in taxes. Mompreneurs who work on a freelance or consulting basis for several different clients should make sure they're classified as independent contractors rather than employees. If the IRS assigns you employee status, it can mean a heftier tax bill for you and your client. As an employee, you lose some of the beneficial home business deductions we talked about on page 219, and your employers have to pick up half of your Social Security taxes—an expense they may not think is affordable or worthwhile.

You can work to protect your status by following these guidelines:

✓ Get a contract or letter of agreement for each project you accept. The language should state that your company, not you as an individual, is responsible for completing the project. Specify that you can hire assistants and take on other jobs while you're working for that client.
✓ Establish a name for your company to show that it's a separate entity. Independent contractors can become corporations or LLCs to protect themselves. If you don't want to incorporate, the least you should do is obtain a doing business as (d/b/a) certificate (see page 206).
✓ If you work primarily for one client, try to get paid on a per-project basis instead of by the hours or days you put into the job.

✓ Become familiar with both the current federal and state requirements for independent contractors. Check out www.irs.gov for definitions.

KEEPING THE IRS OFF YOUR BACK

How do you stay on the good side of the IRS? Take a look at our list of dos and don'ts:

Do pay yourself a salary that's in line with the kind of work you perform.

Don't claim your salary as a business deduction. Your wages are your profits and cannot be tax-deductible unless you incorporate.

Do keep accurate and complete records of all business expenses for five years. These include credit card bills, invoices, receipts, and canceled checks.

Don't run your business at a loss year after year to take advantage of large deductions. If you don't make a profit three years out of five, your venture will be considered a hobby by the IRS, and you may end up in worse financial shape.

Do save tax returns and real estate and retirement fund records for as long as you have the space. Some experts recommend saving these indefinitely.

Don't forget to jot down travel and entertainment dates and expenses in a daily diary or appointment book.

Do deduct gifts bought for business purposes that cost under $25 each.

Don't be late with quarterly payments on estimated taxes.

Do use your credit card for business purchases. You'll get an automatic copy for your tax files, and the interest is deductible as a business expense.

Don't neglect to make changes on your return if you should divorce. Alimony is deductible to the spouse who pays and taxable to the one who receives it. Child support is not deductible or taxable.

KIDS AND TAXES

Come tax time, moms who work from home have a couple of other things to think about besides the child-care credit (see page 222).

The Nanny Tax, enacted in 1994, relaxes the tax rules for moms who pay baby-sitters and housekeepers less than $1,200 annually and for all domestic employees under eighteen years of age. Even if your 17-year-old high school baby-sitter earns $3,000 a year, you are not responsible for paying taxes.

However, au pairs, nannies, and others who work primarily as such are not excluded and require Social Security witholding on your part.

Are you responsible for paying taxes on your mother or best friend? Technically, you are, especially if you want to take the child-care credit. Relatives and friends must be given a 1099 to allow you to deduct the money you paid for their services on your tax return.

Hiring your children to help with the business can make a dent in your taxes. Since kids under the age of nineteen are in a lower tax bracket than their parents, they pay less in state and federal income taxes. As a bonus, you can deduct their wages as a business expense, and they can put their earnings into a college fund. To keep the IRS happy, make sure you pay your kids reasonable wages.

Tax-free college funds are a smart way to save for the future while cutting your tax bill. One program allows you to buy Series EE savings bonds for each child that mature in the years they will be in college or graduate school. The bonds accumulate tax-free interest; when you cash them in at maturity, the entire amount must go toward tuition. Speak to an investment counselor periodically to keep abreast of other choices.

ONLINE TAX HELP

Check out these sites to download tax forms or seek advice:

- ✓ www.irs.gov
- ✓ www.quicken.com
- ✓ www.riahome.com

WHEN TO HIRE AN ACCOUNTANT/TAX ADVISOR

Every home business requires accounting and administrative work from time to time—some more than others. Even if you're good with numbers, don't think you have to do it all. CPA Betty Kohls Stehman recommends "getting rid of what you don't like or don't want to do, and focus on the things you do well. The money you spend on a professional may save you thousands. It also gives you more time to devote to your business, which can mean more money in your pocket." We recommend calling on an accountant or tax advisor familiar with home businesses to:

- ✓ Prepare your tax return, at least for the first year or two you are in business.
- ✓ Evaluate whether or not you qualify for the home office deduction.

✓ Recommend IRA/SEP/Keogh options, channeling your investments into tax-deferred plans that best meet the needs of your family.

✓ Determine the best structure for your business. A good accountant will weigh the pros and cons of sole proprietorships, incorporation, LLCs, and partnerships.

✓ Compute your estimated taxes.

✓ Advise you in a year when there are big IRS changes for the self-employed.

✓ Explain what to do when and if you're ready to hire help. As a home business owner with employees, your tax responsibilities increase.

✓ Assist you in figuring out the tax implications and changes when you move from a corporate job to a home-based business (or vice versa).

✓ Hold your hand if you're audited.

INSURANCE: WHAT KIND AND HOW MUCH?

Many mompreneurs figure that since they're working from home, they can rely on their homeowner's or renter's insurance to cover any mishaps. Unfortunately, some have found out the hard way that this isn't always the case.

"Policies that are adequate or appropriate for the home don't always cover the insurance needs of a business," says Denise Binday-Koslowsky, vice president of Advocate Brokerage Corp. in New York. "As a result, many home business owners are improperly or underinsured." Besides, home-based businesses can be subject to risks other than fire, storms, and theft. Depending on your line of work and the size of your business, you may need liability, health, disability, malpractice, and additional auto insurance, as well as workers' compensation.

Insurance companies are responding to the growing home business market with new and different types of policies. To help steer you in the right direction, the Insurance Information Institute (www.iii.org) offers this overview.

Property and Liability Insurance

This should be your first priority. While homeowner's policies do cover damage to all the rooms in your house, many pay a maximum of $2,500 for business equipment in the home and $250 away from the premises. That may be enough for a mom who does weaving or writing from her home, but it's not much when you consider the cost of today's technology. Business-related liability can also be a problem. Although your homeowner's policy may apply to guests who are injured on your property, it probably doesn't extend to the messenger who trips on your front walk while delivering a package. Extra liability insurance can also protect you against lawsuits from dissatisfied clients or customers and the possibility of closing down shop due to damage to your home.

There are three basic ways you can increase your coverage to protect your home business:

1. Add endorsements or riders to your existing homeowner's or renter's policy. For example, you can extend the coverage for business equipment by getting an endorsement for a higher limit: about $10,000 to $15,000 in the home and $1,000 to $1,500 off the premises. Some companies also offer riders for limited liability, covering injury to customers or clients in your home, for example. But to qualify with some insurance companies, your home-based business may have to be "incidental" or gross less than $5,000 a year. Riders are inexpensive—$40 extra per year—but do not usually include higher-risk areas, like product and advertising liability. If you're a home day-care provider, you're responsible for purchasing separate homeowner's liability insurance for an annual cost of about $70.

2. Get an in-home business insurance policy. For about $200 a year you can insure your business property for $10,000; this price usually includes general liability coverage, too. However, if you're in the type of business that may need more protection, you can purchase anywhere from $300,000 to $1,000,000 worth of liability coverage. The cost of your premium will depend on the amount of coverage you get.

   An in-home business policy also acts as "business interruption insurance." In the event that you cannot work because of damage to your house, the policy will cover lost income and ongoing expenses (including payroll if you have employees) for up to one year. There's also limited coverage for loss or destruction of equipment, records, or valuable papers; accounts receivable and other money; and inventory both onsite and offsite. According to Jeanne Salvatore, vice president of consumer affairs for the Insurance Information Institute, some companies that offer in-home business policies require you to also purchase your homeowner's and car insurance from them, so check with the companies that are already insuring you first.

3. Buy a businessowner's package policy, or BOP. Like an in-home business policy, a BOP covers business property and equipment, loss of income, extra expenses, and liability—but on a much broader scale. These policies were designed for home-based businesses that may operate in more than one location or manufacture products in another facility. Not surprisingly, premiums are higher, too—about $300 to $500 a year with a deductible. But BOPs are still a good deal for the amount of coverage they provide.

Car Insurance

Your personal automobile policy will probably cover the business driving most mompreneurs do, but there are exceptions. If you transport a lot of products, pay frequent visits to customers, or drive employees around in a van, you may need a business auto policy to protect you from accidents during those times. It usually costs 20 percent more to add business use to your personal auto policy; check with your car insurance provider about this option.

Insurance for baby-sitters who drive your car can be added to your existing auto policy, or you can extend the liability coverage of your homeowner's policy to your car by adding a rider; some insurance companies offer this often less expensive alternative.

Umbrella Policies

If your assets exceed the amount of your homeowner's and auto insurance, umbrella policies are recommended. If you're doing business as a sole proprietor or in a partnership, any lawsuit against your home business can put your personal assets at risk (Incorporating is another way to protect your assets; see pages 214–216 in this chapter.) For home-based business owners, umbrella policies generally cost $180 to $230 a year for $1 million worth of liability insurance and about $75 to $100 more for each additional million dollars of coverage. That may sound like a lot of coverage, but people are suing for astronomical amounts these days. Some policies protect you against libel or slander claims, as well as bodily injury to a client, customer, or supplier. To buy an umbrella, contact the agent who handles your auto and homeowner's insurance; most will provide a discount for this extra coverage.

Product Liability

Most businessowner's policies also cover product liability. For a company that manufactures or produces anything that's consumed, touched, or used, product liability insurance is a must. If your business insurance doesn't include any or enough of this coverage, you may have to purchase a separate policy.

Professional Liability or Malpractice Insurance

Known more formally as Miscellaneous Errors and Omissions Insurance, malpractice insurance covers you for the professional mistakes you might make on the job. When we hear *malpractice insurance,* many of us immediately think of doctors and lawyers, but home business owners may benefit from this professional liability insurance as well. It's the equivalent of product liability insurance for service-oriented businesses. Computer consultants, investment counselors, columnists, and masseuses are just some of the home-based businesspeople buying these policies now.

This type of insurance is a bit pricey—about $750 to $2,500 per year—but can be worth the investment. After a little sleuthing, Susan Belkin, an attorney with a practice in her home, found out that part-time malpractice coverage is also available at a reduced cost. Since it's a bit unconventional for mompreneurs, you may have to purchase it through a smaller, independent broker.

Health Insurance

Health insurance is necessary for you and your family if your spouse is not covered through his workplace. Without the reforms in health care we've been promised, buying health insurance can be quite costly. Premiums start at about $5,000 a year for a comprehensive family plan when purchased directly or through an insurance broker; lower-cost policies offering bigger deductibles and less coverage are also available.

Unfortunately, carriers are not anxious to cover one- and two-person businesses. They tend to limit the small business rate to enterprises with three to fifty employees, leaving a lot of home-based entrepreneurs out in the cold. Recently, insurance firms have picked up the slack a bit, as more reasonably priced HMOs and Preferred Provider Plans become accessible to individuals. Several national companies have been formed to find clients the best health insurance deals. Quotesmith Corporation (www.quotesmith.com) is a popular one. (See chapter 11.) Still, there are too many self-employed workers paying too much for premiums or doing without health care coverage altogether.

The best plan of action is to become part of a group that can purchase insurance at a cheaper rate. Many professional organizations, unions, nonprofits, and other networks have health insurance packages available to members at group prices. There are also several associations for the self-employed: The U.S. Federation of Small Businesses, Inc., the Small Business Service Bureau, and the National Association for the Self-Employed all offer medical coverage (and other benefits) to members. (See chapter 11.) Another alternative is to band together with other mompreneurs or home-based workers and form your own group.

Disability Insurance/Workers' Compensation

You and/or your employees will be covered for loss of income due to illness or injury by this type of insurance. Sole proprietors who work from home may find it difficult to purchase disability. However, if your business is well established and you can show tax returns to prove it, you'll have an easier time. Count on spending about 2 percent of your gross income to buy a disability policy that will enable you to receive up to 60 percent of your yearly earnings while you are recuperating. If you hire an employee, you may need to purchase workers' compensation insurance to take care of injuries or illness suffered on the job; each state has its own laws regarding this coverage. If your business is incorporated, you can cover both your employees and yourself with a workers' compensation policy.

Life Insurance

Life insurance is an extra that some work-at-home moms forgo, particularly if Dad is the major breadwinner in the household. However, if your family depends on your income for their lifestyle and well-being, it's not a bad idea to purchase a policy. If you think you contribute a minimal amount to the family finances, consider the other services you offer voluntarily. Cooking, cleaning, driving, and child care could certainly cost a bundle if someone had to be hired to replace you.

There are several options to purchasing life insurance, from the low-cost savings bank type to policies that can double as tax-deferred retirement funds. Look into the alternatives with one or more insurance agents, an investment counselor, or by calling the National Insurance Consumer Help Line at 1-800-942-4242.

The insurance needs of mompreneurs are a lot like our tax situations: Every home business is unique. Weighing all the risks and benefits is an important first step in determining your coverage. Then contact an insurance agent knowledgeable about the home business market to customize a package to fit your needs.

FINDING A BROKER

Now that you know how important business insurance is, how do you obtain it? Some firms don't handle it, others think home-based ventures are too risky, and some worry about businesses that store large inventories at home. Experts advise to first approach the company that already handles your home and/or auto insurance. Even a reluctant agent is more apt to offer business insurance if he or she knows your track record and has dealt with you before. If your broker can't write you a policy, try a smaller independent or storefront insurance agency. Or ask for a referral from another mompreneur or a professional or trade organization.

Don't Steal My Idea!

Mompreneurs are certainly a clever bunch. In our survey, we found mothers who launched businesses by inventing everything from specialty publications to baby toys to incredible edibles to computer software. Many learned along the way how important it can be to protect an original concept, service, or product.

Texan Gail Frankel is a good example. Her company, Kel-Gar, Inc., sells juvenile products primarily through catalogs and specialty retail stores. Throughout the creation and marketing of Stroll'r Hold'r, the invention that launched her company, Frankel learned by trial and error how to legally protect her concept. She began by studying trademark and patent law, drawing up a confidentiality agreement with her designer, and going through the process of applying for a patent on the prototype. Once the invention was out on the shelves, her legal chores still weren't over. Early on, Kel-Gar was embroiled in a lawsuit with Safety 1st, Inc.—a much larger manufacturer—for patent infringement over a product similar to Stroll'r Hold'r.

How did Frankel get through all these legal hassles? Having a tax attorney for a husband helped a little, especially when it came to networking with the right professionals. But her willingness to research every facet of her audience and business, along with a good dose of perseverance and trust, positioned Kel-Gar for success. Following are the steps you should take to safely bring your idea to market:

- ✓ Discuss the concept with people you really trust. Family, personal friends, and close business associates can act as your informal test market and provide feedback. If you feel paranoid about one of these people stealing your idea, be vague.
- ✓ Develop the concept into a business plan or prototype. Although it's possible to complete this step on your own, it often makes sense to ask knowledgeable friends or consultants for help. At this point, you may also have to talk to industry suppliers, potential backers, and others who may be involved in developing the product or service.

Attorneys recommend that each person you meet with sign a confidentiality agreement to discourage them from leaking information or publicly discussing your project.

✓ Produce a sample to test the waters. Frankel brought a prototype of the Stroll'r Hold'r to focus groups composed of mothers like herself. This give-and-take resulted in several revisions and improvements to her product before the design was finalized. Again, have a confidentiality agreement available for each focus group participant to sign.

✓ Give your concept a name and conduct a trademark search. Once you name your product or service, you'll want to prevent another entrepreneur from using the same name. To begin, you should conduct a computerized federal trademark or trade name search. This can be done for you by a law or search firm, or you can do it yourself electronically through www.uspto.gov. The search will reveal whether or not your product's name has already been registered with the government for another business venture. If you're in the clear, proceed to the next step.

✓ Apply for federal trademark registration. As far as patent law is concerned, a trademark can be a word, name, symbol, or any device that identifies goods or services. Trademarks are registered with the United States Patent and Trademark Office (PTO) in Washington, D.C. (See chapter 11.) You can register on your own for an application fee of $325 or use an attorney for the price of the basic fee plus hours billed for the paperwork. The advantage to hiring a patent or trademark attorney is that he or she can help you through any legal entanglements that may develop along the way.

✓ Use your trademark in connection with your product or service. Normally, the PTO will issue a certificate of registration twelve to eighteen months after receiving your application. In the interim, you can use your trademark, noting the ™ symbol after your product's name. Once you receive a certificate, you can use the ® symbol.

✓ Apply for a patent, if necessary. Patenting a product protects it from being duplicated and marketed by someone else—to a certain extent. For many inventions, only the design of the product can be patented, not the idea itself. Patents are exclusive for only seventeen years. If you're willing to accept these limitations, the next hurdle is the patent process itself. It takes an average of 18 months and can cost anywhere from $1,000 to $3,000. Before you jump in, it might be wise to get the opinion of a respected patent attorney; he or she can evaluate your prospects and eventually guide you through the patent process as well. To apply for a patent, contact the U.S. Patent and Trademark Office.

✓ While you're waiting for your patent, you can protect your invention with a disclosure letter. This document should include a detailed written description of your product, be signed by two witnesses, and be notarized.

WHAT IS A COPYRIGHT?

Trademarks protect names, patents protect inventions, and copyrights protect artistic and written work. This includes all published material (books, magazines, newsletters, etc.), literary writings, cartoons, illustrations, musical scores and songs, and computer software. *An idea cannot be copyrighted.*

Applying for a copyright doesn't take as much time or money as a patent or trademark. You submit the material you want to protect, printing a copyright notice somewhere on the work. Your name and the date it was produced or published should appear, too. Then you send your creation in to the U.S. Copyright Office in Washington, D.C. (See chapter 11.)

MOMPRENEUR® HALL OF FAME

SARAH EDWARDS
Co-author of the Best-Seller *Working from Home* and
Other Books About Home-Based Businesses, Santa Monica, California
Mother of One

Sarah Edwards and her husband, Paul, are famous across America as self-employment experts. Together, they have written books, hosted various TV and radio shows, and advised millions of current and potential home business owners through seminars, magazine columns, and the web. Although they always wanted to work together, the couple never dreamed their own business would grow out of the home office boom.

Sarah Edwards was actually the first partner to begin working from home, back in 1974 when her son was seven years old. At the time, she was employed in the Head Start program at the regional level and "began to feel increasingly uncomfortable with someone else being a full-time caretaker for my child." Trained as a psychotherapist, she was able to make a fairly smooth transition from the outside workplace to home, setting up a private practice in a spare room of her California house.

Meanwhile, Paul Edwards was running his political consulting business from an office in downtown Los Angeles but would start his day working from home. He began spending more and more time in his home office, eventually finding it expedient to move his secretary home, too. Working side-by-side in their separate home offices on separate endeavors, the Edwardses came up with the idea of writing their first book. "So many people were becoming interested in working from home," says Sarah Edwards, "and Paul and I wanted to work together. So in 1981, we decided to make this our life's work."

It wasn't long before the couple became leaders of the home business movement, giving speeches, presenting workshops, producing audio- and videotapes–in short, doing all they could to inform the nine-to-five crowd that "it wasn't necessary to mortgage your day to someone else. We wanted to let everyone know that there was another choice out there," recalls Sarah, "and that working from home really provides the ultimate security." Through the years, their message continues to ring true. For the most part, home-based workers are able to create the lifestyle they want in a less-risky, less-stressful environment than corpo- rate employees or entrepreneurs who have built businesses outside the home.

How can mompreneurs minimize risk and preserve that unique lifestyle? Sarah offers some tried-and-true advice for both new and sea- soned home workers who want to protect their interests. To begin, she recommends lining up a personal information network or support sys- tem of professionals who can be there when you need them most. The three top people in this network are an attorney, an accountant or tax advisor, and an insurance agent. Next on the list, in no particular order, are a computer/web consultant, information researcher, investment counselor, marketing and advertising specialist, public relations special- ist, and professional organizer. Even if your budget or plans don't include using these experts right away, it helps to develop a relationship with them in advance so you're not scrambling for names when you're in a pinch.

Sarah Edwards is also a strong proponent of all home businesses obtaining a local business license. "Getting a business license can be especially beneficial for mothers who are working from home," she feels, "because it helps you and everyone else take your business more seriously." (For more on licensing, see pages 212–213.)

She also advocates that home-based businesses claim their home office tax deduction. "Don't be intimidated by the IRS," advises Sarah. "Take the deduction if you qualify, and use the money you save to build your business." It pays to consult with an accountant to figure out just what you can deduct.

(continued)

Largely through the efforts of advocates like Paul and Sarah Edwards, home businesses are being widely recognized and respected today. The powers that be can no longer ignore this growing segment of the work-force; banks, insurance companies, and even the government are becoming much more attentive, but there's still room for greater recognition and improved services, and mompreneurs can actively do their part. "Make your community aware of the contributions home businesses can bring to the area," urges Sarah, "like extra revenues through income tax, licensing, etc." These efforts can result in more advantageous zoning laws, insurance packages, and networking opportunities. Don't think you can't have an impact on a higher level as well. Toward that end, Edwards offers these final words of advice: "Write your congressman, advocating positive changes for home businesses." With millions of self-employed home workers out there, they'll listen.

9

Growing Up and Branching Out

We've come a long way since those early days when we were novice mompreneurs, nurturing squirming newborns and fledgling businesses. Over the years, we've seen our kids and our enterprises through countless stages—many of them remarkable, a few of them nearly unbearable. Through it all, we've seen our home businesses blossom along with our children, guided and shaped by our loving hands.

We could never have predicted the changes we'd see in our babes and our businesses, nor the complete control we'd feel over our careers. You, too, will pass through many phases of mompreneurship as you direct your venture toward adulthood.

MOMPRENEUR STATISTICS

Will We Still Work at Home One Year from Now?

Yes	92%
No	3%
Not sure	5%

Five Years from Now?

Yes   65%
No   8%
Not sure   27%

CHANGES AND CHOICES

Each day, you'll face important decisions and new challenges that affect the course of your home business. At some point, for example, you may have to decide whether it's wiser to specialize or diversify. You might add a support staff or a partner. Perhaps you'll even team up with your husband or kids. You may dabble in a few different types of businesses before you settle on the one that's most profitable and personally fulfilling. Or after years of cultivating one successful business, you might sell it and start another one. You could abandon life as a business owner altogether and return to the traditional workforce. We also know some mompreneurs who opt to close or sell their businesses just so they can devote themselves to full-time mothering.

THE SUCCESS METER

How's your business doing? Where is it headed? Is it growing in the right direction? To answer these questions, make periodic success checks so you can evaluate your goals and monitor your business growth. Most mompreneurs say that they gauge their success against these four factors: happiness, time, money, and achievements.

Happiness

Do you still love what you do? Does your business continue to provide you with the family flexibility and personal and professional fulfillment you desire? Are you sufficiently challenged by your work without being constantly overwhelmed by it? Are you able to keep your hands on the components of the business you enjoy most? Judith Bliss, CEO of Mindplay, an educational software company in Tucson, Arizona, does a self-evaluation once a year. "I ask myself, 'Am I happier this year than last year?' and then figure out why or why not. Then I think about what circumstances might have changed during the year and adjust my priorities accordingly."

Time

Are you comfortable with the amount of hours you spend on business? Are you still achieving a work/family balance that's acceptable to you? Can you handle the workload alone, or do you need additional help? If you already have a staff, is it big enough? What else can you do to manage your time better? "I work very hard, but I love it," says PR woman Lisa Ekus, who says sixty-hour work weeks are typical for her. Still, one of her goals is to carve out more leisure time. She'll do it by relying more on her excellent support staff and limiting her workload to just forty or fifty projects a year. Because of time constraints, "we can't take on everything," she says. "So we pick and choose the projects we want to work on. That commitment to top-quality projects has led to our enormous credibility in the business."

Money

Are you generating a sufficient profit? Are you making enough money for the amount of time you put into your business? Are you getting a reasonable return on your initial financial investment? Are your overhead and out-of-pocket expenses affordable? "Keep tuned in to these issues," says toy designer Ruth Wimmer. Know how much time, energy, and money you're willing to commit to your business and whether it's a worthwhile investment, the Denver, Colorado, mom adds.

Achievements

Are you meeting your business goals? Are your clients and customers satisfied? Is your staff happy? Are you getting appropriate recognition for your work? Are you attaining your business vision? When Judith Bliss evaluates the achievements of her educational computer software business, she focuses on how much she's helping children with learning differences. It's been her goal from the start, when she designed computer games to help her learning-disabled son with his reading and writing. "I want to keep on coming up with software products that teach kids as well as increase their self-esteem," she says. "I want to bring people to understand that learning disabilities are really learning abilities." Bliss is certainly getting the job done. She has a million-dollar business and was a past winner of the Women of Enterprise Award, a prestigious event sponsored by Avon Products, Inc., and the U.S. Small Business Administration (SBA).

Shaping the Business

Prepare to make many modifications to your business plan as the years go by. Most mompreneurs start out with a certain vision, then find themselves adjusting the focus as they become seasoned business owners. Only with time and entrepreneurial experience can you recognize what works and what doesn't from a business and a family standpoint.

A PATTERN FOR SUCCESS

Dolores Maes was a stay-at-home mom looking for a way to make some money yet be home with her two preschool boys. A sewing business seemed the logical fit for her background and skills. She had always had a talent for sewing and design and had recently taken some business courses and a seminar in fashion illustration. She started slowly, first by doing custom sewing and alterations from her home in Peralta, New Mexico. She spent just $60 to get the first business going. "I remember because I used my grocery money to make business cards and buy paint for an outdoor sign. It was the best $60 I ever spent."

Once that took off, she opened a home boutique and sold and rented her one-of-a-kind bridal gowns and prom dresses. The boutique lasted six years, until the long hours and the rigorous demands of the retail business proved too much for Maes and her family. "It was so hard dealing with the public," she says. The sewing was intricate, and customers would call her at all hours. "I just burned out."

So she took time off to reassess her goals, and opened her new business, D'Marie, a home-based company that manufactures uniforms, aprons, and bibs for restaurants and hotels. A $500 loan from ACCION of New Mexico helped buy the new sewing machines Maes needed to get D'Marie off the ground. At first, she had just local accounts, but orders began pouring in from all over the state. Maes even had requests from hotels in Las Vegas.

SUCCESS STRATEGIES: Maes hired five workers to do the bulk of her cutting and sewing, making it possible for her to fill large orders and make more money. Farming out most of the sewing also allowed her to concentrate on what she likes best—designing.

BIGGEST WORK/FAMILY CHALLENGE: "Sometimes clients want to meet with me in my office, and I'd rather not have them come to my house. So I always suggest we meet somewhere else, like a restaurant. It just sets a better image."

FUTURE GOALS: "To get contracts with national chains—a pipe dream, but possible—and to be a freelance designer for clothing companies. And I will continue to travel outside my little town to the fashion markets in L.A. and Dallas, just so I can keep on increasing my design knowledge."

STICKING WITH A SPECIALTY

For Lisa Ekus, who runs a cookbook public relations firm in Hatfield, Massachusetts, the key to success was specialization, even though she started out as more of a generalist. When she first opened her home-based public relations firm, she was handling all types of book publicity jobs for her former employer, Crown Publishing Company. She worked exclusively with Crown on a retainer basis for about two years on a variety of book promotion projects, including a few cookbooks. Little by little, she started expanding her client base to include independent authors and other publishers. Her early projects were diverse, but Ekus quickly discovered that the cookbooks were the ones she liked best. "I had found my niche," she says. "I just loved promoting cookbooks and working with the authors."

Evidently the cookbook authors loved her, too, and word of her unique services quickly spread throughout the culinary profession. Before long, she was handling just cookbooks and food-related clients, and Lisa Ekus Public Relations became well known as the only publicity firm around to specialize exclusively in the area of food. "I didn't set out to find the hot trend. I did it because I loved it. I was fortunate to be there at a time when publishers recognized that cookbooks were an area that could bring in tremendous revenue," she says. "There was lots of money to spend, and cookbook sales began to boom. And we were there."

And she's still there today. Lisa Ekus is a major player in the food industry. Her company has gained international recognition and represents a celebrity roster of cookbook authors and publishers, as well as a number of major food corporations. Business has ballooned over the last several years, and all the while Lisa Ekus has retained her niche in the food industry. She says that each year business has grown in volume and profits, yet virtually 99 percent of it remains focused on food.

Though her rise seems rapid, Ekus says that her business philosophy is actually based on the principle of slow, careful growth. She refused to take a line of credit on the business until she was established for five years, and it took her nearly two years to make her first hire. Whenever she takes on additional projects or expands in new directions, she tries to manage with her existing staff first, before increasing her head count and investing in extra equipment. "I never build the business based on an idea," says Ekus. "I make sure the idea can go before

I add more staff, even if it stresses us a bit. I've seen companies say, 'I'm going to expand here and here and here,' and they double and triple staffs, and then they're out of business. I always make sure I have more work than overhead."

Today, Lisa Ekus has a staff of employees and a spacious office facility in a converted barn located on the same property as her house.

What's next? Expansion beyond cookbooks is a definite. The company has started to do personal representation of very big-name culinary figures and restaurants, something Ekus says she resisted for a number of years. "I tend to let the business guide me," she explains. "I'll go down a number of roads simultaneously but follow them only partially, seeing what makes sense financially and timewise." Some ideas take off and go galloping down the road, while others wind up making no sense at all. No matter which road Lisa Ekus Public Relations travels next, one thing is for certain: It will have something to do with food.

Diversification Within a Niche

While specialization is the way to go for some businesses, others thrive on branching out. These companies usually start out quite simply—with a single idea for a product or service—then gradually expand over the years in new directions. That's how it was for Amy Kalman Epstein of The Straight Edge, Inc., which manufactures those colorful and educational Read a Mat Kids' placemats that have become mealtime lifesavers for moms everywhere.

Epstein came up with her unique business idea while taking an industrial design course. The homework assignment was to invent a new product, she recalls. "My five-year-old, Josh, was a very slow eater and refused to sit still long enough to finish a meal. So I created an illustrated vinyl placemat of the alphabet to keep him occupied during those endless mealtimes," Epstein says. "Josh suggested I add words, and the very first Read a Mat® was conceived." The wonderful result: Josh would eat and learn at the same time.

Epstein's instructor had invited a jury of industry experts to view the students' product prototypes, and Read a Mat® caught the eye of a department store buyer, who promised to carry it if Epstein could produce it. She was 8½ months pregnant at the time. Since she was about to go on maternity leave from her full-time urban planning job, it was a very low-risk venture. If it didn't work out, she had a job waiting. But Epstein never went back: The Straight Edge, Inc., was born the same year as daughter Abby.

Over the years, Epstein has looked to her children's interests and hobbies to discover new ideas for her ever-growing product line. She quickly expanded beyond the preschool market by creating illustrated placemats targeting grade school topics like the solar system, marine life, and multiplication tables. "I was often inspired by the subjects my children were studying in school," she says. But Epstein carefully controlled the growth of The Straight Edge so it wouldn't overtake her family life. "Raising great kids was more of a priority for me than my bottom line, and that guided how my business grew," she says. Once the operation got too big for her home, she moved just three blocks away so Josh and Abby could easily stop by after school.

Today, her company boasts a diversified line of educational products for children of all ages and includes Read a Mats®, Write a Mats®, Color a Mats®, and a variety of puzzles and books. How does she know what will work and what won't? "Walk your ideas around and ask questions," advises Epstein. "I've found an incredible spirit of helpfulness from buyers at stores, neighboring exhibitors at trade shows, and other parents—all of whom have given me great suggestions for improving and merchandising my products." Epstein also makes sure she reads all the letters she receives from customers. Not only does she find new directions to pursue, but she feels an enormous sense of gratification for her mission. "I've received millions of letters from parents saying that my placemats have taught their kids how to read—right at their kitchen tables."

MAKING MINOR ALTERATIONS

Your business doesn't have to go through big-time changes for it to be successful. Sometimes growth means just making a few nips and tucks here and there. After almost seven years in the desktop publishing business, Loraine Goodenough had enough data to evaluate her marketing plan and improve it. So on the second anniversary of the launch of her *Rainy Day Communique,* a marketing newsletter sent free of charge to customers and potential clients, she announced its demise. "After carefully analyzing my business goals and the effectiveness of my various marketing tools, I have determined that the *Rainy Day Communique* (RDC) is not earning its keep," she said in a letter to friends, clients, and loyal readers. "Many readers have said they love to read my newsletter, but the revenue directly attributable to the RDC after two years is not enough to justify the postage, materials, and time involved. Large corporations are not the only ones who downsize an overhead function like marketing to make more efficient use of finite resources," the owner of Rainy Day Business Services said. "This does not mean I'm going out of business. This does not mean I am slowing down my business. It means I am changing the focus of my business. My success is built on helping others succeed by writing and designing effective communications." By making this small change, Goodenough could concentrate on what she does best.

NURTURING YOUR BUSINESS CAN HELP NURTURE THE WORLD

When Vicki Esralew searched for nonviolent computer games for her three-year-old son, Jack, she came up empty-handed. Almost every piece of software she found promoted fighting or destruction. So with no background in software development, this self-proclaimed "mom on a mission" worked with a couple of techies in the basement of her house and produced "Jack's House"—an interactive game for the preschool set that promotes self-esteem and positive family bonding in a kid-appealing format. "I knew I could successfully market an entertaining and educational computer game without using violence as a theme," says Esralew. Her conviction led to the start-up of Kids Count Entertainment, a company dedicated to the production of multimedia products that help children grow and learn without the intrusion of violence. From the very beginning, way before she grew her business into a million-dollar-plus enterprise, Esralew donated 10 percent of her yearly profits to children's charities.

Kids Count Entertainment has since evolved into the Vickilew Company. The product line has shifted from the entertainment of children to the empowerment of families, but its focus on social responsibility remains as strong as ever. "As Kids Count grew, so did my awareness that parents were hungry for tools and information that would enable them to flourish in their role as parents and enrich their children's lives by laying a foundation for positive, esteem-building learning," says Esralew. Through her website, www.vickilew.com, she continues to offer groundbreaking software, workout videos, sleep tapes, and educational products, all supported by content-rich articles and resources endorsed by experts and embraced by moms. "I'm trying to create an environment, a sense of family, where children and adults can come to reach their full potential," she states. "My vision is to be the premier family resource site for the next generation."

CHANGING COURSE AND EXPLORING NEW FRONTIERS

Sometimes mompreneurs start with one idea but wind up in a completely different enterprise than the one they'd originally planned. There are others who cultivate one successful business and then yearn for a change of pace and a new entrepreneurial endeavor. Whether you're just shifting course or embarking on a new venture, each business move you make will be a stepping stone for future accomplishments. For example, Toby Myles of Olney, Maryland, ran a successful home-based graphic design and illustration business for several years with her husband, Jim, before deciding she needed a change of pace. So Myles, a longtime fitness buff, tapped into her passion and started her own personal training business.

Jane Monjar Bayer's business started off in one direction till she steered it in another. When she first got married and moved from California to Germany, she was on the lookout for home-based job opportunities. "I had worked for seven years as an aerospace engineer at McDonell Douglas and was burned out with my job because it involved lots of travel and eighty-plus-hour weeks. I needed more balance in my life," she says. At that point, it seemed most practical for the aerospace engineer and corporate pilot to explore other opportunities within her field. So she began doing engineering consulting for companies in Munich. She did this for about a year, till she had a baby. It was then that she realized that she wanted to get out of the aerospace industry altogether yet convert those skills to a new and different career that could be done from home.

With a friend of hers, Bayer began running a catch-all business called American Lifestyle Consultants from her home in Germany. "Everything American is popular over here," Bayer explains. "People were always asking me about American Christmas celebrations and birthday parties and traveling to California. It gave me this idea." The friends paired their skills and developed a company offering travel seminars, flight tutorials, personal training, party planning, television production, and other miscellaneous services—all with a distinctively American flavor. With two successful television projects in the works, American Lifestyles Consultants finally began making some real money. "If someone had told me years ago that I would be creating and selling television ideas to channels in Germany, I would have thought they were crazy," Bayer says. "It really proves that through hard work and determination, you can really do anything you set your mind to." This pilot's soar to success shows something else, too. When you begin your travels through mompreneurship, you never know where you might wind up.

Your current home business may be the springboard for a future enterprise. Lisa Ebbesen certainly proved that to be true. After ten years of running a successful day-care business in her Petaluma, California, home, this mompreneur was ready for a change. She got out of the child-care business and opened up a home-based word processing firm instead. But she didn't let her years of child-care experience go to waste. Ebbesen parlayed that knowledge to land assignments for her new company, where one of her major goals was to publish a newsletter for home day-care operators. Who would better understand the clients' needs than a mompreneur who was a day-care provider herself?

Connie Hallinan Lagan also used her previous mompreneur experience to forward a new business idea. Her first home venture, a crafts enterprise called Creations by Connie, sparked the idea for a second home-based business called the Entrepreneurial Center for Small Business Development. As executive director of the center, Lagan drew upon her own experiences as an entrepreneur and offered advice and support to hundreds of small business owners, many of them moms. She's come a long way from the days when she worked on her crafts projects while her four daughters played at her feet with cast-off scraps of fabric. Years have passed, her girls are confident career women, and Connie Hallinan Lagan is the inspiration for many other moms hoping for home-based success.

THE MOMPRENEUR GROWTH CHART
IS IT TIME TO . . .

HIRE A STAFF? COULD BE, IF:	MOVE BUSINESS OUTSIDE? COULD BE, IF:	SELL THE BUSINESS? COULD BE, IF:	RETURN TO A STAFF JOB? COULD BE, IF:
You're finding it impossible to do it all yourself.	The business has invaded every square inch of your home.	It's no longer fun for you.	You yearn to return to your prebusiness career or tackle a new one in the corporate world.
Business has really taken off, and you need extra help.	You need to expand staff and have no more room to do it.	You don't feel challenged.	You need health insurance and other benefits.
You can afford salaries and extra equipment.	You can afford to pay rent and additional overhead expenses.	Your company or equipment is attractive to buyers.	You want the security of a set salary and schedule.
You're increasingly frazzled and never seem to have enough time.	You're no longer able to effectively separate your business and family life.	You sense the time is right for a lucrative deal.	You can't deal with the isolation any longer.

HIRE A STAFF? COULD BE, IF:	MOVE BUSINESS OUTSIDE? COULD BE, IF:	SELL THE BUSINESS? COULD BE, IF:	RETURN TO A STAFF JOB? COULD BE, IF:
The business is constantly cutting into your family time.	Your kids are growing older and more independent.	You're feeling restless and ready to explore new frontiers.	Your children are older, and you don't need as much job flexibility.

BEEFING UP BUSINESS AND STAFF

It's wonderful to have a booming business, but not so wonderful to have to handle those ever-increasing duties all by yourself. As your business grows, you may find it necessary to recruit employees to lend a hand with the business.

Think about what duties you could delegate to someone else. Do you need help with the administrative tasks? Could you use a hand with the sales and marketing? Are there specific duties that are beyond your realm of expertise and require the experience of a hired specialist? By filling in these gaps with staff, you'll be freer to focus on what you do best.

You may not have to splurge on a full-time person; a part-timer or an independent contractor who works on a per-project basis may suffice. It's also possible to simply get a temp or lease an employee from a staff-leasing firm.

When evaluating whether you can afford to add employees, don't just think about what it will cost you. You've got to look at what you'll save by having a support system. Learn to put a dollar amount on your own time, stresses Gail Frankel, owner of Kel-Gar, Inc., a juvenile products company in Dallas, Texas. "You might be amazed at how much it's costing your company for you to handle everything yourself," she says. It's really cheaper to hire good people to do simpler tasks, she adds, so you can be free to deal with the things that demand your expert attention.

Early on in her business, Frankel realized she needed assistance with her order entry process. She hired a part-time person and slowly increased the staff member's hours over the years. "For my particular business, what's most important is developing more product," she points out. "In order for me to be free to continue to do that, I need someone else to take up the slack."

A good way to test the waters before actually hiring outside help is to tap into the talents of family members. If they're willing and energetic, they can lend a hand during the start-up stages or crunch times while you determine whether a permanent employee is necessary. But don't expect them to do it for free. Offer a small salary or other incentives to make it worth their while.

Joy Sacramone's first helpers in her housecleaning business were actually her daughters, who were around the ages of fourteen and eleven when she got started. Sacramone, who was a single mom, already had a full-time job at a state agency in Massachusetts. She wanted to send her girls to private schools, so she cleaned houses at night to drum up the money for tuition. As Sacramone tells it, "I said to the girls, 'This is for you to go to private schools, so you've got to help me. I can't do it alone.' I took them with me to people's houses, and they helped me clean. They were really very good."

Mother and daughters did such a great job that they came to the attention of a reporter for the *Boston Globe,* who wrote an article about them. From that article, Sacramone got over 100 calls, from which she culled a list of about twenty-five houses. Realizing that she and her daughters couldn't tackle those alone—after all, Sacramone still needed her day job with the state in order to survive—she hired one woman to help her. The two would clean homes around 6 in the morning so Sacramone could head to her full-time job afterward. Sacramone was lucky enough to have her mom living upstairs, to help make sure her daughters got out the door on time to school every day. At night, Sacramone would take the girls with her and get a few more houses done.

Those early, short-staffed days were really hard, she recalls. She'd leave her house in the morning wearing her cleaning duds and carrying her office clothes with her so she could change at the client's. "I remember my mother watching from the window and calling, 'Why are you doing that, Joy? Can't you get a real job ?' " Even her kids were worried that their friends might find out they were cleaning houses. "It was embarrassing for everybody," she says.

But her perseverance paid off, and soon Sacramone had so many customers she was able to quit her day job and expand her cleaning business. She gave it a clever name, Joy of Cleaning, and went about hiring more staff. "I put an ad in the paper that said, 'Housecleaning is not easy. If you are energetic and are really willing to work, call me.' " She gathered a wonderful team of women, many of whom are still with her today.

"I don't clean houses myself anymore because I really have a good force of women," Sacramone says. She pays them well, "because they're the best," but she thinks it's her family-friendly philosophy that makes her workers so loyal. From the start, Sacramone made a point of hiring mothers and letting them know their schedules could be flexible. "When I worked at my full-time job, the hardest thing was not being able to go to my daughters' school plays or field trips," she says. "So I tell my staff members, 'If you come to me and say you need Wednesday off because your daughter's going to be in a school play, you've got it off.' My staff has always told me that's the reason they've stayed with me so long. They know I understand that the kids really do come first."

HIRING HINTS

Things to do before you make your first hire:

Develop a job description. What do you need your employee to do? Write the specific duties down on paper so you're clear on what you want before you start looking for someone.

Establish a work schedule. What hours will your staff member work?

Start slowly. It's best to start with a part-time staffer so you can gauge how much help you really need and how much of a payroll your business can carry.

Consider hiring high school or college kids. The career centers at local schools can help you locate affordable part-time help and can also help you fill full-time positions during summers and other vacation periods. You may even be able to arrange for a college intern who earns credits and a small stipend for assisting you. Some might work for free, though many mompreneurs feel it is exploitative not to offer some kind of salary. If you hire an intern, however, make sure you assign the student more than just your grunt work. Internships are designed to be a learning experience and will be most successful if you can offer your interns the chance to handle rewarding responsibilities like letter writing, proposal planning, troubleshooting, design work, computer consulting, and any industry-specific tasks.

Spread the word that you're hiring. Tell everyone you can think of: friends, relatives, business associates, even your dentist. They just may know someone who's perfect for the job. If you advertise for the position, remember to tap into trade journals and association bulletin boards as well as newspapers.

Don't look for a clone of yourself. Hire people who are different from you, urges small business specialist and former cookie baker Cathy Bolton. They will bring a fresh perspective to the business and may even "teach you better ways to do things," Bolton says.

Find someone who can wear many hats. You'll want your workers to be able to handle a variety of duties. "My secretary actually baby-sat on occasion," admits Judy Lederman of JSL Publicity and Marketing. When you work at home, your staff may have to do a lot of pinch-hitting in several different areas.

Be explicit about job duties. Don't spring any surprises on your employees. Be clear about what on-the-job duties they can expect. If you think you might need your staff member to baby-sit occasionally, say so in the interview process, but also emphasize that this would be a rare occurrence. It's helpful, too, to find out what things the person hates to do, suggests Judy Lederman. Make sure that potential employees understand that they'll be working with kids around, she adds. Your staffers are going to have to cope with toys, noise, distractions, and other consequences of working for a mompreneur.

Check liability and legalities. Make sure your homeowner's insurance covers on-the-job mishaps, and be aware of the tax implications of having employees. (For more on this, see chapter 8.)

Be family-friendly. Offer the best perks you can, even if they're not monetary. One of the best benefits you can share with your workers is a family-friendly policy that allows employees to have flexible hours. It will pay off greatly and reward you with a staff that's loyal and eager to work hard.

DADDY JOINS THE COMPANY

That business you started solo could eventually lead to a joint venture with your husband. In the course of our research, we've met many mompreneurs who've happily partnered up with their spouses to run the business together.

Toby Myles knew all along that her husband, Jim Paterson, would one day join her home-based graphic design firm. "We went into our marriage with this in mind," she says. When they were in art school together, they'd collaborated on several projects and discovered they were a great team. They bought a house with ample room for a joint office, intending to one day merge Toby's design skills and Jim's illustration talents into a full-service graphic design/illustration company.

The plan was for Toby to get the business off the ground first. They didn't have kids yet, she explains, and figured they should get the business established before starting a family. She quit her job at a local design studio and started doing freelance work from home. Little by little, she developed her client base. In the meantime, Jim kept his full-time job (and benefits) at a local trade association but arranged to work from home about half of the time. This enabled him to take on freelance illustration work (something his employer had no problem with) and cultivate his own stable of clients. As time went on, Toby built up the business and brought in the bulk of the revenue, designing corporate logos and marketing materials. Occasionally, she'd freelance out any illustration work to her favorite resident artist, Jim.

Four years and two children later, Jim finally joined the company full-time. They incorporated and called their firm Myles and Paterson. It offered a complete menu of design, illustration, and writing services and enabled them to offer clients a much wider range of services than before.

That doesn't mean the couple worked jointly on everything. Though they shared some clients—companies with both design and illustration needs—the majority of their work fell into the "his" or "hers" categories, depending on the area of expertise needed. Each spouse retained an independent set of clients. Toby concentrated on design work for large corporations such as power companies, public relations agencies, and accounting firms that required design expertise. Jim mainly did illustrations for newspapers, trade association magazines, and ad agencies. His writing background allowed him to offer certain editorial services as well.

"As we added to our family, our business grew," Toby Myles says. "Not necessarily in the amount of work, but in the quality of the projects. We were consistently able to do better each year in terms of income." Working together allowed Myles and Paterson to achieve a lifestyle they loved.

Sometimes husbands help out from the sidelines, without officially being part of their wives' businesses. When Elise Ravenscroft first began wooing potential clients for her desktop publishing company, she brought her spouse along with her to the pitch meetings. "By providing a team approach with a large base of knowledge (my husband worked for a printing company), we were able to handle most questions on the spot, rather than have an 'I'll get back to you' attitude," the Maryland mother notes. What Elise didn't realize, however, was that many of the clients she talked to just assumed that it was her husband who was running the show, not her. "In a time of what we want to believe of as equality for all, most companies prefer talking to a man," she says. Even though her husband would defer many questions to his wife during the meetings, people would turn to him for the explanations about the business's capabilities and advice on desktop publishing jobs. "Many found it hard to believe that he was not the genius behind the scene," she recalls. Still, having her husband's input early on helped Ravenscroft snatch the start-up projects she needed to get the business up and running. Those meetings taught her that she'd need to increase her confidence as well as her printing knowledge if she wanted to stay successful. She's made an effort to learn the ins and outs of the printing world so she no longer has to depend on her husband's expertise.

Ravenscroft now attends meetings by herself and has an excellent sense of what people want and may need to know. She became an expert in every area of her business. And though she occasionally turns to her husband for help with prepress problems, she is her own boss!

MILLION-DOLLAR BABY

Jody Kozlow Gardner and Cherie Serota were both marketing executives at New York's upscale Henri Bendel department store when they conceived the idea for a unique line of maternity wear. "There was a distinct lack of chic clothes available for moms-to-be," says Serota who was pregnant at the time. "We thought someone should invent a maternity wardrobe made up of hip, basic black mix-and-match pieces." She and Kozlow Gardner would go out for coffee after work and sketch clothing designs on the coffee shop napkins. Their vision: the Pregnancy Survival Kit—stretchy black leggings, skirt, dress, and tunic, bundled together in a little white box, and sold on main floors of department stores to catch the eyes of all shoppers. They decided to pursue their venture and call their company Belly Basics.

By networking with everyone they knew, they located a sample maker for the clothing patterns and a printer to do the packaging. To protect their idea, a lawyer friend suggested they make even closest friends sign a confidentiality agreement and that they trademark their product and company names. Once the prototype was ready, the partners lined up a contractor who could quickly manufacture it if necessary and they began to shop their idea around to department store buyers.

They took the Pregnancy Survival Kit to Bloomingdale's, where a buyer flipped over the groundbreaking concept. Bloomies launched seventy of them on (appropriately enough) Labor Day weekend. By Monday they were sold out. Bloomingdale's chairman called them into his office and told them, "I want to make this a million-dollar business by Christmas." And he did.

Today, Belly Basics has instant name recognition with moms all over the world. The company's line has expanded to include sweaters, jackets, pants, jeans, dresses, workout wear, accessories, diaper bags, hosiery, and even skincare—all sold internationally in department stores, boutiques, and online at Bellybasics.com. The partners have even authored a book called *Pregnancy Chic: The Fashion Survival Guide* (Villard Books). "We knew we'd really made it when women started telling us they wanted to get pregnant just so they could wear our clothes!" they laugh.

SUCCESS STRATEGY: "Take everything step-by-step," recommends Kozlow Gardner. "We tried to focus on one detail at a time, like the clothing label or the box design. That way the obstacles didn't seem so insurmountable."

BIGGEST WORK/FAMILY CHALLENGE: Serota recalls the time she had to bring her three-year-old along to a big meeting with a Nordstrom buyer. "Jody had just given birth and was home with her newborn, and I was in between baby-sitters." To keep her son Stephen quiet through the meeting, Serota enticed him with candy. "There I was, shoving chocolate into his mouth while I tried to get a few sentences in with the buyer so I could sell our line. Stephen kept asking for more, so finally I gave him the whole bowl. I had to sacrifice my son's teeth for the business! We got the order, but after the buyer left Stephen was bouncing off the walls with a sugar high!" Fortunately, clients are usually understanding at times like these, say these mompreneurs. After all, their product *is* all about being a mom!

FUTURE GOALS: To fulfill their mission statement to "provide everything a pregnant woman needs" and follow her through every stage of mommyhood. Serota and Kozlow Gardner will continue to tap into their own experience as parents (they now have five children between them!) to create clever products that moms can't live without, such as the "Mommy Tote," a chic bag with pockets for stashing kids' snacks and sippee cups.

MAKING YOUR HUBBY YOUR BUSINESS PARTNER: TIPS FOR A WINNING RELATIONSHIP

Do you take this man to be your lawfully wedded business partner? Do you promise to love him and cherish him in slow times and busy times? In profit and in debt? With child care and without? Till death do you part—or at the very least, until you decide to close down or sell off the business?

Before you say "I do," think carefully about the commitment you're entering into. A successful husband/wife business partnership is just like a marriage. It requires lots of loyalty, communication, and mutual admiration and respect.

We've talked to lots of successful couples who have told us how they keep their marriages and their businesses running smoothly. Here's what they say are the keys to success.

Start with a Solid Foundation

Make sure you and your husband have a good personal relationship, cautions Sarah Edwards, who with her husband, Paul, co-authors books on home-based businesses. "If your relationship is troubled, running a home business together won't save your marriage."

Agree on the Basics

You and your husband should share the same basic vision for the company. Discuss how much time, money, and energy you're willing to invest in the venture, and be sure the two of you are in total agreement, advises Allan Ferguson, who founded an infant toy company with his wife, Ruth Wimmer. Wimmer adds that it's essential to keep negotiating and talking about these things over the years to make sure your goals remain the same. "We've tuned in with one another on all these issues throughout the years we've been in business. And our decisions for the future all hinge upon how much we are willing to commit," she says.

Define Your Roles

"Establish what each of you likes to do so you can separate the responsibilities clearly," suggests Toby Myles who launched a Maryland graphic design firm with her husband Jim Paterson. "There was no competition between us because we divided our talents."

Write Yourself a Job Description

When Allan Ferguson and Ruth Wimmer first teamed up to form their company, they actually wrote job descriptions for themselves. Wimmer would be in charge of the product research, design, development, and shipping. Her husband handled the sales and marketing. They agreed to tackle certain areas together, such as the general planning, financial analysis, and packaging issues. Having job descriptions has helped them delineate and refine their duties over the years they've been in business together. When drawing up the boundaries, just remember that you're equal partners, counsels Sarah Edwards. "A couple should come into their home business as peers. One shouldn't be the helper and the other the boss."

Lean on Each Other

Pinpoint your own weaknesses and strengths as well as your partner's. Then know the areas where you can best help each other out. "It's advantageous to bring different personalities and abilities to the business," says Ferguson, "so that as partners, you complement each other." His wife is a "real good editor," he says, so he'll often have her read over the marketing materials he writes. Of her husband, Wimmer says, "He has a great analytical mind and the ability to sum things up. He can look at a situation and assess it and figure out where to go with it. And that's something I'm not as good at. We really are a good balance for one another."

California couple Liana and Svante Rodergard also used their differences to benefit their business. In running their Emeryville computer exporting firm, they learned exactly in which areas they could rely on each other for support. Liana Rodergard describes her husband as a great salesperson with terrific people skills. But, she says, she's a better judge of character. So Svante Rodergard frequently ran people by her for a thumbs up or thumbs down.

Give and Accept Criticism Graciously

It's not always easy to accept your partner's assessment, particularly when it is different from yours and is offered in the final hour of a deadline. You'll both have to learn when to critique and when to keep quiet. At the beginning of their business partnership, Myles and Paterson found themselves seeking each other's project approval at the last minute. This led to a few late-night conflicts. To avoid these, the couple began involving each other more at the onset of a design job. "We'd brainstorm together at the start," says Myles, reviewing each other's ideas and thumbnail sketches first and offering feedback. "Then we'd go our separate ways," Myles says.

Pick Your Battles

"It's important to put petty disagreements aside and focus on the success of the business," says Wimmer. "This is not the place to battle with your spouse." Joanne Walthall, a New Yorker who imports picture frames and home accessories with her husband, agrees. "I try not to get into a competitive thing with my husband, because we're both very competitive people. I often back off, unless it's something I feel very strongly about. For example, when we started the business, he wanted to rent showroom space in a building on Fifth Avenue, but I wanted to keep our overhead down by being home-based. I finally convinced him to stay home. If you don't argue about too many things, it's easy to win a few."

When you have opposing views on a matter, Ruth Wimmer suggests you think about whether it is going to make a difference in the business, and then figure out how much to dig in your heels regarding your own perspective. If you can't come to agreement, it's helpful to consult with an objective third party who can offer advice so it won't "be a one-to-one split vote." The advisor could be a friend or family member, a fellow business owner or colleague, or your accountant or attorney. Just make sure that it is someone you trust and respect, who will offer you both an impartial opinion, Wimmer and Ferguson stress.

Keep the Lines of Communication Open

Ongoing communication with your spouse is essential. Running a business together requires a lot of active listening. "Express things as they come up," advises Liana Rodergard. "Don't fume about stuff."

One of the perks of working side-by-side, mentions Toby Myles, is that it gives you the opportunity to banter with each other during the day and problem-solve together. Although this informal repartee does keep you connected, it's also a good idea to set aside regular times for more extensive shop talk. When they can, Joanne Walthall and her husband, Stuart Kramer, schedule morning meetings in the dining room, where they discuss the day ahead with coffee cups in hand. If you have pressing business or family issues to attend to, it's helpful to get out of the house and do it on neutral territory. "When we really needed to discuss something, we'd go to lunch," says Liana Rodergard. Toby Myles and Jim Paterson also found lunch dates a great way to get a change of scenery and key into each other's feelings without phones ringing and faxes whirring in the background.

Designate Your Workspace

"To maintain your own sanity, establish a separate, clearly defined workspace from your spouse," advises Sarah Edwards. That could mean working from separate offices or having your own work stations in a common space. Joanne Walthall and Stuart Kramer started out with two desks in the same workspace, a small maid's room off the kitchen. Her messiness drove him crazy, so she moved her desk to the den on the complete opposite side of their New York City apartment. She now has the computer and a view of the Hudson River. He has the fax machine. They both have phones and their own set of files.

If you're in the same room, set the boundaries for which equipment and areas you will both use. The Rodergards worked from separate desks and phones in the dining room, but shared the use of the PC. Myles and Paterson worked directly across from each other in the basement. Each had their own desk, computer, and file cabinet, but they shared the printer, fax, and copy machine. Both had easy access to a center table, which housed envelopes, stamps, packing tape, and other supplies. "Jim joked that I took over more of the space," laughs Myles, "but I'd say it was because I was there first."

Tolerate Each Other's Work Styles

Is he a neat freak while you've got paper piled in every corner? You're going to have to learn to put up with each other's work habits. Because her husband is a night person who often works evenings, Ruth Wimmer learned that their schedules were likely to vary. The couple is careful not to draw rigid lines about work hours. Another mompreneur grew to accept the fact that her husband and business partner wasn't as organized as she was. You must simply respect each other's styles and treat one another like grown-ups.

Share the Parenting Responsibilities

"If you work together, you have more empathy for each other's situations," says Liana Rodergard. You also have more flexibility to split the parenting and child-care duties. "Running a business together allowed us both to raise our daughter," says Wimmer, who notes that she and Ferguson are equal partners in parenting as well as in business. "We give each other breaks with the child-care," says Liana Rodergard. Myles and Paterson have each taken one full day off a week to spend with the kids. Raising a child together prepares you well for running a joint business adds Joanne Walthall. She says that solving conflicts with a two-year-old really taught her and her husband how to work things out in the business.

Know When to Turn Off the Work

The danger of working with your spouse is that it becomes even more difficult to separate work from family life. You'll have to find little ways to keep the business from becoming all-consuming. "We try to avoid business talk at the dinner table," says Allan Ferguson. Myles and Paterson didn't go back to their offices till after the kids were in bed. They also tried not to discuss work on the weekends. "We'd just say, 'We're not going to talk about it,' and the first person to talk about business had to give the other a back rub. It usually worked," says Toby Myles.

BABY ON BOARD

Did you ever dream that the little baby who inspired you to become home-based could one day help you run your company? As your business and kids mature, you may find your offspring ready and willing to do more than merely lend a hand with the stapling or the collating. When they grow up, some children become pivotal players in their moms' businesses.

Ann Clark's cookie-cutter business has always been focused on the family. This Vermont mom found so much joy in baking cookies with her children that she decided to start a business that would help other families share that special bond. Her company, Ann Clark, Ltd., produces cookie cutters in the shapes of animals and other whimsical designs. Each one is tied with yarn and accompanied with a homespun hand-decorated card featuring one of Clark's family cookie recipes. "Our cutters give people a warm and fuzzy feeling," says Clark. Popular with collectors, the cutters are also frequently bought by working parents who are looking for ways to create traditions and carve out family time. Ann Clark, Ltd., has grown from a small home-based enterprise to a $2-million-a-year empire, run from manufacturing headquarters in Rutland, Vermont. Yet the company remains a family affair. Son Ben now runs the business, daughter Elizabeth handles promotional products, and Clark focuses on creating new product ideas.

Tracia Ledford's daughter, Katelyn, grew up working alongside her mom. As Tracia developed columns and crafts for national magazines and trade publications, her preschooler sat beside her and dabbled with her paints and supplies. At holiday time, the two would collaborate on Christmas ornaments and other hand-crafted gifts for friends and family. Once Katelyn was school-age, venturing into a Mom and Me design business was a logical step. Their work has been featured in magazines, children's how-to books, and on television crafts shows.

Katelyn enjoyed making crafts and "was able to express her creativity through our work," says her mother. The youngster learned lots about television and magazine production and the discipline required to run a business. She experienced the thrill of seeing her work in print and on TV and reaped some monetary rewards as well. A paint company that sponsored Katelyn's designs paid the youngster in savings bonds, helping her build a nice little nest egg for her future. Will that future include staying in the crafts business? Not even her mom can predict that one, but you can be sure that Tracia Ledford will never force her daughter to continue something that's no longer fun. "It's important that she likes what's she's doing," her mom emphasizes.

That's an essential point to keep in mind when you work with your kids. Even if you involve your children in your day-to-day operations when they're young, don't expect that they'll automatically want to be part of the business as adults. Though both of Joy Sacramone's daughters grew up helping their mom with her house cleaning service, only one of them has made the business a career. "My younger one had no desire to do this for a living," Joy Sacramone notes. But eldest daughter Laureen Hadley became a bona fide partner in the business. Not only that, she's a full-fledged mompreneur, too. Today, Hadley runs a branch of Joy of Cleaning out of her own home in Salem, Massachusetts, which allows her ample time to be with her daughter, Olivia.

Moving Up and Out

Not all successful mompreneurships can remain at home, however. When a business really takes off, it also has a tendency to take over every nook and cranny of your house. You can reach the point where moving out is the only solution if you want your business to continue to grow.

If you have a product-based service, you may be able to move just part of the business to a warehouse facility while keeping your central business operations at home. That's what Hannah Vago did with her New Rochelle, New York, gift basket business. She used her home-based office for processing orders and other paperwork and handled assembly and shipping from a warehouse that she rented in a local shopping center.

How do you know when it's time to move the business completely out of the house? It wasn't one telltale sign but rather a bunch of little things that told Judy Lederman her publicity and marketing business had grown too big for her Irvington, New York, home. She had to climb over her secretary to reach the file cabinet. Her block filled up with cars whenever she conducted a client meeting. She was constantly trekking to the attic and basement to retrieve office supplies. Her pens and pencils were buried under Barbie accessories, Lego blocks, and plastic spiders (thanks to her three kids). Lederman frequently signed for FedEx packages in crayon. Then there were the times that her children burst into client meetings stark naked or ran in terror from the "fax monster." The real breaking point came one day when her husband was home sick with the flu. The poor guy was trying to rest, and phones were ringing and secretaries were scurrying around in every part of the house. "He thought he was having hallucinations of being back in the office," Lederman says. Shortly after that, Lederman moved her business to a commercial space not too far from home. JSL Publicity and Marketing had a spacious Southwestern-style office, and the Lederman family had their home to themselves once again.

The space crunch was the main factor that drove Gail Frankel to relocate Kel-Gar, Inc., her Dallas juvenile products company, to commercial space. After five fruitful years of working from home, she had more product and staff than ever before, and she was just running out of room to put it all. The move outside has rewarded her with more than just space. It's allowed a physical separation of work and family life. At home, "the business had become all-consuming," she says. "It was very hard for me not to run into my office and answer the business phone or check the fax machine," even if it was late at night. With an outside office, she finds it easier to turn off at the end of the day.

Oklahoma T-shirt designer Judy Fisher also found that moving her business out of the house helped put a barrier between business and family duties. As her silk-screened T-shirt emporium grew, she found herself stressed out trying to please her husband, kids, and customers all at the same time. "A lot of my time with the kids was spent saying, 'Let's hurry, I've got to print these shirts by 2!'." The business was quickly blossoming beyond her control. Luckily, a unique opportunity arose to change things. She heard about an incubator program at a government-run vocational-technical center about fifteen miles from home. The program gave small businesses an affordable way to rent retail space. Fisher was able to set up a rent-free space at the center for six months and then pay just a small monthly rent after that. With the help of a low-interest loan from a SEEDS program, she bought more equipment and operated from there for about three years, before relocating to a shop in her hometown.

Setting up a booth at major crafts shows also helped keep the orders rolling in. Because her time was limited, Fisher only attended very large shows that attracted crowds of over 100,000. "I used to do a lot of small ones and spend lots of weekends and holidays away while someone else raised my kids." But focusing her energy on just eight large shows instead helped conserve her precious, irreplaceable family time.

When you move your business out of the house, you'll be able to expand and explore, yet you'll always have the option of returning home again one day. When Ruth Wimmer and Allan Ferguson began developing their high-contrast baby toys from home, Ruth's desk was crammed beneath the furnace ductwork. It didn't stay there for long. The award-winning black-and-white toys became so popular that the couple had to move to larger outside quarters twice in ten years. Before they sold their company, they had a corporate office in Denver, Colorado, not far from where they live, but that's not where you'd find this husband-and-wife team. They had come full circle and both ended up back in their home offices, away from the main business location.

EXPERIMENTAL BUSINESS SEES EXPLOSIVE GROWTH

To daughter Kelly and sons John and Evan, Jennifer Moorehead is simply "Mom." But to the hundreds of children who participate in her after-school science clubs, Moorehead is known by her scientific nicknames: "Jupiter Jen," "Jenergy," and "Jenifang." That's because this Blue Ball, Pennsylvania, mompreneur can usually be found launching rockets, demonstrating the principles of physics, and dissecting fascinating creatures to an audience of captivated grade-schoolers.

Started in September of 1999, Moorehead's company, Science Explorers, Inc., offers a variety of hands-on science literacy programs, with titles such as *It Takes Guts* (a tour through the human body), *Mission Control* (exploring space and its outer limits), *I Spy Science* (investigative science at its best), and *Serendipity Science* (cool science that was discovered by accident). Moorehead also offers summer science camps, as well as science-themed birthday parties.

Schools provide the meeting space, and parents pay the program fees. "Kids learn early on that science can be fun," says Moorehead. "And the parents get excited because their kids can come home and give them a whole dissertation on the water molecule."

SUCCESS STRATEGIES: In an attempt to raise start-up capital, Moorehead entered the Ben Franklin Business Plan Competition, sponsored by Ben Franklin Technology Partners (www.bftc-cnp.org), an economic development agency that provides funding and start-up support to fledgling companies in Pennsylvania. The winner of the contest would receive $25,000 for business development. Along with nine other finalists, Moorehead was required to present her business plan to a foreboding panel of judges that included bank officials, venture capitalists, and accounting executives. "My husband stayed home with the kids, but my father came along for moral support," she says. "I felt like my dad finally saw me as a grown-up that day." As her proud papa looked on, Moorehead whizzed through a PowerPoint presentation detailing her business. Then she wowed the judges by whipping out ingredients like lemon extract, purple cabbage juice, and raw meat and conducting some hands-on science experiments. She won the coveted prize. Today, Moorehead's company, Science Explorers, Inc., employs over twenty part-time teachers, as well as several full-time staffers (including a curriculum writer who works from home). Though she still hosts some of the school presentations herself, she's delegated most of those duties so she can now focus her efforts on running and growing her business.

BIGGEST WORK/FAMILY CHALLENGE: Fitting her staff, kids, dog, and boxes of scientific supplies into her small home-based office. "We were all squeezed into the converted garage, and the kids were constantly getting into my inventory of experiments and trying to create explosions and make slime while I was trying to work." Finally, she found it necessary to move her business out of the house and into roomier rented space. But she still works frequently from her home office. "I have glass doors that separate my office from the rest of the house," she explains. "When I need quiet, I lock the doors on my side, so I can keep an eye on the kids without them being able to barge in." Still, Moorehead admits that the solution isn't sound-proof. "There have been many times I've been on business calls and the kids have gotten too rowdy." What does she do? "I hold up giant cue cards that say things like 'Please Be Quiet!' or 'Stop Hitting Your Sister!' "

FUTURE GOALS: To expand Science Explorers through the web and eventually offer franchise opportunities nationwide.

TWELVE THINGS TO CONSIDER WHEN MOVING YOUR OFFICE OUT OF THE HOME

"Taking your business out of the home is one of the scariest moves you can make," says Judy Lederman, of JSL Publicity and Marketing in Irvington, New York. But there are some strategies that can help you leave home without having a nervous breakdown, she says. She should know. She moved her business out of her home and into a spacious and homey new corporate setting and is now home-based again. She suggests you ponder these important points when making your move:

1. *Consider your long-term plan.* Use your past history to determine the future of your business. Think about your company's growth to date. Have you been expanding steadily and turning a solid profit? Ask yourself where you expect your business to be in five years. This will help you determine how much space you will need and how much money you should be spending.

2. *Calculate how much space you'll need.* Based on your long-term business projections, figure out how much space you'd need immediately, two years from now, and five years down the road. If you can afford it, get yourself a big enough space to grow into.

3. *Research the cost of rental space.* It helps to know the going rates for different types of commercial space in your area. Check the real estate listings and network with fellow business owners to get a feel for what's out there and how much it costs.

4. *Figure out what you can afford.* Before actually looking for rental space of your own, carefully figure out your typical monthly operating costs as a home-based business. Then add on the estimated amount you might spend on rent. This gives you a good starting figure with which to work. Will you be able to carry it? Don't forget that you'll also need to factor in money for extras like office furniture and equipment.

5. *Search for office space that's close to home.* The transition to an outside office will be much easier on you and the kids if you're just minutes away from home and school. Don't be discouraged if there are no real office buildings in your town. Some smaller businesses may have storefronts you can rent. Just walk in and ask.

6. *Factor in your other needs.* Of course, space and price are most important, but there are other essential things to consider when renting. You should make sure your landlord has a good reputation for taking care of the tenants. You'll also want to check that there's ample parking. And don't forget to find out whether there's adequate climate control and access to a cleaning service.

7. *Don't use a commercial realtor.* If you're looking for space under 2,000 square feet, you're better off hunting on your own. Commercial realtors usually deal with clients who need huge blocks of space. While they may show you spaces in large buildings, it's likely that commercial realtors have saved all the juicy spots for their bigger clients. You could end up with a pricey out-of-the-way office on an undesirable floor. You'll get a better deal and probably a nicer space if you go directly to the buildings you're interested in and start asking questions.

8. *Know what you're getting.* When you find a space you like, be sure you're clear on what amenities and responsibilities come with it. Read your lease carefully, have your lawyer review it, and keep in mind that everything is negotiable. Remember, too, that you're likely to give up many of the conveniences you enjoyed at home: the kitchen one room away, the powder room down the hall, a security system or air conditioning, and evening and weekend access.

9. *Have a decorating budget.* You'll want to have enough money set aside to decorate your new digs tastefully. You can cut costs by doing it yourself, but if you don't have an artistic flair or too much time, it's best to hire a professional. Figure out what you can afford to spend on decorating and then find a professional decorator who can deliver the look you want without going over your limit. Clear your décor with your landlord before you proceed.

10. *Have dependable child care.* The stress and upheaval of moving your office outside the home can be tough on you and your family. You'll be relying even more on your caregiver for support, so make sure your child-care situation is solid. If it's not, you, your family, and your business are all likely to suffer.

11. *Market your move.* Make sure people know you've expanded into a bigger and better space. Send out press releases on your new office and your staff. Consider throwing an opening party to celebrate with all your customers, vendors, and clients. If you can afford to, purchase promotional items to let people know your new address. Now more than ever, you will need new business to keep your company solvent, so don't be shy about spreading the word.

12. *Hang in there.* A move is like starting your business all over again. You'll have lots of new bills to get used to—rent, phone, and computer lines—and it will take some time for you to adjust to the higher operating costs of commercial space. You'll feel a change in your work/family routine, too, once your children are no longer a scream away from your office. Eventually, you'll get comfortable with this new phase of mompreneurship. With lots of hard work and a little luck, your business will continue to grow as the years go on.

SELLING THE BUSINESS

Why in the world would you want to sell the business you've raised from infancy through adulthood? There can be many reasons, but the answer we hear most often is that it was simply time for change.

After ten years of running Write Away, an invitation, calligraphy, and personalized stationery business from her Scarsdale, New York, home, Pat Kornfeld had had enough. The challenge was fading, and the need to have a home-based business was no longer as urgent now that her children were older and more independent. "In a retail business like mine, you must make each person feel like the only customer, so I went all out to do this. It eventually took its toll on my three children." Kornfeld decided she was ready to get out of the business altogether and set out to sell her enterprise. Similar circumstances led Cathy Bolton to sell her Oklahoma gourmet bakery. "I got to the point where I was tired of managing people," she says. "The fun part of the business was gone."

Both mompreneurs found buyers completely by luck. "Through word of mouth, I heard that the woman who ran the local shipping/postal box franchise that I patronized was selling her business and looking for something new to do," recalls Kornfeld. "I asked if she was interested in buying Write Away, and she was." Cathy Bolton figured she'd just wait and see if she got any nibbles on her business and was prepared to wait quite a while. "My timetable was to phase out in about six months," she says. One day, a gentleman came into the shop, she explains, and made an outstanding offer on her equipment, which he would use for a business he had elsewhere. The only caveat, Bolton says, was that the man needed the ovens and other gourmet machinery in just one month. Bolton would have to close up shop much sooner than she had expected. "I felt like I was betraying my customers," she says of the town members who were so supportive of her all along. Still, the offer was too good to pass up. At the same time she finalized the sale, Bolton also sent postcards out to all her customers, telling them she was closing and thanking them for their loyal patronage.

Kornfeld and Bolton contend that knowing what your business is worth and what components of it you're willing to sell are the keys to a smooth sale. "To figure out my asking price, I consulted with my financial analyst husband and itemized all the components of the business (computer, calligraphy system, books from the printers, etc.)," says Kornfeld. "The hardest part was putting a value on my business name." But she did, and the deal was finalized. Cathy Bolton wasn't interested in putting a price on her name. "I wasn't going to sell my name or my recipes," the owner of Cathy's Cookies, Etc. notes. She calculated what her equipment was worth so that she'd know a good offer when she heard it.

There's no foolproof formula for knowing when the time is right for selling. "It's really an intuitive thing," says Bolton. "I just had a gut instinct that it was time." Adds Allan Ferguson, who sold the juvenile products company he ran with his wife, Ruth Wimmer, "You have to know when to hold 'em and know when to fold 'em." Of course, you also have to consider market and financial factors and have insights into what the business needs and whether you're prepared to give it, he says. Most of all, you have to key into your personal evolution over the years you've been in the business, says his wife and partner, Ruth Wimmer. "When I stopped having fun, I knew it was time to wrap up the business and start learning new things."

RETURNING TO THE TRADITIONAL WORKFORCE WITH A NEW UNDERSTANDING

Where do former mompreneurs head after they've exited their businesses? Many reenter the traditional work world on either a part-time or full-time basis and find that they have a wealth of knowledge and experience to bring to the job.

About a year after she got out of the baking business, Cathy Bolton returned to the traditional workforce in a full-time job that seemed tailor-made for her. She took a position as a small business specialist at a local technology center, where she worked one-on-one with people who wanted to start businesses, taking them from the idea stage to preparing the business plan to strategic planning and developing operations manuals. Part of the job also included speaking to groups and associations about small businesses, something she's always loved and had done as a businesswoman.

This full-time job gave Bolton a new forum for her entrepreneurial experience and brought her talents to the attention of many powerful people. She was appointed as a delegate to the White House Conference on Small Business and was invited to make a presentation to the Oklahoma House of Representatives' Special Committee on Small Business. She is also the recipient of the Small Business Administration's Women in Business Advocate Award at both state and regional levels. "Home-based business has provided me with a world of opportunities," Bolton says.

Suzanne Israel Tufts is another mompreneur who proved that home business skills are a valuable commodity in the regular work world. This New Yorker was running a home-based consulting firm, specializing in nonprofit organizations and government affairs, before she joined the American Woman's Economic Development Corporation (AWED) as president and CEO. AWED is an organization that supports women entrepreneurs and offers workshops and conferences that teach businesswomen to realize their moneymaking potential. "I think the AWED search committee felt that I could bring the real-world experience of running a business to their organization," Tufts says. Tufts has firsthand knowledge of the challenges that women business owners face. "I've been a lawyer, worked on campaigns, been in a senior government position, and still I had a hard time pricing my own services and negotiating for consulting contracts," she says. "You can have all kind of technical skills, but knowing how to run a business is completely different."

In her high-profile position as president of AWED, Tufts uses many of the skills she cultivated when running her own firm, such as program development, risk management, and coalition-building. Now that she's back in the corporate world, she's passing along her knowledge and helping other women discover the enormous power of entrepreneurship.

SELLING YOURSELF BACK TO THE TRADITIONAL WORK WORLD

Leaving your business to return to corporate life? Remember to emphasize your mompreneur skills when interviewing for new positions. "Once you've run a business, you are the most responsible worker a company could ever want," notes Suzanne Israel Tufts. Cathy Bolton agrees. "Look at the full range of experience you've gotten in running a business," she says—from bookkeeping to troubleshooting to marketing to management.

When a potential employer asks "Why should I hire you?" Cathy Bolton says these are the important skills to play up in your answer.

Strategic Planning

You're an expert at developing a course of action and following it through.

Self-Starting Abilities

You're disciplined, focused, and hardworking. You don't need anyone else to motivate you to get a job done.

Problem-Solving

You're a pro at finding creative ways to solve problems that come up on the spur of the moment. You're quick-thinking and adaptable, with a desire to find solutions that will best benefit the business.

People Skills

You've dealt with many different types of people, all with their distinct personalities. Your interactions with clients, vendors, employees, customers, and other business professionals have given you great insight into the right and wrong ways to manage people. You're a terrific listener.

You've Constantly Got Your Eye on the Bottom Line

You're used to looking at things in terms of dollars and cents. When you make decisions, you always keep finances and cost-effectiveness in mind. And you certainly know how to stick to a budget.

LEAVING HOME?

Prepare Yourself and Your Family for the Big Move

Whether you're relocating your business to commercial office space or shutting it down completely so you can work outside the home, the change can be hard to get used to. When Suzanne Israel Tufts accepted her full-time job as the president of the American Woman's Economic Development Corporation (AWED) after years of running her home business, she found it was quite an adjustment. It was especially hard for her daughter, Abigail, who was used to having Mommy around. In the beginning, Tufts says her daughter would ask, "Can't you stay home with me?" and "Why are you going to the office?"

Here's how to help make the transition easier for everyone involved: *Let your kids know what to expect.* "I spoke to Abigail about it almost a month before I went back," Tufts says. Explain what the work day will be like for both of you. Make sure the kids understand who will be caring for them while you're working. Be honest about how things will change, but also stress the positives of the new arrangement. It helps to plan some special events or outings with your children before your new job starts.

Phase in slowly. Tufts's first week on the job was a partial one. "I needed that as much as my daughter," she says.

Expect it to be rough at first. "It's really like going back to running a marathon when you haven't worked out," Tufts explains. "You underestimate the amount of effort that getting out of the house takes. It's going to take you a few weeks, if not months, to get back in the swing of it."

Keep an upbeat attitude. "Treat this as something normal, exciting, happy, and vibrant," encourages Tufts. Your enthusiasm will spread to the whole family.

Find work/daytime rituals to connect you to your kids. Tufts and Frankel talk with their children by phone every day after school. "It's something my mother started with me," says Tufts. "No matter what I was doing, at 3:00 when I came home, I called my mom and told her what went on during the day." Traditions like this can ease the separation anxiety for both you and your children. Frankel also finds it helpful to have the kids lend a hand at the office whenever possible. She has them come in and help out with the copying and other jobs and also involved them in the decorating of her new office. Her two boys had a big say in which of their drawings, photographs, and other home mementos would look best in Mom's new space.

Learn to leave the office at the office. "Don't make your home your office," cautions Tufts. One of the wonderful perks about working outside the home is that you can leave the work there at the end of the day.

As Frankel says, when you're at home, "There's always something that you could do."

CRISSCROSSING

For moms who aren't yet ready to give up their businesses completely to return to the traditional nine-to-five workforce, there is a way to have the best of both worlds. We call it crisscrossing. Crisscrossing is moving back and forth between self-employment and the traditional work world. It's a luxury of mompreneurship that allows you to keep your foot in the corporate door until you're ready to reenter it permanently. Crisscrossing gives you the chance to try out different types of full- or part-time jobs, yet still have your business to fall back on.

For us, crisscrossing has been a quick fix for those periods when we've felt especially isolated and begun fantasizing of what it would be like to be in the full-time ranks once again. From time to time in our careers, both of us have taken freelance magazine projects that required us to work on-site for months at a time. We found these opportunities offered us an exhilarating and financially secure way to mingle with our colleagues in the corporate world again—all without having to give up our home businesses. Other mompreneurs have discovered the same.

Ann McGrath Condon, a freelance writer in West Hartford, Connecticut, is always on the lookout for part-time jobs or short-term projects that can supplement her home-based work. "As a former news reporter and editor, I miss being in the thick of the news every day," Condon says. So crisscrossing helps her beat isolation and keeps her connected to the pulse of the newsroom and the regular work world.

Janie Winkler's been crisscrossing since the beginning of her word processing business. The Evanston, Illinois, mom set up shop at home when her kids were both in school full-time. To supplement self-employment, she also took a part-time job with a publishing company, thinking she'd only keep it till the business took off. In the mornings, she worked at the publishing company, and in the afternoons and evenings, she ran her home business. She's had the same arrangement for the past several years. "My out-of-the-home job helps me maintain contact with other professionals and keep up-to-date with computers and technology," she says. Her kids are young adults now, yet Winkler is reluctant to relinquish her work-at-home freedom. "I still enjoy the afternoons of being my own boss. There are times when I take a ride on my bike or do some gardening and then do the work in the evening."

Crisscrossing is a way to see if you're really ready to be a nine-to-fiver again. Perhaps you're tempted to get a traditional job but uncertain of how you'll feel about working on a set schedule. Maybe you're wondering whether you'll be able to work for someone else after all these years of being your own boss and calling the shots for your company. You might even be curious about how you could bring your entrepreneurial skills back into the corporate work world. Crisscrossing helps you learn the answers to these questions. It gives you a look at the opportunities that are out there and helps you find the best full-time job to fit your post-mompreneur lifestyle.

For graphic designer Nancy Danahy, crisscrossing taught her what she wants and doesn't want in a regular job. After working on her own for nearly two years, the graphic designer concluded that a staff job would give her a chance to get health coverage, build up retirement benefits, and get a lift up the corporate ladder. When she was offered a job as an art director at a communications/public relations firm, she took it on a four-week trial period, "with one week nonpaid leave in the middle to accommodate my son's spring break." During the trial period, she kept some of her freelance design projects, though this meant working nights and weekends. Danahy was glad she did, because the full-time job turned out to be much more production-oriented than she had counted on. "I wanted something that was more art direction/design," she says. Since she'd been hired, the company's needs had changed, and she found that they really wanted someone who could make constant calls to vendors, get updates on jobs, and liaison with the account directors. So she submitted her resignation and with half an eye open for another full-time job, worked from home again. Ever the shrewd mompreneur, she capitalized on the experience. "The owner asked me if I would be interested in freelancing for them, since my design style pleased them." Danahy has proven that even when a position doesn't work out, crisscrossing can lead to new possibilities and future job prospects down the road.

How do you go about uncovering crisscrossing possibilities? Ann Condon suggests mompreneurs watch the help wanted ads and post your résumé on online job boards. "I've seen some positions that were either for home-based people or could be tailored to such. Because I read the classifieds, I started working part-time as the director of a newspaper by and for inner-city teenagers," Condon says. She was also lucky enough to land periodic work with the Associated Press, where she worked before she had her first child. She continued her great relationship with her former boss and often works for the AP coordinating election coverage. "This way, I keep my hand in the business I love the most, and the company knows that I haven't disappeared. Maybe someday I'll go back."

What's in Your Future?

When we asked the mompreneurs in our research pool what they planned to do next, we heard lots of interesting answers. The majority intended to be mompreneurs forever, either continuing to work from home or expanding the business to outside office space. A good number planned to return to the full-time corporate world when their kids reached school age. Teaching and public speaking is another area many of the moms seem to be headed in. Several have told us they'd like to pass their skills along to others by teaching community classes, college courses, or hosting business seminars. Some plan to go back to school, either getting a degree that relates to their business or pursuing a new direction. Cathy Gallagher, the mompreneur who ran a childbirth education service, enrolled in nursing school. Her business experience being a labor coach taught her that she really wanted to work full-time in a hospital helping people.

We've met a secretary who longs to work in an orchid nursery, a floral arranger who might get into massage therapy, and a CPA who'd like to be a lawyer or a psychologist. Public relations woman Andrea Disario says any future business of hers will be directed specifically to the needs of the working mother. She'd like to start a new agency with family-friendly policies and flexible work schedules so she can accommodate other time-pressed parents.

We've spoken to million-dollar mompreneurs and mothers who are well on the way to being millionaires. We've also met plenty who simply dream of hitting the jackpot. We've enjoyed our conversations with all of them and have been energized by their successes and their aspirations.

Where will mompreneurship lead you? Who knows—but it's going to be an exciting journey. The roads are limitless. Your choices are boundless. And your trip will be powered by a very important fuel: flexibility. As a work-at-home mom, you'll have the freedom to forge a new work style. Once you do, you'll uncover countless career opportunities for the future. Isn't it great that mompreneurship can give you so many choices?

MOMPRENEUR® HALL OF FAME

LILLIAN VERNON
Chairman of the Board and CEO, Lillian Vernon Corporation,
Rye, New York
Mother of Two

In 1951, Lillian Vernon was a housewife pregnant with her first child. She was also a budding businesswoman with an idea for a unique service. She would sell bags and belts by mail from her Mount Vernon, New York, home and personalize them for customers free of charge. Using $2,000 of wedding gift money, she purchased her products and advertised her services in *Seventeen* magazine. The ad was small, but it brought in $32,000 worth of orders. A business, called Vernon

Specialties Company, was born, and soon after, so was a baby named Fred.

The energetic mompreneur devoted all her time to bringing up the baby and the business. "I was always busy, and it was challenging to constantly juggle my schedule," she says. "Balancing the conflicting demands of having a family, maintaining a home, and working were never easy."

In a few short years, both her family and her company had expanded. By 1957, Fred had been joined by baby brother David, and Vernon Specialties Company had over 125,000 customers. The business had grown so successful that Vernon had moved it out of her home and into rental space nearby. In addition to belts and bags, she now also sold combs, buttons, pins, and cuff links and showed off her product line in a spiffy sixteen-page catalog.

Today, the company is a multi-channeled empire with a spacious corporate headquarters in Rye, New York, and a state-of-the-art National Distribution Center in Virginia Beach, Virginia. Lillian Vernon Corporation publishes nine specialty catalogs, packed with giftware, household, gardening, gourmet, office, Christmas, and children's products. Shoppers can also browse and buy at Lillian Vernon outlet stores, as well as two online sites (lillianvernon.com and RuedeFrance.com). The catalog company processes more than four-and-a-half million orders a year. Ninety percent of Lillian Vernon customers are women.

Vernon says that being a mom has certainly helped her understand the needs of her shoppers. She learned firsthand what kinds of toys kids like to play with and what types of household gadgets a mother might find handy. Motherhood also taught her how to effectively head a company. "Running a home is like running a small business. They both require good management skills, knowing your priorities, expecting the unexpected, and, of course, learning to juggle a full plate of tasks at one time," the mail-order maven says.

When growing a home-based business, Vernon suggests mompreneurs start small and set realistic short-term and long-term goals. If at all possible, "keep your business separate by making sure you have a special area in your home set aside for work. This will keep your family from confusing work time with personal time," she advises, particularly when your children are young. Once your kids get older, recruit them to help you with your business, if they're interested. As teenagers, Vernon's sons often accompanied their mom to the office during the busy Christmas rush. "We would help out any way we could," says David, "stuffing envelopes, packing products, and filling cartons." Once the boys were

(continued)

out of college, they came on board full-time. Fred started working in the marketing department, and David took a job as national sales manager of the wholesale division. Their responsibilities grew along with the company. Until the mid-1990s, Fred was running Lillian Vernon Corporation with his mom. David is still on board, heading up the public relations department.

But Vernon still has plenty of say in the day-to-day dealings of the company she founded. She recently celebrated her fiftieth anniversary in business and is still the CEO. After all, it is her baby.

10

Special Section:
Cash in a Flash!

Are you one of those moms who doesn't want to launch a full-scale home business but still yearns for a flexible, scam-free way to earn a little money? Or maybe you're looking to boost your family's income while you get your home business off the ground? Well, you've come to the right place!

We've rounded up the ten most family-friendly ways to earn money from home—all requiring minimal time and financial investment. Though you can't expect to make a bundle, you *can* bring in enough cash to pay for a night or two out with your husband or to cover your monthly phone bill or car payment. New Yorker Annette Rodriguez earns quick cash auctioning off toys on eBay and uses it to pay for toddler gym classes for her daughter. "I call it my play money," she says, adding, "there are many opportunities out there for moms to make money." The trick is figuring out how to uncover the most reputable and time-efficient options.

To help you do that, we've talked with moms across the country and asked them to share their favorite quick-and-easy moneymakers. We've listed our top picks here. A few of them—like online auctions or scrapbooking—can even be developed into a full-fledged business as your children grow. So read on and discover how you can earn some fast cash!

BEFORE YOU GET STARTED . . .

Watch out for scams. There are many companies that prey on a mother's desire to be home with her kids, warns Jeanette Lisefski, founder of The National Association of At-Home Mothers in Fairfield, Iowa. Be especially wary of any get-rich-quick ads or e-mails promising that you can earn hundreds of dollars a week or more working from home. Here's how to protect yourself from disreputable offers:

✓ Proceed with caution. Use your common sense when evaluating any work-at-home opportunity. If the claim sounds too good to be true, it usually is.

✓ Don't pay up front. Beware of ads requiring you to send in money for additional work-from-home information, lists of hiring companies, or starter kits (such as those for home crafts or envelope stuffing).

✓ Do a background check. Research the reputability of the company to see if there have been any complaints lodged. Before getting involved with any work-at-home opportunity, check with the Better Business Bureau (www.bbb.org), Scambusters (www.scambusters.com), the National Fraud Information Center (1-800-876-7060; www.fraud.org), and/or the offices of the Attorney General and Department of Consumer Affairs in the state in which the company is located.

Assisting Realtors at Open Houses

Job description: Welcome prospective buyers at real estate open houses and hand out sales materials.

Moneymaking potential: Approximately $10 an hour, for about 6 hours of "house-sitting."

Flexibility factor: Open houses are usually held on weekends, so a family member or neighborhood teen can watch your kids while you work.

Success secret: "I offer to do brochures, newsletters, and other mailings for an extra fee," says Michelle Giesey of Elgin, Illinois, because realtors don't have time for these tasks. And while not required, a real estate license is a bonus, she adds. Then you can try to sell the house and earn a commission.

Start-up strategy: Call local realtors and offer your services.

CLEANING SERVICES

JOB DESCRIPTION: Clean private homes, apartments, and small businesses on a per-project basis, offering one-shot deals such as "Spring Cleaning," "Back-to-School Specials," and "Freshen Up for the Holidays." Should have a high energy level and be well organized.

MONEYMAKING POTENTIAL: $10 to $30 per hour or $100 and up for a thorough top-to-bottom seasonal job. Most three-bedroom, two-bathroom homes take about four hours to clean; apartments can take as little as two hours. Some clients like you to use their cleaning supplies, others prefer you to bring your own. Buy the basics in economy-size containers at a wholesale club and dilute them yourself to save money.

FLEXIBILITY FACTOR: Most customers will allow you to choose your own hours, so you can work around your children's school schedules. Rebecca Thyne, co-owner of White Glove Cleaning Service in Wappingers Falls, New York, works mornings while her twin boys are in school, often teaming up with another mom. The two of them get an average job done in two hours, leaving Thyne plenty of time to pick up her children at 1 P.M. A thorough spring cleaning will take more time but can be spread over a couple of days. Some moms bring teenagers along to help out (with a client's permission), but babies and young children should be left with a child-care provider; being around cleaning equipment and products without constant supervision can be risky, and you'll be too busy getting the job done to pay complete attention to them.

SUCCESS SECRET: Discuss all your responsibilities up front so there are no surprises once you get underway. "People often ask you for extras in the middle of a job and I feel guilty saying 'no.' But I don't like clients to take advantage of me," says Thyne. Her solution is to agree on exactly what tasks are to be done down to the last detail. If cleaning the windows is on your list, for example, you even have to specify whether you are responsible for both the inside and outside of the panes! Keep in mind that grease-encrusted ovens, moldy bathrooms, and neglected basements will require a little more elbow grease, and price the job accordingly.

START-UP STRATEGY: A few weeks before you're ready to work, make flyers and go door-to-door in your town and adjoining communities promoting your services. Thyne also suggests advertising in the Pennysaver or another local give-away publication. Spring and fall cleanups will probably get a good response, so be prepared. It may be wise to team up with other moms to share and speed up jobs.

CONSIGNMENT SALES

JOB DESCRIPTION: Sell secondhand clothing, furnishings, toys, and children's equipment at community consignment sales or shops. June Adelsberger, a mom of two from Fairfax Station, Virginia, makes a profit on her kids' cast-offs at a twice-yearly sale sponsored by her child's preschool.

MONEYMAKING POTENTIAL: You and the shop owner or sale sponsor split a percentage of the item's final price. "Community consignment sales are more profitable than consignment stores," notes Adelsberger. Most consignment stores in her area take 50 percent of the cost, she says, while at the preschool sales, 70 percent goes into her pocket.

FLEXIBILITY FACTOR: Gathering the items you plan to sell and dropping them off at the consignment site is easily done with the kids alongside you.

SUCCESS SECRET: You'll maximize your moneymaking potential if you have enough things to sell several times a year. Adelsberger says maternity clothes, children's furnishings, and baby equipment are always in demand—as long as they're in good condition.

START-UP STRATEGY: Be on the lookout for sales sponsored by churches, synagogues, schools, and other organizations. These are often advertised in PTA and church/synagogue newsletters and local newspapers and parenting publications, as well as on community bulletin boards. Also check out the growing number of parents' online consignment shops such as Mothers' Online Thrift Shop (www.motshop.com), Clever Moms Coupons and Online Resale Shop (www.clevermoms.com).

DECORATING HOUSES FOR THE HOLIDAYS

JOB DESCRIPTION: Assist busy families and/or elderly people in decorating their homes for the holidays. Services can include installing indoor and outdoor lights, customized tree-trimming, gift-wrapping, and the removal/inventory/packing up of decorations. "Many times people get so caught up in the holiday rush, they often wish they had someone to do the hard parts for them," says Kim Nocera, who runs a home-based business called Partyz for You (www.partyzforyou.com) in Newtown, Pennsylvania.

MONEYMAKING POTENTIAL: Anywhere from $100 to $300 per home for complete seasonal decorating and removal; $50 or $150 for tree-trimming. Nocera's party-planning business branched out into holiday decorating a couple of seasons ago, and she now decks out offices and storefronts as well as private homes. She's also addressed and mailed out holiday cards for businesses and individuals. "You can focus on one aspect of holiday decorating or offer several services," Nocera suggests. "And you don't have to limit yourself to the month of December. Just think of all the other holidays in the year . . . New Year's, Mardi Gras, Valentine's Day, St. Patrick's Day, Easter, 4th of July, Halloween, Thanksgiving, and many more!"

FLEXIBILITY FACTOR: You'll be more efficient if you can get child-care coverage and devote an uninterrupted chunk of time to each client. If your children are very young, they shouldn't tag along for safety reasons—installing lights and hanging fragile ornaments on a tree can be downright dangerous with youngsters underfoot. Older children, however, can pitch in and help—provided the homeowner gives her OK. Elderly clients may really enjoy seeing kids around the house, but most shop and business owners would probably prefer you to do the job solo. Nocera has had no trouble arranging her hours around her son's and daughter's schedules, and she points out that moms can take on as many or as few houses or businesses as they choose.

SUCCESS SECRET: Market yourself as an extra pair of hands during stressful times. "I try to help minimize the holiday hustle-bustle that seems to overwhelm many people," says Nocera. "My goal is to help people concentrate more on the meaning of the holidays and the memorable times that come with them—not the stress, which for most, includes decorating." While it's not necessary to be artistically inclined, it's essential to have an enthusiastic attitude that conveys your own sense of joy about what you're doing.

START-UP STRATEGY: Make up a flyer advertising your services and distribute it six to eight weeks before the major holiday season; a few weeks before other celebrations. Canvas neighbors, friends, and local businesses that could use your services; aside from the markets mentioned above, singles who travel extensively and newlyweds are two other groups to target. Word of mouth is the best way to drum up business! You don't need many supplies to get going—scissors, tape, nails, hammer, heavy twine, and a stepstool or ladder should do the trick. Many times, clients want you to use their own decorations. If you're required to purchase materials, be sure to keep receipts and tack your expenses onto your bill. Scour party stores for inspirational ideas and end-of-season sales on merchandise you can put away for next year.

FOCUS GROUPS AND MARKET RESEARCH SURVEYS

JOB DESCRIPTION: Offer your opinion on products and services via mail-in and online surveys or through online or in-person focus groups. Online surveys and focus groups often have to do with high-tech or Internet-related products and services such as computer software or Personal Digital Assistants (PDAs). In-person groups usually cover a broader range of topics. For example, New Jersey mom Mary Ann Chaneski has participated in several in-person focus groups, where she's tested baby wipes, skincare products, commercials, TV shows, and investment strategies. She once took part in a month-long diaper study—it paid $100, plus a free supply of diapers. In return, she had to keep a diary of how often she changed her son, plus stop by the market research offices for a few minutes twice a week to answer questions and have him checked for diaper rash. She received payment at the completion of the study and deposited the money in her baby's savings account. "His first paycheck!" Chaneski says, laughing.

MONEYMAKING POTENTIAL: Surveys pay from around $2 to $10 but usually take only a few minutes. Focus groups last at least an hour and pay from $25 to $100, depending on the product and budget. However, some surveys and focus groups offer coupons, gift certificates, point systems, or prize drawings instead of cash, so make sure you understand how you'll be rewarded for your time. But don't rule out quick nonpaying phone surveys; these can sometimes lead to future income. "I've been called by diaper and baby food companies for my opinion and then asked to attend focus groups for pay," says Amy Speck of Walkersville, Maryland.

FLEXIBILITY FACTOR: Surveys can be completed in spurts, around the demands of your kids. Focus groups require sustained concentration and child care. Chaneski does many of her focus groups in the evening, when her husband is home to baby-sit.

SUCCESS SECRET: Companies find you through new-mom mailing lists, so fill out warranty cards and consumer questionnaires. Also approach the market research departments of local beauty companies to see if they need product testers. Paula Krueger, a mom of two from Arlington Heights, Illinois, samples shampoos for Helene Curtis. Diana Salto, a mom of three from Lake Ronkonkoma, New York, has tested soaps and skincare creams for a nearby health and beauty testing lab. "Some of the best leads come from word of mouth," Salto says, so plug in to your mom network. She heard about the skincare testing opportunity by chatting with another mom in the stands at their children's swim meet.

START-UP STRATEGY: Assignments can be sporadic, so "register with several market research companies at once to increase your earning potential," advises Capri Dawson, co-founder of Money4Surveys (www.money4surveys.com), a site that lists market research firms and current surveys and focus group opportunities.

MYSTERY SHOPPING/SECRET SHOPPING

JOB DESCRIPTION: Visit stores, restaurants, banks, and other establishments and discreetly evaluate the service through questionnaires that rate factors like helpfulness, safety, and cleanliness. After registering with a mystery shopping company, you'll receive occasional assignments with specific instructions. "I was sent to a toy store to see how quickly someone helped me," says Stacey Gustafson of Superior, Colorado. At a pizzeria, she once had to count the pieces of sausage on her slice. Julie Rogers, a Campbell, California, mom, has had a variety of mystery shopping assignments—from applying for credit cards, to mailing things at the post office, to having the oil in her car changed.

MONEYMAKING POTENTIAL: Anywhere from around $5 for a supermarket or fast-food evaluation to up to $100 for complicated, time-consuming tasks like opening a bank account or assessing the service at an airport ticket check-in counter. "But most pay in the $20 to $40 range" and include additional incentives such as free dinners, movies, baseball games, or groceries, says Rogers, who offers a free newsletter at her mystery shopping website Mom!Mom!.com (www.mom-mom.com). "I've had my carpet cleaned and the shock absorbers on my car replaced—all for free," Rogers says. Be aware that some companies don't pay cash—instead they'll offer coupons, free products or services, or gift certificates. Yet these perks have value, too, notes Rogers, and can save your family money in the long run.

FLEXIBILITY FACTOR: Kids are welcome, and "you make money going places you might have gone anyway," says Betty Taylor of New Braunfels, Texas, who has evaluated burger joints, video stores, and service stations with her toddler in tow. With online mystery shopping, you won't even have to leave the house! Most mystery shopping assignments (whether online or off) will require at least thirty minutes of "shopping time" and another thirty minutes to fill out the form.

SUCCESS SECRET: "Keep careful records of any out-of-pocket expenses, such as gas and car mileage," cautions Rogers. Mystery shoppers work as independent contractors, and you will be able to write off many of your nonreimbursable expenses on your taxes.

START-UP STRATEGY: Register with several companies to increase your job frequency. For an extensive list, contact the National Center for Professional Mystery Shoppers (813-984-6907, www.ij.net/nationalms), Mom!Mom!.com (www.mom-mom.com), and DotCom Mommies (www.dotcommommies.com). For online mystery shopping, sign up with Target Surf (www.targetsurf.com).

ONLINE AUCTIONS

JOB DESCRIPTION: Sell new, used, and handmade items for profit on Internet auction sites such as eBay. Post a photo, description, and opening price, and wait for bids to roll in. Most sites charge about 50 cents for listings, plus take a small percentage (usually around 5 percent) of your final selling price.

MONEYMAKING POTENTIAL: It depends on what you sell and how often. Laura Goetz, a mom of two from Dubuque, Iowa, has made as much as $400 a week selling collectibles she bought at yard sales for pennies. She once purchased a set of 1959 paper dolls in a tattered box for 50 cents and made a $39 profit. "But there are also weeks I earn nothing," she notes. "It's almost like the stock market," adds New Yorker Annette Rodriguez. "You have to get out there, see what's hot, and try to make a quick profit." Rodriguez stocks up on hot new toys and then auctions them off at holiday time when they become hard to find in stores. One season she was lucky enough to find the much-sought-after PlayStation 2 before Thanksgiving in ToysRUs. She bought it for $300 and auctioned it off for over $600!

FLEXIBILITY FACTOR: "I shop on our way to the park, input items online after my daughter goes to bed, and often check on bids with her on my lap," says Rodriguez. "Having a child makes it easier to know which toys are in high demand," she adds.

SUCCESS SECRET: Do your homework before you start selling. "Familiarize yourself with the collectible market," advises Goetz. Reference books like *Garage Sale Annual* and *Flea Market Trader* will help you recognize hot items and their value. (Goetz always keeps copies of these in her car.) "Stuff from the 1970s is particularly popular right now," says Goetz, who has turned a quick profit selling glass grapes and Garfield the Cat memorabilia. Jewelry, vintage clothing, and sewing patterns seem to be perennial strong sellers. But keep abreast of current trends, too. Virginia mom Beth Schumann started out auctioning Beanie Babies. But after that market went flat she began selling special edition Barbies, which eventually grew into a thriving business for this enterprising mom.

START-UP STRATEGY: First visit auction sites like www.ebay.com, www.amazon.com, and www.yahoo.com to learn the process and see what's profitable. Then scoop up bargains at tag sales, close-outs, garage sales, flea markets, thrift shops, and wholesale distributors. Before you set a price for your treasures, look at completed auctions to learn the going rates for items similar to yours, advises Goetz. She suggests using comprehensive search sites like BidXS.com (www.bidxs.com) for comparison shopping. Another hot tip: "Start your auction on a Sunday evening," Goetz urges. Most auctions last a week, she explains, so you want yours to start and end on a weekend, because that's when most people are surfing. For more advice about online auctions, check out these resources: *Discards to Dollars* (www.koovy.com), Laura Goetz's informational and inspirational website, and *How to Sell on eBay* by Annette Graf, a how-to book available at www.annetteonline.com.

Party Helper/Server

Job description: Assist with parties and other events held in private homes or public spaces as a server, kitchen helper, hostess, bartender, or coat checker. Servers usually set up tables and chairs, pass hors d'oeuvres and drinks, tend the buffet table or provide sit-down food service, and help clean up. Kitchen helpers may be asked to heat up food, arrange serving platters, wash dishes, and clean up the kitchen. A hostess is responsible for greeting guests and making sure an event runs smoothly. Each job requires courtesy, patience, and stamina.

Moneymaking potential: Expect to earn $15 an hour and up, plus gratuities, with four hours minimum at an event.

Flexibility factor: Most events take place at night and on weekends, when a spouse or teen is more available to assume child-care responsibilities. Linda Yerby, founder of Rent-A-Hostess, Inc, (http://rent-a-hostess.baweb.com), in the greater Washington, D.C., area, often hires moms to staff parties. "This kind of opportunity is perfect for mothers because they can do it on an 'as needed' basis without getting penalized when they can't work. If I call one mom and she's not available, it's no problem—I just call the next one on the list," says Yerby. Serving at parties is also a painless way to keep in touch with the work world and a pleasant way to interact with other adults.

Success secret: Project a positive attitude and a professional image. Friendly, efficient service and a pleasant personality will get you asked back again. Clients expect you to be accommodating, considerate, and well-groomed.

Start-up strategy: Contact caterers in your area; they usually have "on call" positions available. Yerby suggests looking in the Yellow Pages for listings. Banquet facilities and restaurants with party rooms are also good possibilities, as are wedding consultants and party planners. Yerby is planning to franchise, offering moms the chance to buy into a flexible, home-based business that "won't clean out the bank account." So there may be a Rent-A-Hostess coming to your area soon!

PRODUCT DEMONSTRATIONS/MERCHANDISING

JOB DESCRIPTION: Demonstrate products at trade shows, fairs, and retail stores; hand out samples at supermarkets and specialty shops. Requires an outgoing personality and the willingness to be on your feet for hours.

MONEYMAKING POTENTIAL: About $10 to $15 an hour, with four hours minimum.

FLEXIBILITY FACTOR: Since you'll be working out of the house, you'll need child-care coverage. Trade shows are usually held during the week in major metropolitan areas, so plan for child care if your children aren't school-aged. Product sampling or merchandising often takes place toward the end of the week and on weekends, says Ellen Gellert, founder of Goodie Givers, a mom-owned business in Chappaqua, New York, that hires demonstrators. "The weeks around the holidays are an especially busy time," she adds.

SUCCESS SECRET: Target juvenile product shows and family-oriented events to showcase your parenting experience, advises Iris Kapustein, owner of Tradeshow Express in Boynton Beach, Florida. "Who better than a mom to demonstrate a stroller?" Tap into passions, too. For creative types, there are crafts and gourmet shows, while handy moms may enjoy demonstrating products at housewares and automotive shows. Popular merchandising opportunities include food, cosmetics, and fashion accessories.

START-UP STRATEGY: Obtain a list of upcoming shows from your city's convention and visitor's bureau, or go to www.expoguide.com. Pick shows that fit your schedule and interests, and call the listed contacts about potential jobs. Also register with temporary help agencies like Nationwide Convention Services (1-800-553-8855). For merchandising leads, check out the National Association of Retail Merchandisers at their website, www.narms.com. Mom Elizabeth Linnerman, host of two merchandising forums—www.topica.com/lists/merchandiserslisthere and www.delphi.com/merchandising—suggests you choose the type of work you're interested in, such as product demonstration or point-of-purchase displays. Posts will be listed under those categories on both her site and the NARMS website.

SCRAPBOOKING

JOB DESCRIPTION: Capitalize on a scrapbooking hobby by creating heirloom photo albums for others to purchase.

MONEYMAKING POTENTIAL: Completed books usually range in price from $60 to $100 or more, depending on the length and complexity; most scrapbookers charge about $10 per page. But many moms find it more cost-efficient to set hourly fees. Amy Saleik, of Fort Wayne, Indiana, charges between $15 and

$20 an hour for her services. Make sure you charge enough to cover your scrapbooking expenses—materials like fancy papers, templates, and stickers can be quite pricey.

FLEXIBILITY FACTOR: Scrapbooking is a social activity that's often done in groups. If you get together with other mommies, your children can play together while you create the keepsakes to sell. As your children get older, they can even join in your hobby. "My six-year-old daughter, Ashley, loves to work alongside me, creating little books of her own," says scrapbook aficionado Stacey Gustafson.

SUCCESS SECRET: Test the waters by entering scrapbook contests. Gustafson has won over $400 in cash and prizes for her original designs. A page she created to commemorate her daughter's ballet-themed birthday party earned her a $100 check! Check out contests sponsored by local scrapbooking stores and crafts magazines like *Creating Keepsakes* (www.creatingkeepsakes.com) and *Memory Makers* (www.memorymakersmagazine.com). Websites such as Cock-a-Doodle Design (www.cockadoodledesign.com) also have monthly contests. Eventually your hobby might even grow into a full-fledged business, as it did for Bardstown, Kentucky, stay-at-home moms Robin Magruder and Alison Davis. They started scrapbooking for the fun and camaraderie. But today they also teach scrapbook classes and run CutoutCrazy, where they sell creative supplies. "You never know when your little moneymaker will turn out bigger than expected!" agrees Diane Lillie of Austin, Texas. She took the art of scrapbooking high-tech, with a business called I'm the Baby.com, where she sold electronic scrapbooks (ranging in price from $40 to $150) for parents who wanted to create an online archive of their baby's photos and milestones.

START-UP STRATEGY: For inspiration and supplies, check out scrapbooking stores as well as websites that specialize in the art, such as the Scrapbook Mania Community at MSN.com (www.msn.com), and the Scrapping 4Others board at Yahoo!Groups (www.yahoogroups.com).

TEACHING COMMUNITY-EDUCATION COURSES

JOB DESCRIPTION: Offer courses in your field of expertise at your local adult-education center, community college, or youth centers. Diane Lillie has taught seminars for the local school district and Austin Community College. "I put together short three-to-six-hour programs on things I know about, like web design, writing résumés, and creating family histories," she says.

MONEYMAKING POTENTIAL: Rates vary according to where you live, so check local adult-ed catalogs to get a feel for what is being charged for different courses. Lillie's community college pays her $50 an hour for her in-class time, and $50 per student for teaching online courses. Robin Magruder and her partner, Alison Davis, charge $25 a person per class (including supplies) to teach scrapbooking classes at the local adult-education center.

FLEXIBILITY FACTOR: Courses are usually offered at night, so a spouse or family member can baby-sit. And there's no long-term commitment required. "If you want to take a semester off—like I did to have a baby—there's no problem at all," Lillie says.

SUCCESS SECRET: This can be a great way to market an existing business. Magruder and Davis publicize their courses on their scrapbooking e-commerce site and spread the word about their website when they're teaching.

START-UP STRATEGY: Call your local school districts and town or city hall to find out where and when community-education courses are offered. Then review course catalogs to see what's currently on the agenda. "Think about ways to convert your own talents, hobbies, or previous work experience into interesting programs," advises Lillie, and then send a written proposal and résumé to the dean of the continuing education department. Though Lillie had experience in résumé writing, her community college already had a teacher for that course. So she came up with a new spin on the idea and proposed an outline for a course called "Creating Online Résumés." The college loved the idea and added Lillie's seminar to the next semester's roster of classes. Now she even teaches an online version of her course.

WHAT ABOUT DIRECT SALES?

Thinking of selling cosmetics, cookware, partyware, toys, vitamins, or some other type of direct sales product? Wondering if this qualifies as a quick-cash option? While many moms create full-fledged home businesses around direct sales (see chapter 2), some manage to do this kind of work on a very part-time basis, fitting it in when they need to boost the household income. But remember: Income depends on time invested. If you plan to work less than 10 hours a week, don't expect to make more than $5,000 a year!

Amy Robinson, Manager of Marketing Communication at the Direct Selling Association, maps out these success strategies to help you decide if direct sales is for you.

✓ **Assess your personality.** Are you comfortable selling things to individuals and groups?
✓ **Research the company.** The focus should be on selling a product— make sure earnings aren't based solely on recruiting other salespeople.

Starter kits should be fairly inexpensive and include training materials. Avoid companies that make you buy large inventories or don't allow you to return unsold products. Screen companies through the Direct Selling Association (www.dsa.org).

✓ **Pick a product you're passionate about.** It's easier to sell people on something you use and believe in! Moms are flocking to companies with family-friendly merchandise, like Discovery Toys, Pampered Chef, 1-800-PartyShop, and Watkins.

11

Resources:
The Mompreneur®
Survival Kit

All the tools you need to get your business up and running.

ASSOCIATIONS
For Home Business Owners and/or Women Entrepreneurs

American Association of Home Based Businesses; www.aahbb.org
AT&T Women in Business; 1-800-537-8700; www.att.com/wib
Center for Women's Business Research; 202-638-3060; www.nfwbo.org
Homebased Working Moms; 512-266-0900; www.hbwm.com
Home Office Association of America; 1-800-809-4622; www.hoaa.com
Mother's Home Business Network; 516-997-7394; www.homeworkingmom.com
National Association for Female Executives (NAFE), 1-800-634-NAFE; www.nafe.com
National Association for the Self-Employed (NASE); 1-800-232-NASE; www.nase.org
National Association of At-Home Mothers; www.athomemothers.com
National Association of Women Business Owners; 1-800-55-NAWBO; www.nawbo.org
Netpreneur Exchange; www.netpreneur.org
Small Office/Home Office (SOHO); 1-800-495-SOHO; www.so-ho.org

Women, Inc.; 1-800-930-3993; www.womeninc.org
Women's Forum; www.womensforum.com

BOOKS
For Work-from-Home Moms

The Frazzled Working Woman's Practical Guide to Motherhood by Mary Lyon (Starburst Publishers, 1997).

How to Raise a Family and a Career Under One Roof by Lisa M. Roberts (Bookhaven Press, 1997).

Mompreneurs® Online: Using the Internet to Build Work-at-Home Success by Patricia Cobe and Ellen H. Parlapiano (Perigee, 2001).

MothersWork: How a Young Mother Started a Business on a Shoestring and Built It Into a Multimillion-Dollar Company by Rebecca Matthias (Currency, 1999).

The Stay-at-Home Mom's Guide to Making Money by Liz Folger (Prima, 1997).

The Work-at-Home Mom's Guide to Home Business: Stay at Home and Make Money with WAHM.com by Cheryl Demas (Hazen Publishing, 2000).

Working at Home While the Kids Are There, Too by Loriann Hoff Oberlin (Career Press, 1997).

General Business Books

The Best Home Businesses for the 21st Century: The Inside Information You Need to Know to Select a Home-Based Business That's Right for You by Paul and Sarah Edwards (JP Tarcher, 1999).

Bringing Your Product to Market by Don Debelak (John Wiley & Sons, 1997).

Business Know-How: An Operational Guide for Home-Based and Micro-Sized Businesses with Limited Budgets by Janet Attard (Adams, 1999).

Entrepreneur Magazine: Starting a Home-Based Business by Inc. Staff/Entrepreneur Media (Wiley, 1999).

Her Venture.com: Your Guide to Expanding Your Small or Home Business to the Internet—Easily and Profitably by Priscilla Y. Huff (Prima, 2000).

The Home Office and Small Business Answer Book: Solutions to the Most Frequently Asked Questions About Starting and Running Home Offices and Small Businesses by Janet Attard (Owl Books, 2000).

The Home Office Solution: How to Balance Your Professional and Personal Lives While Working at Home by Alice Bredin and Kirsten M. Legatree (Wiley, 1998).

Honey I Want to Start My Own Business by Azriela Jaffe (Career Press, 1997).

More 101 Best Home-Based Businesses for Women by Priscilla Huff (Prima Publishing, 1998).

101 Best Home-Based Businesses for Women by Priscilla Huff (Prima Publishing, 1998).

Patent It Yourself, 8th Edition by David Pressman (Nolo Press, 2000).

The Shoestring Entrepreneur's Guide to the Best Home-Based Businesses by Robert Spiegel (Griffin, 2000).

The Small Business Money Guide by Terri Lonier and Lisa M. Aldisert (John Wiley & Sons, 1998).

Steps to Small Business Start-Up: Everything You Need to Know to Turn Your Idea into a Successful Business, 4th Edition by Linda Pinson and Jerry Jinnett (Dearborn Trade, 2000).

Woman to Woman: Street Smarts for Women Entrepreneurs by Geraldine A. Larkin (Prentice Hall, 1993).

The Work at Home Sourcebook, 7th Edition by Lynie Arden (Live Oak Publications, 1999).

Working from Home: Everything You Need to Know About Living and Working Under the Same Roof by Paul and Sarah Edwards (JP Tarcher, 1999).

Working Solo, 2nd Edition: The Real Guide to Freedom and Financial Success with Your Own Business by Terri Lonier (Wiley, 1998).

CAREER ADVICE AND SUPPORT

Associations/Organizations

American Franchisee Association/Women in Franchising; 1-800-222-4943; www.franchisee.org. Clearinghouse of information on home-based franchises; provides programs, help, and protection to franchisees.

At Home Professions; 1-800-359-3455; www.at-homeprofessions.com. Offers learn-at-home courses on starting specific small businesses.

Catalyst: Research and Advisory Organization to Advance Women in Business; 212-514-7600; www.catalystwomen.org.

Direct Selling Association; 202-347-8866; www.dsa.org. Checklist of reputable direct sales companies and information for those interested in pursuing this field.

Families and Work Institute; 212-465-2044; www.familiesandwork.org. Offers support and information for working parents.

Idea Café; www.ideacafe.com. Lively site for insight into different business options and resources for starting up.

New Ways to Work; 415-995-9860; www.nww.org. Information on setting up alternative and flexible work arrangements.

Work/Family Directions; 1-800-477-0543 or 617-673-3100; www.wfd.com. Provides consultation and referral programs to corporations, businesses, and nonprofits to create better work/family balance.

Work Options Resources; 808-948-2255; www.workoptions.com. A home-based consulting firm specializing in resources and help in setting up flexible work arrangements for individuals and employers.

Books

The Crafts Business Answer Book and Resource Guide: Answers to Hundreds of Troublesome Questions About Starting, Marketing, and Managing a Homebased Business by Barbara Brabec (M. Evans and Co, 1998).

Finding Your Perfect Work: The New Career Guide to Making a Living, Creating a Life by Paul and Sarah Edwards (JP Tarcher, 1996).

Home Business You Can Buy: The Definitive Guide to Exploring Franchises, Multi-Level Marketing, and Business Opportunities Plus: How to Avoid Scams by Paul and Sarah Edwards (JP Tarcher, 1997).

Let's Go Into Business Together: 8 Secrets to Successful Partnering by Azriela Jaffe (Career Press, 2001).

Turn Your Talents into Profits by Darcy Sanders and Martha Bullen (Pocket Books, 1998).

CHILD CARE
Agencies/Associations

American Camping Association; 765-342-8456; www.ACAcamps.org. A clearinghouse and information service on the nation's camps.

Childbirth and Postpartum Professionals Association (CAPPA); 1-888-548-3672; www.postpartumdoula.com. Helps you find postpartum caregivers (doulas) and offers training and certification for those interested in becoming doulas.

Child Care Action Campaign; 212-239-0138; www.childcareaction.org. Nonprofit organization that takes an active role in expanding the supply of quality, affordable child care and offers resources for parents.

Child Care Aware; 1-800-424-2246; www.childcareaware.org. A clearinghouse that directs parents to local agencies, which in turn can recommend family day-care homes, summer programs, child-care centers, and in-home caregivers.

International Nanny Association (INA); 856-858-0808; www.nanny.org. Support organization for nannies and the families that employ them; can refer you to nannies and placement agencies.

NannyShare.com; www.nannyshare.com. If you're interested in sharing a nanny with another family, this site helps you link up with compatible families in your area. You can browse the listings for free or post an ad of your own for about $30.

National Association for the Education of Young Children (NAEYC); 1-800-424-2460; www.naeyc.org. Directed mostly toward professional educators, this organization also has some literature for parents on choosing early childhood programs.

National Association for Family Child Care; 515-282-8192; www.nafcc. org. Resources and support for family child-care providers.

National Association of Child Care Resource and Referral Agencies (NACCRRA); 202-393-5501; www.naccrra.org. Helps link parents with local agencies that can recommend caregivers in different areas of the country.

National Child Care Association; 1-800-543-7161; www.nccanet.org. An association for those who own and/or operate a licensed, private child-care/preschool program.

National Child Care Information Center (NCCIC); www.nccic.org. Sponsored by the Child Care Bureau and U.S. Department of Health and Human Services, this site connects you to child-care resources nationwide.

National Cooperative Business Association (NCBA); 202-638-6222; www. neba.org. Provides tips on forming a child-care co-op.

National School Age Care Alliance; 617-298-5012; www.nsaca.org. Membership organization representing 8,000 members and 35 affiliated state organizations that provide school-age care for children up to age 14.

Safe Sitter; 1-800-255-4089; www.safesitter.org. This national program helps prepare baby-sitters through child safety courses and is especially important if you'll be hiring a pre-teen or teen to watch your kids.

Zero to Three: The National Center for Infants, Toddlers, and Families; 202-638-1144; www.zerotothree.org. Information on finding the best care for infants and toddlers.

Books

The Anxious Parents' Guide to Quality Childcare: An Informative Step-by-Step Manual on Finding and Keeping the Finest Care for Your Child by Michelle Ehrich (Perigee, 1999). This valuable resource offers step-by-step advice on finding the caregiver who is right for your family.

The Babysitting Co-Op Guidebook: Building a Community Support Network by Patricia McManus (Diane Publishing Co., 1993).

Handbook of Child and Elder Care Resources (Diane Publishing Co., 1997).

Summer Fun: The Parents' Complete Guide to Day Camps, Overnight Camps, Specialty Camps, and Teen Tours by Marian Edelman Borden (Checkmark Books, 1999).

E-ZINES AND NEWSLETTERS

BizTalk; www.biztalk.com
Business Hotline; www.bizhotline.com
Entrepreneur's Start-Ups; www.bizstartups.com
Home Office Magazine; www.homeofficemag.com
Small Business Advisor; www.isquare.com
Working Solo; www.workingsolo.com
ZD Net Small Business Advisor; www.zdnet.com/smallbusiness

FINANCING

Agencies/Associations

ACCION International; 617-492-4930; www.accion.org. This economic development agency provides small amounts of seed money for disadvantaged women and minorities.
Association for Enterprise Opportunity; www.microenterpriseworks.org. Lists micro loan programs.
Ben Franklin Technology Partners; 717-234-1748; www.benfranklin.org. Helps Pennsylvania businessowners start and build their companies.
Count-Me-In; 1-888-856-9806; www.count-me-in.org. A national loan fund that provides small business loans and scholarships to qualifying businesswomen.
Department of Commerce, Office of Business Liaison; 202-482-3942; www.doc.gov. Provides information on business assistance programs offered by all federal agencies.
U.S. Small Business Administration Loan Programs; www.sba.gov. Includes Low-Doc Program for Securing Loans, SBA Express Revolving Lines of Credit, and Women's Loan Pre-Qualification Program.

Banks That Believe in Women

Bank of America Small Business Investment Company; www.BankofAmerica.com/community. Provides loans and equity investments for minority- and women-owned businesses.
Fleet Bank Women Entrepreneurs' Connection; 1-800-CALL-FLEET; www.fleet.com. Provides loans for women-owned businesses in the Northeast.

Venture Capital and Angel Funding

AngelMoney; www.angelmoney.com. Provides seed capital and start-up investors.

Seraph Capital Forum; www.seraphcapital.com. Angel network for business-women in the Pacific Northwest.

Venture Capital Resource Library; www.vfinance.com. Helps locate funding sources.

Viridian Capital Partners; www.viridian-capital.com. Women-run venture capital firm specializing in start-ups in technology and health-care fields.

WomenAngels; 202-342-1627; www.womenangels.net. Funding sources for businesswomen in the Mid-Atlantic United States.

Women's Growth Capital Fund; 202-342-1431; www.womensgrowthcapital.com. Invests in businesses in early or expansion phases.

IMAGE BUILDING

Websites

Organization by Design; 1-800-578-3770; www.dressingwell.com. Get an e-mail newsletter and helpful tips, courtesy of expert Mary Lou Andre.

Books

Reinventing Ourselves After Motherhood: How Former Career Women Refocus Their Personal and Professional Lives After the Birth of a Child by Susan Lewis (NTC/Contemporary Publishing Company, 2000).

Soloing: Realizing Your Life's Ambition by Harriet Rubin and Avram Miller (HarperCollins, 1999).

INSURANCE

Digital Insurance; www.digitalinsurance.com. Online source for comparing policies and quotes from various insurance companies.

Health Insurance Association of America; 202-824-1849; www.hiaa.org. Clearinghouse of health insurance information.

Insurance Information Institute; 1-800-942-4242; www.iii.org. Provides unbiased, up-to-date information on all types of insurance needed by home business owners.

Insurance Noodle; www.insurancenoodle.com. An online source specializing in business insurance.

Insurance Web; www.insweb.com. Compare quotes and policies from different carriers on this comprehensive site.

Quotesmith; 1-800-556-9393; www.quotesmith.com. Comparison shop for all types of insurance on this easy-to-navigate site.

MAGAZINES

Entrepreneur; www.entrepreneur.com. With both print and online versions, this magazine offers practical advice and inspirational articles for all business owners.

Entrepreneur's Business Start-Ups; www.bizstartups.com. Published by *Entrepreneur* magazine and geared to newbies launching a small or home business.

Home Business Journal; www.homebizjour.com. Tax tips, website development help, telephone selling strategies, and other practical information.

Home Business Magazine; www.homebusinessmag.com. Timely information helpful to home business owners.

Inc. magazine; www.inc.com. Trendy and topical information for growing companies.

PC Magazine; www.zdnet.com/pcmag. Comprehensive source for choosing hi-tech equipment and software.

Victoria magazine; www.victoriamag.com. Features entrepreneurial success stories in its "Turn Your Passion into Profits" series.

Working Mother magazine; www.workingmother.com. Published monthly, with lots of articles devoted to balancing work and family life, plus an annual "Best Companies in America" guide every October.

MARKETING
BOOKS

The Anatomy of Buzz: How to Create Word-of-Mouth Marketing by Emanuel Rosen (Doubleday, 2000).

Bringing Home the Business by Kim Gordon (Perigee, 2001).

How to Market a Product for Under $500: A Handbook of Multiple Exposure Marketing by Jeffrey Dobkin (Danielle Adams Publishing, 2000).

Linda Radke's Promote Like a Pro: Small Budget, Big Show by Linda Radke, et al (Five Star Publishing, 2000).

Mastering Guerilla Marketing: 100 Profit-Producing Insights You Can Take to the Bank by Jay Conrad Levinson (Houghton-Mifflin, 1999).

Six Steps to Free Publicity by Marcia Yudkin (Plume/Penguin, 1995).

Smart Speaking by Marcia Yudkin and Laurie Schloff (Plume/Penguin, 1992).

Starting from No: Ten Strategies to Overcome Your Fear of Rejection by Azriela Jaffe (Dearborn, 1999).

The Way of the Guerilla: Achieving Success and Balance as an Entrepreneur in the 21st Century by Jay Conrad Levinson (Houghton-Mifflin, 1998).

Websites/Associations

Direct Marketing Association; 212-391-9683; www.the-dma.org.

Gorilla Marketing; www.gorillamarketing.com. Thrifty marketing techniques.

Guerilla Marketing Online; www.gmarketing.com. Tips from the famous original guerilla marketing team.

Idea Marketers; www.ideamarketers.com. Resource for inexpensive marketing ideas.

The Mom Pack; www.mompack.com. A cross-promotion venture founded by and for mom-owned businesses.

Mother-Owned and Operated; www.m-oo.com. A co-op marketing group that focuses on services and products offered by stay-at-home moms.

One-to-One Marketing; www.1to1.com. Strategies and articles from the reputable Peppers and Rogers group.

Promote Yourself; www.promoteyourself.com. Articles and advice for promoting your business.

Publicity Hound; www.publicityhound.com. Newsletter and articles on promoting your business with a small budget.

Small Business Now; www.smallbusinessnow.com. A website full of marketing ideas for mompreneurs.

Trade Show Database; www.tsnn.com.

NETWORKING

Association of Internet Professionals; 1-800-JOINAIP; www.association.org.

Business Network International; www.bni.com. The well-regarded, national word-of-mouth business referral group.

Her Planet; www.herplanet.com. Resources for business owners and other women, plus a very supportive community.

MATCH: Mother's Access to Careers at Home; 703-764-2320; www.freestate.net/match. A metro-Washington, D.C., networking and advocacy group for mothers with home-based businesses.

Mothers + More, 630-941-3553; www.mothersandmore.org. A group for "sequencing mothers" who have taken time out of their careers to raise their children.

Mommy Co., www.mommyco.com. Online source that helps work-from-home moms form offline support groups.

Trade Association Directory; www.pueblo.gsa.gov/crh/trade.htm. A comprehensive guide listing trade and professional associations across the country.

Webgrrls International. An online networking group offering support and information to women working online and in traditional businesses.

Yahoo!; www.yahoo.com. Search the Yahoo! web directory under Business and Economy/Organizations/Trade Associations to find a group catering to your speciality.

OFFICE SET-UP/SUPPLIES

Business Cards; designyourowncard.com. Business cards in an instant, all done electronically with input from the customer.

MacMall; www.macmall.com. Everything for the Macintosh computer user, including hardware, software, and peripherals.

MicroWAREHOUSE; www.warehouse.com. Computers, scanners, and other equipment for the office.

Mobile Mall; www.mobile-mall.com. One-stop shopping for laptops, cell phones, digital organizers, and other portable devices.

NEBS; www.nebs.com. All kinds of business forms, including checks, invoices, etc., as well as custom labels, business cards, envelopes, etc.

Office Depot; www.officedepot.com.

Office Max; www.officemax.com.

Papers Plus; www.paperplus.com. Specialty papers for letterhead and brochures.

Printing for Less.com; www.printingforless.com. Letterhead, brochures, post-cards, and more are available at this website.

Quill Office Products; 1-800-982-3400; www.quill.com. Order everything from paper clips to file folders, file cabinets, furniture, computer monitors, and digital cameras at this one-stop source.

Stamps.com; www.stamps.com.

Books

Ergonomic Living: How to Create a User-Friendly Home and Office by Gordon Inkeles and Iris Schencke (Simon and Schuster, 1994).

101 Home Office Success Secrets by Lisa Kanarek (Career Press, 2000).

Practical Home Office Solutions by Marilyn Zelinsky (McGraw-Hill, 1998).

ONLINE SITES FOR WORK-AT-HOME PARENTS

Bizy Moms; www.bizymoms.com

Club Mom; www.clubmom.com

Entrepreneurial Parent; www.en-parent.com

iVillage Work Channel; www.ivillage.com/work

Main Street Mom; www.mainstreetmom.com

Mompreneurs® Online www.mompreneursonline.com
Moms Help Moms; www.momshelpmoms.com
Mom's Network Exchange; momsnetwork.com
Moms Online; On the Oxygen website; www.momsonline.com
ParentPreneur Club; www.parentpreneurclub.com
Slowlane: The Online Resource for Stay-at-Home Dads;
   http://slowlane.com
Work-at-Home Dads; www.wahd.com
WAHM: Work-at-Home Moms; www.wahm.com

PROTECTING YOURSELF AND YOUR BUSINESS

Attorney General's Office, U.S. National Organization site; www.naag.org
Find out how to contact the U.S. Attorney General's office in your state.
Better Business Bureau; 703-276-0100; www.bbb.org. If you're considering
investing in a business opportunity, check here to make sure there are no
complaints against the company.
Lawphone; 1-800-255-3352; www.lawphone.com. Pre-paid legal services
plan for small businesses.
Name Protect.com; www.nameprotect.com. Trademark research, protection,
and name monitoring services.
National Fraud Information Center; 1-800-876-7060; www.fraud.org. For
investigating and reporting suspected scams.
Nolo Self Help Law Center; www.nolo.com. Legal advice on a wide range of
business issues.
U.S. Copyright Office/The Library of Congress; 202-707-9100; www.
loc.gov/copyright. For registering copyrights on your work.
U.S. Patent and Trademark Office; 1-800-786-9199; www.uspto.gov. Use this
site to do patent and trademark searches, find patent/trademark attorneys,
and apply for patents or trademarks.

START-UP SUPPORT

ABC Small Business Center; www.abcsmallbiz.com. State-by-state review of
licensing requirements, zoning review, forms to file, etc. to get your business going.
American Express Small Business Services; www.americanexpress.com. A
wealth of resources for home and small business owners.
Association of Small Business Development Centers; www.asbdc-us.org.
Refers you to small business development centers in your area.
American Women's Economic Development Corporation; New York, NY;
917-368-6100. Helps women gain the skills and motivation to become suc-

cessful entrepreneurs through peer support, business counseling, and high-quality training programs.

Biz Office; www.bizoffice.com. Links to dozens of small and home business sites.

BizWeb 2000; www.bizweb2000.com. Online resource center for small business start-ups.

The Entrepreneurial Edge; www.lowe.org. Sponsored by the Edward Lowe Foundation, this site offers helpful resources on every aspect of entrepreneurship from business plans to venture capital.

EntreWorld: Resources for Entrepreneurs from the Kauffman Center for Entrepreneurial Leadership; www.entreworld.org.

Innovation Assessment Center at Washington State University's Small Business Development Center; 509-358-7765; www.sbdc.wsu.edu. Helps inventors determine if their idea is marketable.

Inventors Assistance League; 877-IDEA-BIN; www.inventions.org. Hand-holding and advice for and by inventors.

National Business Incubation Association; 740-593-4331; www.nbia.org. Lists hundreds of small business centers across the country that provide administrative support, communications facilities, and space for conferences and client meetings.

National Chamber of Commerce for Women, Home-Based Business Committee; 212-685-3454. Helps women research, write, and reach their business plan and career path goals; offers valuable pay comparison profiles for various professions.

National Women's Business Council; 202-205-3850; www.nwbc.gov. Public policy and advocacy group, has a database of women business owners who offer assistance, training, and other help to start-ups.

Online Women's Business Center; www.onlinewbc.org. Resources for planning, financing, and building your business. Can refer you to a local Women's Business Center in your neighborhood for in-person help.

ParentWise; www.parentwise.com. An online resource and incubator for mothers of invention—run by a mom herself.

SCORE; www.score.org. Small business counseling by retired executives.

U.S. Small Business Administration; 1-800-8-ASKSBA; www.sba.gov.

Wisconsin Innovation Service Center; 262-472-1365; http://academics.uww.edu/BUSINESS/innovate/innovate.htm. New product and invention assessment.

TAXES AND RECORDKEEPING
Agencies/Associations

All Small Biz; www.allsmallbiz.com. Tax and incorporation information plus direct links to the SBA site.

Digital Daily; www.IRS.gov. The online IRS guide to income tax regulations, forms, and publications.

Internal Revenue Service; 1-800-829-3676; www.irs.ustreas.gov. Get forms for all your tax needs, plus information on small business tax classes in all fifty states.

Nanny Tax, Inc.; 212-867-1776; www.nannytax.com. Payroll tax compliance service for employers of domestic help.

Quicken; www.quicken.com. Forms to download and tips for doing taxes.

Books

Minding Her Own Business, 3rd Edition: The Self-Employed Woman's Guide to Taxes and Recordkeeping by Jan Zobel (Adams Media Corp., 2000).

Tax Planning and Preparation Made Easy for the Self-Employed by Gregory L. Dent and Jeffrey E. Johnson (Wiley, 1996).

Telecommuting and Other Flexible Work Options

Associations

International Telework Association and Council; Washington, D.C.: 202-547-6157; www.telecommute.org.

Books

101 Tips for Telecommuters: Successfully Manage Your Work, Team, Technology and Family by Debra A. Dinnocenzo and Ronald Fetzer (Berrett-Koehler Publishing, 1999).

The Virtual Office Survival Handbook by Alice Bredin (John Wiley and Sons, 1996).

E-Books

Flex Success: A Blueprint and Planning Guide for Getting a Family-Friendly Work Schedule, sold exclusively through www.workoptions.com.

Job Resources

DotCom Mommies; www.dotcommommies.com. This website targets moms who may not have extensive professional experience, yet want a scam-free way to work from home.

Flexible Resources, Inc.; 212-697-3867; www.flexibleresources.com. An employment agency that places experienced professional in flexible work arrangements, including part-time, job share, telecommuting, and project assignments. Based in Greenwich, Connecticut, the company also has offices in New York City, Boston, Los Angeles, and New Jersey.

FlexTime Solutions; 973-763-6603; www.flextimesolutions.com. An interim staffing firm that specializes in placing marketing, communications, and public relations professionals in project, part-time, and flex-time jobs in New Jersey companies.

GET A MOM; www.getamom.com. Online job placement network for professional mothers in technology, legal, and accounting fields.

Jobs and Moms Resource Center; www.jobsandmoms.com. Offers resources, advice, and helpful links for moms in search of new career directions, flexible work options, and home-based information. Also links you to career counseling services through telephone coaching and online courses.

MoneyMakin' Mommy; www.moneymakingmommy.com. This website offers an extensive list of telecommuting and other work-at-home jobs across the nation.

Telecommuting Jobs; www.tjobs.com. Online job board specializing in telecommuting opportunities.

Telework Connection; www.telework-connection.com. Telecommuting job opportunities, products, and other resources.

WAHMFest; 877-271-5218; www.wahmfest.org. Annual job expo available in several states; connects parents with legitimate work-at-home opportunities and business resources.

Womans-Work; www.womans-work.com. This website helps professional women across the United States find alternative work arrangements such as job-sharing, telecommuting, and part-time positions.

Workaholics4Hire.com; www.workaholics4hire.com. Online listing of jobs for telecommuters.

Online Support Sites for Teleworkers

About.com's Telecommuting Center; http://telecommuting.about.com.

Gil Gordon's Telecommuting, Telework, and Alternative Officing; www.gilgordon.com.

June Langhoff's Telecommuting Resource Center; www.langhoff.com.

TIME MANAGEMENT AND ORGANIZATIONAL STRATEGIES
Associations

National Association of Professional Organizers; 512-206-0151; www.napo.net.

Books

The Family Manager's Everyday Survival Guide by Kathy Peel (Ballantine, 1998).

Be Your Best: The Family Manager's Guide to Personal Success by Kathy Peel (Ballantine, 2000).

A Housekeeper Is Cheaper Than a Divorce by Kathy Fitzgerald Sherman (Life Tools Press, 2000).

Organize Your Home Office: Simple Routines for Setting Up an Office at Home by Ronni Eisenberg and Kate Kelly (Hyperion, 2000).

Organizing from the Inside Out: The Foolproof System for Organizing Your Home, Your Office and Your Life by Julie Morgenstern (Owl Books, 1998).

Time Management from the Inside Out: The Foolproof System for Taking Control of Your Schedule and Your Life by Julie Morgenstern (Henry Holt, 2000).

The Work-at-Home Balancing Act: The Professional Resource for Managing Yourself, Your Work and Your Family at Home by Sandy Anderson (Avon Books, 1998).

Index

Page numbers in **bold** indicate tables.